Reading Still Matters

Reading Still Matters

What the Research Reveals about Reading, Libraries, and Community

Catherine Sheldrick Ross,
Lynne (E. F.) McKechnie, and
Paulette M. Rothbauer

LIBRARIES
UNLIMITED™

An Imprint of ABC-CLIO, LLC

Santa Barbara, California • Denver, Colorado

Library of Congress Cataloging in Publication Control Number: 2017051877

ISBN: 978–1–4408–5576–4 (paperback)
 978–1–4408–5577–1 (ebook)

22 21 20 19 18   1 2 3 4 5

This book is also available as an eBook.

Libraries Unlimited
An Imprint of ABC-CLIO, LLC

ABC-CLIO, LLC
130 Cremona Drive, P.O. Box 1911
Santa Barbara, California 93116-1911
www.abc-clio.com

This book is printed on acid-free paper ∞

Manufactured in the United States of America

Contents

Preface

It has been more than 10 years since the publication of *Reading Matters: What the Research Reveals about Reading, Libraries, and Community* (2006). *Reading Matters* has been cited in both scholarly and professional publications and is held in the collections of many public and academic libraries in North America and internationally. Colleagues teaching in MLIS programs have written to tell us that they have put sections of the book on syllabi for courses dealing variously with reading, readers' advisory, public libraries, and children's and young adult (YA) literature. But these colleagues say they want an update. During the last 10 years, there has been a burgeoning of new research about the reading experience in all its many facets. Some international groups and associations concerned with reading for pleasure have formed to sponsor conferences and publish proceedings on aspects of pleasure reading. This new book provides a roundup of new work together with a restatement of what has *not* changed. As was the case with *Reading Matters*, the new book is written for people interested in reading and in the role that reading plays in people's lives. We continue to focus on the intersection of reading, libraries, and communities and expect our primary audience to be library staff, library trustees, and students in Library and Information Science (LIS) programs. But we also hope our book will be relevant to parents, teachers, and community members who have an interest in reading, especially pleasure reading.

Library staff, in particular, have a gut feeling that reading is a Good Thing and that libraries should play—and do play—a vital role in promoting it. But library staff often find it hard to explain *why*. This book helps them know why and will help them articulate the why to others—such as to board members and trustees who mistakenly think that libraries are improved when popular materials, including bestsellers, series books, comics, and romance titles, are downplayed. Teachers and parents sometimes need to be reassured of the value of pleasure reading, a domain where libraries have taken a lead role. What the research shows is that people become readers by doing lots of reading of extended text; that what motivates novice readers is the pleasure of the reading experience itself; and that libraries, schools, and communities need to support pleasure reading by making the books accessible, by helping readers choose books, by celebrating and modeling the love of reading, and by creating communities of readers—either face-to-face or in an electronic environment—who share the excitement of books. Yes, education and learning are crucial to an individual's successful negotiation of the challenges of life in a modern economy. But first comes the pleasure of reading, which is the cornerstone for all those other desirable outcomes such as academic success, civic engagement, and so on.

Since our first book, *Reading Matters*, research on reading and the reading experience has multiplied, and we have tried to include the new material that we have found most useful, thought provoking, or interesting. New research has been published on long-standing areas of interest such as the history of books and reading, the experience of audiences and readers, popular genres of reading, the value of popular culture, book clubs, communities of readers, and the role of libraries in promoting literacy and reading. Improvements in the technology for listening to audio books and reading on screens have expanded readers' participation in new ways of reading. As a consequence, the definition of what constitutes the reading experience itself has changed, and we advocate a broadly inclusive definition. Some new concerns have moved to center stage, including the following: research on reading and the brain, digital reading, multiliteracies, and shared reading and therapeutic practices.

There is an embarrassment of riches here, but the literature is scattered and fragmentary, published variously in scholarly journals and in monographs from the various disciplines of education, literary studies, cultural studies, media studies, history, sociology, psychology, and LIS. For our first book, we were guided by the conviction that library-oriented readers would benefit from having an accessible single source that draws together the scattered findings that relate to reading and the library's role in fostering reading. Although many useful books and websites are available on leisure reading, most focus on one or another specialized aspect of reading—for example, guides to genre fiction, handbooks for reading groups, guides to collection development, how-to-do-it advice on readers' advisory, self-reports by avid readers on a year of reading. Or they focus on one or another segment of the reading public—for example, children or YA readers or romance readers or science fiction readers. This book takes a synoptic approach to pleasure reading. It includes the entire lifespan of the reader from childhood through adolescence to adult and a broad spectrum of reading formats and genres. Teachers and students in LIS programs have told us that they have found the book useful in their courses and personally encouraging to themselves as enthusiastic readers. Therefore, the goal of *Reading Still Matters* remains the same as before: to provide a map to the research findings, organized according to themes that are central to people interested in the intersection of reading, readers, and libraries.

In *Reading Still Matters*, about 80 percent is new text. We have cut sections dealing with issues that seem no longer contentious or that haven't changed since the first book, specifically sections on the so-called fiction problem, reading as a transaction, series books, the boy problem, reading high and low, and how adult readers choose books. We refer you to *Reading Matters* for coverage of these topics. In addition to updating and substantially rewriting almost every section to emphasize work published in the past decade, we have added new sections on the following: digital reading, readicide, multimodalities and multiliteracies, the popularity of YA literature, comics, special communities of YA readers, censorship and prohibited reading, and therapeutic reading. Because so much has changed about the technologies for reading, we discuss digital formats throughout the book and stress the ways in which print is currently cohabiting with other media. Readers now have many choices about the kinds of materials they read and what formats they choose, often becoming deeply attached to one or another format and hostile to others. We end the book with a gift for avid readers—all of you—an annotated list of enjoyable novels that center, in one way or another, on the pleasures of reading.

All three authors have done extensive empirical research on real readers who read for pleasure. Therefore, to illustrate various themes and issues, we have been able to draw upon data gathered in our own research. Lynne McKechnie has been engaged in a longitudinal, ethnographic study of the role of the public library in the life of 30 girls. The children were four years old at the beginning of the study, which involved three kinds of data: observations and tape recordings of each child's visit to the library, diaries kept by mothers of the uses made of the library materials in the week following the library visit, and interviews with mothers. Lynne just completed an observation and interview study of 20 children from 2 through 12 about their e-reading practices and is doing an in-depth case study of one of them (Stella, now five years old) to situate her e-reading within her full reading life. Paulette Rothbauer continues to study the reading interests of older teens and young adults to explore their experiences of reading as they come of age in hyper-mediated cultures. She draws from over 70 interviews that she and her students have conducted with readers between the ages of 16 and 24. Catherine Ross studies adult readers who read for pleasure and at last count had over 300 open-ended interviews with avid readers. In these interviews, readers reflected on such topics as factors that fostered reading in childhood, how they choose books for pleasure reading, the role of reading in their lives, their preferences and dislike for various genres, and how they feel about rereading books. In this book, we use data from our own research so that the voices of real readers can be heard.

In addition, we have included cameo pieces from two outstanding researchers—Kathleen Schreurs, who recently successfully defended her LIS PhD thesis at Western, and Lucía Cedeira Serantes, a former doctoral student at Western and now an LIS faculty member at Queens College, CUNY—whose doctoral research has involved interviewing special kinds of pleasure readers. Kathleen Schreurs, who has contributed the case study in section 1.4, studies the implications of digital and electronic culture on reading and writing. She has done case studies focusing on the writing practices of literary authors, emphasizing the role played by electronic tools and forms as well as the shaping role of readers' expectations. Lucía Cedeira Serantes, who has contributed section 3.5 on comics, has a research focus on the intersection of young adults, reading, and public libraries, with an emphasis on reading practices related to comics. She has interviewed 17 young adults between the ages of 16 and 25 with a view to understanding their experience of reading comics and the interplay between identity, culture, and social structures.

We have designed the book so that, if you start at the very beginning and read consecutively, there is an unfolding chronological and linear order. Chapter One, "The Company of Readers," is an introduction to some issues and questions that apply in general to pleasure reading, including the histories of reading, current discussions about reading under threat, new technologies for reading, the various disciplinary approaches to research on reading, and reflections on the value of reading in people's lives. Chapters Two, Three, and Four focus on the reading of particular age groups—children, young adults, and adults, respectively. But we know that readers with a special interest in a particular aspect of reading will want to zero in on the topic of interest. Therefore, each section is more or less self-contained, with selected suggestions for further reading. An extensive index and a system of cross-referencing will allow you to follow a single topic—for example, e-reading, prison reading, or hearing stories read aloud—across different sections and chapters. Therefore, you can start at the beginning or you can dip into the book at whatever section most engages your interest. Either way, happy reading.

Acknowledgments

Thanks are owed to a great many people, starting with the many interviewees in our various research projects that investigated reading for pleasure. We also want to thank the hundreds of MLIS students in our various graduate courses at Western who collaborated by collecting data on the everyday reading of pleasure readers of different ages and types. Lynne thanks the students in her Children's Materials classes over the past 20 years who contributed interviews with children and also especially the many, many children from birth through 12 years of age who participated in studies, sharing their perspectives on their reading. Paulette thanks the students in her Young Adult Materials class over the past 10 years for their insights, and especially the class of fall 2016 for their interviews with young adult readers. And Catherine thanks the 276 interviewers in successive offerings of Genres of Fiction and Reading, who recruited the avid readers, interviewed them, and transcribed the interviews. We are especially indebted to Lucía Cedeira Serantes and Kathleen Schreurs, who have shared with us their research findings, respectively, on reading comics and on the digital reading and writing practices of literary authors. All three of our research programs were supported by grants from the Social Sciences and Humanities Research Council of Canada (SSHRC). Thanks also to colleagues and reading experts who have provided support, read sections of this book, made helpful suggestions and corrections, or agreed to be interviewed: Mary K. Chelton, Irene Gotz, Rosanne Greene, Marni Harrington, Anne Marie Heron, Penn Kemp, Melanie Kimball, Cecilie Naper, Cindy Orr, Knut Oterholm, Nancy Pearl, DeNel Rehberg Sedo, Joyce Saricks, Kjell Ivar Skjerdingstad, Jofrid Karner Smidt, Duncan Smith, Åse Kristine Tveit, and Neal Wyatt. And, as always, we thank our editor Barbara Ittner, whose support, encouragement, and good advice has carried us through two editions: *Reading Matters* and *Reading Still Matters*.

Chapter 1

The Company of Readers

Catherine Sheldrick Ross

When it comes to reading, it is the best of times, it is the worst of times. There are more books, magazines, and web pages available than ever before, and there are more readers to read them. But anxieties continue to bubble up about alleged threats to the future of reading posed by technology. In this chapter, we consider themes and topics that apply to reading in general, examine evidence for claims about reading, consider how reading itself has changed from scroll to codex to digital text, and highlight the importance of story, pleasure, and readers' choice.

1.1 Henny Penny and the Case for Reading

A lot of glum experts have been saying for at least 35 years that reading is becoming a dead art—it has been killed off successively by competition from movies, television, video games, the Internet, and smartphones. Reports about reading began to appear with titles that included such terms as "plight," "fate," "at risk," "demise," "death of," "end of," and "elegies." We hear that the introduction of digital media has produced a generalized attention-deficit disorder, leading to the death of the reader and the end of the book. Moreover, people in general—taxi drivers, talk show hosts, and your next-door neighbor—have horror stories to tell about children who can't read or *won't* read, can't spell, or can't write anything longer than a tweet. In 1983, the National Commission on Excellence in Education released a report on schools in America with the alarming title *A Nation at Risk.* Pointing to weakening literacy skills and declining SAT test scores, the report warned that a "rising tide of mediocrity" was threatening America's very future. Newspaper headlines highlighted a "literacy crisis," "plummeting" test scores, and "skills gaps," connecting these perceived literacy deficits to social problems such as unemployment, poverty, and crime. In 2004, the National Endowment for the Arts (NEA) released a major study, *Reading at Risk: A Survey of Literary Reading in America*, with a preface by the then NEA chair Dana Gioia (see sections 3.1 and 4.1 for more on this study). Gioia warned that "the news in the report is dire" and predicted "an imminent cultural crisis." He summed up the report this way: "Literary reading in America is not only declining rapidly among all groups, but the rate of decline has accelerated, especially among the young" (NEA 2004, vii). Even worse, "at the current rate of loss, literary reading as a leisure activity will virtually disappear in half a century" (NEA 2004, xiii).

Changing Our Brains

By the 1990s, social critics were convinced that things were going to hell in a hand basket. The culprit most often fingered was technological change, especially the Internet, multimedia, and screens. Jane Healy's *Endangered Minds* (1990) and Sven Birkerts's *Gutenberg Elegies* (1994) argued that the capacity for reading sustained text was being threatened by competition from the visual media and by the fragmentary nature of the discontinuous hypertext read on screens. Healy claimed that what we now call thinking itself—the ability to pursue the development of an idea, step by step in a logical chain of reasoning, through sentences and paragraphs—is an outgrowth of the linearity of print and is endangered by the shift from reading print to watching screens.

More recently, the debate has heated up with support from neuroscience research. Functional magnetic resonance imaging (fMRI) technology allows researchers to monitor blood flow in the brain as a marker of neuronal activity. Now scientists can observe brain activity and measure the size of various parts of the brain such as the hippocampus, which is associated with memory. New understandings about neuroplasticity have offered a possible explanation of something that Marshall McLuhan claimed some 50 years ago in *The Gutenberg Galaxy* (1967): that we are changed by the technologies we use. The neuroplasticity argument is that the brain is not fixed, as once was thought, but is constantly changing in response to its engagement with the world. Everything we do changes the structure of our brain, whether it is playing a musical instrument, learning a new language, reading screens, or practicing a golf swing. Neural connections that are not reinforced atrophy, while other circuits are strengthened through repeated use. Canadian neuroscientist Donald Hebb summed up this complex process with this memorable shorthand: "Neurons that fire together, wire together" (Doidge 2007, 63). Appealing to the neuroplasticity argument, critics such as Mark Bauerlein (2008), Nicholas Carr (2010), and Sven Birkerts (2015) have argued that we are making ourselves stupid. By repeatedly clicking and surfing our way through websites, spending as few as 10 seconds on each page, we are changing our brains, they claim, and not for the better. In effect, when we make the shift from a print-based to a digital culture, we risk becoming addicted to novelty and speed and correspondingly less capable of sustained, concentrated thought. This is another version of the complaint once made in the early 1970s about *Sesame Street*: that the television program's short segments, quick changes, and high intensity would produce a generation that is overstimulated and easily distracted. But now critics can point to neuroscience as an ally in making their case.

Developmental psychologist Maryanne Wolf (Wolf and Barzillai 2009) has used the term "deep reading" to describe the type of reflective engagement and close reading that she thinks is endangered by the many hours we spend in distracted skimming, scanning, and scrolling. She says, "What we read and how deeply we read shape both the brain and the thinker." In an environment of stable and linear print, Wolf argues, "Little is given to the reader outside the text. For that reason, readers must engage in an active construction of meaning, in which they grapple with the text and apply their earlier knowledge as they question, analyze, and probe." Through this sustained, active engagement, readers develop the right kinds of reading circuits in the brain. In contrast, the "fluid, multimodal" digital reading environment is an "uncensored, unedited maelstrom of anything and everything that is always available and capable of diverting one's attention." Digital reading of hypertext therefore "has the potential to form a more passive . . . learner"—or what Wolf calls the "distracted reader."

Two widely cited books have elaborated upon Wolf's argument about neural circuits, particularly her metaphor of "deep reading," in order to sound the alarm about the distracted reader: Nicholas Carr's book *The Shallows: What the Internet Is Doing to Our Brains* (2010) and Sven Birkerts's *Changing the Subject: Art and Attention in the Internet Age* (2015). In the latter book, the subject that is changing is *us*—the contemporary user of digital technology. In the chapter "You Are What You Click," Birkerts uses such terms as "unregulated floods of information," "inundation," and "deluge" to describe the electronic flows that swamp the digital reader. Clicking through from website to website, the reader gains "amazing lateral speed" but loses depth. "The upshot," says Birkerts (2015, 92–93), is that we have "extraordinary movement between points," a movement that creates an "expectation very much at odds with the narrowing intensity and focus for any more sustained kind of development." Making a parallel argument about the erosion of conversation by digital reading and writing, technoculture researcher Sherry Turkle in *Reclaiming Conversation* (2015) reports that addiction to smartphones has produced people that lack empathy, are panicked by solitude or boredom, connect only superficially with others, can't engage with any depth in face-to-face conversations, and can't focus on anything (even if they want to). In a nutshell, this recent body of critical work offers a series of aligned contrasts in relation to reading: active versus passive engagement, deep versus shallow reading, vertical versus lateral movement, concentrated versus distracted thinking, and slow versus fast.

As evidence of their own rewired brain circuits, a number of people have confessed in print, sometimes in long books, that their concentration is shot. They can't read anything more than a few pages long, they claim. They can no longer read *Middlemarch* (or *The Ambassadors* or *War and Peace*). Nicholas Carr (2008) made his confession in his widely read article in *The Atlantic*, "Is Google Making Us Stupid?" He reported that recently he has had "an uncomfortable sense that someone, or something, has been tinkering with my brain, remapping the neural circuitry, reprogramming the memory." Whereas he used to get easily caught up in a long book, now, he says, "My concentration often starts to drift after two or three pages. I get fidgety, lose the thread, begin looking for something else to do. I feel as if I'm always dragging my wayward brain back to the text. The deep reading that used to come naturally has become a struggle." A *Washington Post* article by Michael S. Rosenwald (2014) quotes Wolf as saying that current students "cannot read *Middlemarch*. They cannot read William James or Henry James. I can't tell you how many people have written to me about this phenomenon."

Despite this worried speculation, the jury is still out. Neuroscientists don't yet know enough about the digital reading brain to say anything definitive. Popularizing accounts of the effects of media on the brain are still dueling it out. On the one hand, there is Mark Bauerlein (2009) in *The Dumbest Generation: How the Digital Age Stupefies Young Americans and Jeopardizes Our Future.* On the other hand, there is Steven Johnson (2005) in *Everything Bad Is Good for You: How Today's Popular Culture Is Actually Making Us Smarter.* In each case, the book's title summarizes its central thesis. Mark Bauerlein, who was a consultant on the NEA *Reading at Risk* (2004) report, summarizes studies beyond the 2004 NEA report that highlight gaps in American students' knowledge and literacy skills. For example, on the 2001 National Assessment of Educational Progress (NAEP) History assessment, more than half of high school seniors "chose Germany, Japan, or Italy over the Soviet Union as a US ally in World War II" (Bauerlein 2009, 17). In a 2006 Geographic Literacy Survey, 63 percent of Americans surveyed could not identify Iraq on a map and 30 percent picked the U.S./Mexican border as the most fortified border in the world (26). Directly linking poor test scores to a decrease in print reading, Bauerlein's book supplies further ammunition to support the 2004 NEA report's conclusion: America faces "an imminent cultural crisis."

Steven Johnson, on the other hand, turns the good/bad polarity on its head. He argues that popular culture—Dungeons and Dragons, geopolitical strategy games such as Diplomacy, video games, TV series such as the multi-threaded *The Sopranos*—has become steadily more challenging, "exercising *different* mental skills that are just as important as the ones exercised by reading books" (23). Johnson points out that video games are hard—that is why there is a large cottage industry devoted to publishing game guides, maps, and cheat sheets. Games require a great deal of persistence, but the promise of rewards—access to new levels, more life, new equipment, new spells—keeps gamers playing. In effect, games are designed to tap into the brain's dopamine reward circuitry (35–38). The benefit is not the content, which often involves either drive-by shootings or princess-rescuing, but the practice gaming provides in certain valuable ways of thinking: decision making, priority setting, and probing and exploration to learn about the limits of the virtual world. Players give their brains a beneficial workout by holding in memory all the nested hierarchical relationships that make the linkage between immediate decision making in the moment and the game's long-term objectives.

As cultural historian Frank Furedi (2015) has pointed out, the creation of hierarchies of different types of readers and reading materials has a long history. The Roman Stoic philosopher Seneca warned that the reading of many books is a distraction and advised readers to digest the books of a limited number of master thinkers. In the nineteenth century, novels, especially romance and adventure stories, were pathologized with metaphors of addiction because they were thought to encourage people, especially women and children, to read excessively and indiscriminately. For centuries, the problem was said to be that people read *too much*. Now, although in comparison with most past periods, people are reading more than ever, the worry is that they are not reading *enough* extended text, their concentration having been weakened by surfing digital text. Furedi remarks, "Socrates' claim that writing weakened the reader's mind anticipates the current crop of internet-related inattention syndromes." Often social anxieties about reading—too much, too little, the wrong way, the wrong stuff—focuses on children, teens, women, and the uneducated.

A Literacy Crisis or a New Era of Reading?

In the meantime, countering this worried talk about plummeting test scores among the young, weakening literacy skills in the general population, and rewired brain circuits, there is compelling evidence that literacy is holding its own or improving. A lot depends, as we shall see in section 4.1, on what counts as reading. Book reading but not magazine, newspaper, or comic reading? So-called literary reading (NEA 2004) but not nonfiction books? Print and eBooks but not audio books? Materials read for pleasure but not assigned reading or work-related reading? Survey findings about what percentage of the population are "readers" depend entirely on how readers are defined. Meanwhile book production and book sales are at an all-time high, although bricks-and-mortar bookstores are in trouble and publishers' midlists are being squeezed. Over the last 200 years, the status of books has changed from being a rare object to being what Ted Striphas (2009, 4) calls "ubiquitous, accessible, and comparatively mundane things." Simon Eliot (2007) described the British Book Market in the nineteenth century as a transition from "few and expensive to many and cheap." At the same time, the literacy rates in North America and elsewhere have steadily been going up (Stedman and

Kaestle 1991). The 1983 Consumer Research Study on Reading and Book Purchasing sponsored by the Book Industry Study Group (BISG 1984, 13) started off with "America is overwhelmingly a nation of readers." Environics (2013) surveyed 1,001 adult Canadians to "gather benchmark data about the amount and type of pleasure reading being done by Canadians" and reported that 95 percent of respondents said they had read for pleasure in the last year, with three-quarters of these pleasure readers preferring books. In a Pew Research survey (Zickuhr and Rainie 2014) of American adults ages 18 and over, three-quarters of respondents reported that they had read at least one book in the past year. Almost 7 in 10 adults (69 percent) reported reading a print book in the past 12 months, while 28 percent had read an eBook and 14 percent had listened to an audio book. And meanwhile more new books than ever are made available each year to readers, not counting the 13 million or so books previously published and still in circulation. Since 2013, more than 300,000 books from traditional publishers have been released each year, with another 700,000 or so self-published books being produced each year, about 60 percent of them through Amazon's on-demand publishing platform, CreateSpace (Bowker 2016). According to Bowker (2013), the number of traditionally published fiction books doubled in a decade from about 25,000 in 2002 to almost 50,000 in 2012.

So what should we believe? Is there a crisis or isn't there? Is reading dying out or is literacy expanding triumphantly? Is on-screen reading killing off the physical book, reading, and all the values, practices, and social relations associated with print culture? Or is it enhancing literacy and making reading materials more accessible, especially in parts of the world where many people do not have access to well-stocked libraries and bookstores? It cannot be denied that the interactive electronic screen culture of e-mail, web pages, online discussion groups, blogs, fanzines, and self-published books provides new opportunities for both reading and writing. The real story turns out to be more complex than a simple either/or account of "national crisis" or "nation of readers." But one thing we can all agree on is that *something* is different in the digital age (Baron 2015). What we read, how we read, and what we count as reading—all these are changing. This change in the reading ecology is important to acknowledge because a so-called literacy crisis occurs (and the news media carry stories of "declining standards") not when fewer people learn to read but when what counts as literacy is redefined. Whereas in the nineteenth century the measure of literacy was being able to sign one's name instead of an X on a document, now expectations are far higher. To be literate in a modern society means not only being able to read documents but also being able to use them effectively in everyday life contexts. As Margaret Meek (1991, 8) has pointed out in *On Being Literate*, "There are different versions of literacy, some much fuller than others, some much more powerful than others."

Literate people make reading and writing work for them. The concept of literacy has quite clearly evolved beyond the ability to meet some arbitrarily fixed standard such as being able to sign one's name or completing eight years of schooling. Literacy, as measured by the NAEP, is viewed as a continuum of skills from very basic to proficient to the most advanced. By standards of 50 years ago, the news is good: some 95 percent of the population in Westernized countries *can* read and understand the printed word. The NAEP, which has tracked literacy in America since 1971, reported, "Compared to the first assessment in 1971 for reading and in 1973 for mathematics, scores were higher in 2012 for 9- and 13-year-olds and not significantly different for 17-year-olds" (NAEP 2012). So the real problem is that levels of literacy achievement are going up, but they are not going up *fast* enough. The literacy demands of a complex, modern society are going up even faster.

The public concern about literacy is justified because so much is at stake. To be literate is to be at home in a world that is thoroughly permeated by texts: job application forms, customs declaration forms, bus schedules, driving tests, operator's manuals, maps, restaurant menus, "best before" dates on perishable food, ingredient labels on packaged food, hurricane warnings running along the bottom of the television screen, birthday cards, advertising, and so on. To lack literacy skills means being shut out of jobs and opportunities. Parents know this and view literacy as an entitlement that schools are expected to deliver. However, literacy is not something that is acquired once and for all in school and then, like an inoculation with occasional boosters, lasts a lifetime. Practice is continually required. Those individuals who are the most successful in school have the credentials to pursue jobs where they practice their literacy skills and put an even greater distance between themselves and people who are struggling to read basic texts.

Gaps and Inequalities and the Story Remedy

Inequalities start early. By the time children are four years old, a huge language gap has already opened up between children with the most exposure to rich language and those with the least. This early language gap has far-reaching knock-on effects on the child's later facility with reading. An ethnographic study by Hart and Risley (1995) revealed that talkative families had spoken 30 million more words to their child in the first four years of life than had the least talkative families (see section 1.5 for more on the Hart and Risley study). We are back to the topic of neuroplasticity. The 30 million word gap is really a story about the child's developing brain. During the critical period of brain development (between birth and age four), a crucial variable is the richness of the language environment in which the child grows. Discussing the Hart and Risley study, Dana Suskind (2015, 49) explained, "Those exposed to more talk had larger vocabularies and faster language processing speeds. And that was true for all socioeconomic levels. It all came down to how well the brain had been nourished with words."

With evidence accumulating on the impact of early language environment on brain development, the American Academy of Pediatrics (AAP) began in 2014 formally to recommend a particularly nourishing form of language exposure: reading stories aloud to children every day, from infancy onward (PBS 2014). Dr. Pamela High is the author of a report that supported new guidelines for pediatricians, recommending that they educate parents about the benefits of daily reading and incorporate reading into office checkups (Neufeld 2014). In an interview on the *PBS NewsHour* (2014), High explained why daily early reading with children is so important: it gives them the undivided attention of a parent or caregiver in a routine, comforting environment, and it gives them enriched language. She elaborates, "We know that the more words that are in a child's language world, the more words they will learn, and the stronger their language skills are when they reach kindergarten, the more prepared they are to be able to read, and the better they read, the more likely they will graduate from high school." Australian literacy expert and best-selling author of children's books, Mem Fox has for decades been a powerful advocate for reading aloud to children. In her accessible and engaging book *Reading Magic* (2001, 13), Fox warns, "Reading problems are difficult to fix but very easy to prevent." Her magic formula? She says, "[E]xperts tell us that children need to hear a thousand stories read aloud before they begin to learn to read for themselves. A thousand! . . . Three stories a day will deliver us a thousand stories in one year alone. . . . We can do it!" (17). Fox's account of reading aloud to children embodies a key element in what fosters early reading and keeps people reading throughout their lives: the pleasure of the experience itself. With struggling learners, she says, all pressure should be taken off the child. Learning occurs best in a low-anxiety environment. "The aim should be to make reading seem as fabulous as it is for most of us: fun, hilarious, thrilling, useful, interesting, amazing, essential, and desirable" (152).

When people enjoy something, they do more of it. Pleasure is what keeps readers reading for the thousands and thousands of hours necessary to produce the bulk of reading experience that creates confident readers. This connection between reading for pleasure and proficiency in reading has been known for a long time. Reporting on adult reading, *Reading in America* noted that a number of findings "underscore the importance of pleasure as the reason for a higher incidence of book reading and more sustained reading in general" (Cole and Cole 1979, 61). Research from the Organisation for Economic Cooperation and Development (OECD 2002) showed that when it comes to a child's educational success, reading enjoyment trumps the family's socioeconomic status. In the United Kingdom, a literature review sponsored by the National Literacy Trust entitled *Reading for Pleasure* (Clark and Rumbold 2006) cites this OECD study and much other research that found that children who enjoy reading do more of it and are more successful in school. In general, people who do not find reading pleasurable tend to view book reading the way most people view preparing an income tax return: that it is hard to do, done under compulsion, and requires long blocks of uninterrupted time. Confident readers, in contrast, find reading effortless. They say that they pick up a book whenever they have a few spare minutes and frequently carry books with them in case they have to wait in line-ups. When they travel, they carry tablets preloaded with hundreds of books to ensure that they will never run out and will always have choices.

Since literacy is a skill requiring practice, this means that those who are already good at reading end up getting the most additional practice. Stephen Krashen (2004) has argued persuasively that the remedy for low literacy skills is what he calls "free voluntary reading," or FVR, which means reading because you want to. FVR is what avid readers do every time they pick up a book to read for pleasure. The connection between voluntary reading and powerful literacy is that people learn to read by reading. Krashen's conclusion is that "those who do not develop the pleasure reading habit simply don't have a chance—they will have a very difficult time reading and writing at a level high enough to deal with the demands of today's world" (Krashen 2004, x).

The Whole Company of Readers

In this book, we examine some of the contending arguments about reading, in an attempt to see where libraries and communities fit in and how they contribute to the dialogue on reading. We don't think it is helpful to take a Chicken-Little, Henny-Penny—the sky-is-falling-in—approach to the research findings on reading. We argue for an expanded definition of reading and readers, generous enough to include the reader skimming hyperlinked pages, the deeply engrossed reader of *Middlemarch*, and the preschool child chiming in on *Rosie's Walk*. The most common image of the reader is the solitary person—intent scholar or entranced novel reader—who is "lost in a book." But reading is also a social activity, as we discuss in section 4.7. It turns out that reading is a remarkably complex and variable behavior, as is evident from the number of words we use to refer to the act of reading—browsing, scanning, skimming, consulting, studying, immersed in/lost in a book, reading for pleasure, reading for information. Louise Rosenblatt ([1978] 1994) has made the case that all reading is a transaction between a reader and the text and furthermore that readers can take different stances toward a text at any given time. One kind of relationship with a text Rosenblatt called "aesthetic reading," which is undertaken for its own sake. In contrast, Rosenblatt introduced the term "efferent reading" to describe a type of reading done in pursuit of some fact or knowledge that can be carried away and used. The stance taken is determined by the reader, not by the text. Everything depends on what the reader wants to do—sink into the world of the book in a prolonged engagement or efficiently and quickly find nuggets of information to be used elsewhere.

We want to include all these kinds of reading and count them all as genuine reading. Which style of reading the reader engages in at a given time depends on the reader's purpose in reading as well as on other factors such as mood, time available, and so on. There is professional reading, reading for pleasure, skimming to find some small usable fact or quotation, immersion in the text to the point of forgetting your physical surroundings, reading for the first time, rereading, silent reading, reading aloud in a shared reading experience, reading alone with the intention of sharing the reading experience with others in a reading group, and no doubt many other kinds of reading. The company of readers includes a motley group: the commuter listening to an audio book, the comic book reader, the literary scholar performing a close reading of *Paradise Lost*, the six-year-old reading a primer, the video game player looking at an on-screen help file, the web surfer using Google to find information about hotel accommodation in New York City, the genre reader of YA novels/romances/urban fiction, and the book club members reading the current year's Man

Booker Prize. Clearly, reading is not a single activity, but many, with different kinds of purposes, satisfactions, and required skills.

Librarians need to value this variety and recognize the role of the library in supporting all these different styles and purposes of reading. Reading is woven into a majority of the activities that libraries consider foundational: reference, collection building, the provision of leisure materials, readers' advisory services, storytelling programs, adult literacy programs, and the like. Similarly, parents and family members need to be aware of the crucial importance of family literacy practices in the making of avid readers. In a large proportion of cases, people who grow up to be enthusiastic and powerful readers come from families where the bedtime story is a crucial part of the nightly ritual of getting ready for bed and where parents themselves read for pleasure and have books and magazines in the house. In other cases, however, where parents may not be readers, it is an aunt or uncle, a neighbor, a teacher, or a librarian who provides the supportive environment for reading by giving books as gifts or by talking about a favorite book.

You will notice that we are insisting on the importance of reading for pleasure, because this aspect of reading has been downplayed in comparison with the value assigned to reading for information or literacy as a practical life skill. Until recently, public librarians have been embarrassed about their role in providing leisure reading materials, especially fiction, that people read for the joy of it. Nor has the idea totally died out that public libraries would have more status if only they would market themselves as educational institutions and not mention pleasure. In a provocative article in "Public Libraries," Bill Crowley (2014, 37) argued that public libraries should say little in public about their role in providing books for pleasure reading and avoid using such words as "recreational" and "leisure." Instead public libraries should emphasize "learning" and "education." In Crowley's view, the way to win over library directors, funders, and taxpayers and bolster the professional status of the librarians is to talk about the long-term benefits of reading, not the immediate pleasure of reading an engaging book. Our argument is that public libraries *do* support literacy and learning, but the way they do this is by providing books and other materials that people actually *want* to read. *The best book for an individual reader, whether a novice or an old-hand, is the one that gets read.* Reading of the chosen book happens in the first place because the reader anticipates some pleasure or reward in the reading. The learning and literacy benefits follow.

Public library users know the value of reading for pleasure—for themselves and for their children. When they think of the public library, they think of it as the place, *par excellence*, to get books—and now increasingly eBooks and audio books. A large percentage of these books are borrowed for leisure reading. For almost 150 years in North America, fiction has quite consistently represented about two-thirds of library circulation—this despite strong efforts in the early decades by librarians to reduce fiction reading and emphasize the information aspects of library service. The Public Library Inquiry in 1950 found that in U.S. public libraries "fiction constitutes 60 to 65 percent of total circulation, ranging from 50 percent or a little less in the largest libraries to 75 percent in the smallest ones" (Leigh 1950, 92). Barbara Hoffert (2016) reported in *Library Journal* that in U.S.

public libraries, fiction accounted for 65 percent of print circulation and 79 percent of eBook circulation.

In short, a major function of public libraries is the circulation of materials for leisure reading, and it always has been. Instead of treating this fact as a shameful secret, we need to celebrate it. Remember those 1,000 stories that a child needs to hear before going to school? Many of those stories will come from the public library. At the other end of reader development, academic librarians are increasingly seeing a role for "popular reading collections" or "browsing collections" for students, staff, and faculty in academic libraries (Dewan 2010, 2015; Gilbert and Fister 2011). The research reviewed in this book indicates that pleasure and free choice are both key elements in the making and sustaining of readers at every age and stage. With their large collections of books and magazines and newspapers that are free to all, promoting leisure reading for all ages is a role that public libraries are ideally suited to fill. It is time for public libraries to stop feeling apologetic and begin to celebrate one of their most important functions: the support of pleasure reading. Since the mid-1980s, this has been happening as public libraries across North America and Europe have recognized that people have a deep need, not just for facts, but for story. In fact, readers' advisor *par excellence*, Joyce Saricks (2015) has suggested that the public library's brand is Story:

> Through stories, our libraries offer something for everyone.... We possess the technology and the tools to help readers find whatever they're looking for and to create their own stories. Sure, we need technology, but stories form the heart of libraries. Isn't it time we acknowledge that Story is our brand?

Case 1: What Does an Avid Reader Look/Sound Like?

Jean (teacher librarian, 44) is one of the approximately 300 readers interviewed for my study of avid readers who read for pleasure. Here's what Jean said in answer to the question, "Can you come up with a summary of the importance of reading in your life":

> I hate to say that reading is everything, but I think sometimes it's more important than people, and that scares me. It is; it's everything. If I don't have a book, I'm bare. I feel like there's something lacking in my life. I cannot be without something to read; and if it's not a book—if I don't have access to a book (which is fairly rare)—then I'll buy a good magazine. But I have to have something. If I have three or four at one time, that's all the better. I remember when I was in school in a guidance class and one of the girls said to the guidance teacher, "I want to become an artist, and my parents won't let me draw. What do I do?" And the teacher said, "If you are going to be an artist, you will draw. Nobody can stop you from drawing." And that's what it's like being a reader. If you're going to be a reader,

nobody can stop you. You are going to be that. That's what reading is to me. I just am. It's part of me.

Comments

Although obviously at the upper end of the scale in terms of committed reading, Jean was not untypical. Like addicts, avid readers in my study talked about laying in supplies, to make sure that they wouldn't be stuck without something to read. They described in compelling terms the way the act of reading itself was an important part of their identity and the way they thought of themselves. For more discussion of the role of reading in people's lives, see section 4.2.

What Libraries and Community Members Can Do

1. Make the public library a place that celebrates readers and booklovers. In turn, they will become the library's most vocal supporters in times when advocates are needed for investment in libraries.
2. If you are an academic librarian thinking about creating a popular reading collection, identify the barriers and work with colleagues to overcome them. Naysayers may argue that they are already too busy as it is, that students don't read anyway, and that academic librarians need to stick to their knitting: research and the curriculum. If they do, point out that accomplished readers become so by doing a lot of reading—both inside and outside of the curriculum. Supporting popular reading advances the academic library's mission of fostering lifelong learning.

To Read More

Krashen, Stephen. 2004. *The Power of Reading. Insights from the Research*, 2nd ed. Englewood, CO: Libraries Unlimited.
Krashen reviews the reading literature conducted in education to make the case that what he calls "free voluntary reading" is the best way for children, less literate adults, and second language readers to become better readers. He argues that direct instruction can never give novice readers enough exposure to language for them to learn to read and spell and develop a rich vocabulary. Rather novices learn to read through exposure to lots of print, which happens most readily when they are reading materials they have chosen and enjoy. A new edition is in the works.

References

Baron, Naomi S. 2015. *Words Onscreen: The Fate of Reading in an Online World*. Oxford: Oxford University Press.

Bauerlein, Mark. 2008. *The Dumbest Generation: How the Digital Age Stupefies Young Americans and Jeopardizes our Future.* New York: Jeremy P. Tarcher/Penguin.

Birkerts, Sven. 1994. *The Gutenberg Elegies: The Fate of Reading in an Electronic Age.* Boston and London: Faber and Faber.

Birkerts, Sven. 2015. *Changing the Subject: Art and Attention in the Internet Age.* Minneapolis, MN: Graywolf Press.

Book Industry Study Group. 1984. *1983 Consumer Research Study on Reading and Book Purchasing.* New York: Book Industry Study Group.

Bowker. 2013. ISBN Output Report for 2002–2012. Available at: http://media.bowker.com/documents/isbn_output_2002_2013.pdf.

Bowker. 2016. "Report from Bowker Shows Continuing Growth in Self-Publishing." Available at: http://www.bowker.com/news/2016/Report-from-Bowker-Shows-Continuing-Growth-in-Self-Publishing.html.

Carr, Nicholas. 2008. "Is Google Making Us Stupid? What the Internet Is Doing to Our Brains." *The Atlantic* (July/Aug): 56–83. Available at: www.theatlantic.com/magazine/ archive/2008/07/is-google-making-us-stupid/306868/.

Carr, Nicholas. 2010. *The Shallows: What the Internet Is Doing to Our Brains.* New York: W.W. Norton.

Clark, Christina, and Kate Rumbold. 2006. *Reading for Pleasure: A Research Overview.* London: National Literacy Trust. Available at: http://www.literacytrust.org.uk/assets/0000/0562/Reading_pleasure_2006.pdf.

Cole, John Y., and Carol S. Cole, eds. 1979. *Reading in America: Selected Findings of the Book Industry Study Group's 1978 Study.* Washington, DC: Library of Congress.

Crowley, Bill. 2014. "Time to Rethink Readers' Advisory Education?" *Public Libraries* 53, no 4: 37–43.

Dewan, Pauline. 2010. "Why Your Academic Library Needs a Popular Reading Collection Now More than Ever." *College & Undergraduate Libraries* 17, no. 1: 44–64.

Dewan, Pauline. 2015. "Reading Trends and College-Age Students: The Research, the Issues, and the Role of Libraries." *Against the Grain* 27, no. 1 (March 27). Available at: http://www.against-the-grain.com/2015/03/v27-1-reading-trends-and-college-age-students/.

Doidge, Norman. 2007. *The Brain that Changes Itself: Stories of Personal Triumph from the Frontiers of Brain Science.* New York: Viking.

Eliot, Simon. 2007. "From Few and Expensive to Many and Cheap: The British Book Market, 1800–1890." In *A Companion to the History of the Book*, 291–302. Edited by Simon Eliot and Jonathan Rose, Oxford: Blackwell.

Fox, Mem. 2001. *Reading Magic: Reading Aloud to Our Children Will Change Their Lives Forever.* San Diego, CA: Harcourt, Inc.

Furedi, Frank. 2015. *Power of Reading: From Socrates to Twitter.* London: Bloomsbury.

Gilbert, Julie, and Barbara Fister. 2011. "Reading, Risk, and Reality: College Students and Reading for Pleasure." *College & Research Libraries* 72, no. 5 (September): 474–495.

Hart, Betty, and Todd R. Risley. 1995. *Meaningful Differences in the Everyday Experience of Young American Children.* Baltimore: Paul H. Brookes.

Healy, J. M. 1990. *Endangered Minds: Why Our Children Don't Think.* New York: Simon & Shuster.

Hoffert, Barbara. 2016. "Trend Turaround: Materials Survey 2016." *Library Journal* (February 15). Available at: http://reviews.libraryjournal.com/2016/03/books/trend-turnaround-materials-survey-2016/.

Johnson, Steven. 2005. *Everything Bad Is Good for You: How Today's Popular Culture Is Actually Making Us Smarter.* New York: Penguin Group.

Krashen, Stephen. 2004. *The Power of Reading. Insights from the Research*, 2nd ed. Englewood, CO: Libraries Unlimited.

Leigh, Robert D. 1950. *The Public Library in the United States.* The General Report of the Public Library Inquiry. New York: Columbia University Press.

McLuhan, Marshall. 1967. *The Gutenberg Galaxy: The Making of Typographic Man.* Toronto: University of Toronto Press.

Meek, Margaret. 1991. *On Being Literate.* London: The Bodley Head.

National Assessment of Educational Progress. 2012. "Top Stories in NAEP Long-Term Trend Assessments 2012." Available at: https://www.nationsreportcard.gov/ltt_2012/.

National Commission on Excellence in Education. 1983. *A Nation at Risk: The Imperative for Educational Reform.* Available at: https://www2.ed.gov/pubs/NatAtRisk/risk.html.

National Endowment for the Arts (NEA). 2004. *Reading at Risk: A Survey of Literary Reading in America.* Research Division Report #46. Washington, DC. Available at: https://www.arts.gov/sites/default/files/ReadingAtRisk.pdf.

Neufeld, Sara. 2014. "Q & A with Dr. Pamela High: Should Reading Be Part of a Checkup with the Pediatrician?" *The Hechinger Report*, July 8. Available at: http://hechingerreport.org/q-dr-pamela-high-wrote-new-literacy-policy-pediatricians-urging-doctors-promote-reading-young-children/.

OECD. 2002. *Reading for Change: Performance and Engagement Across Countries. Results from PISA 2000.* New York: Organisation for Economic Cooperation and Development.

PBS. 2014. "I is for Infant: Reading Aloud to Young Children Benefits Brain Development." June 24. Available at: http://www.pbs.org/newshour/bb/infant-reading-aloud-young-children-benefits-brain-development/.

Rosenblatt, Louise. (1978) 1994. *The Reader, the Text, the Poem: The Transactional Theory of the Literary Work.* Carbondale, IL: Southern Illinois Press. Reprint 2nd ed., Carbondale, IL: Southern Illinois Press.

Rosenwald, Michael S. 2014. "Serious Reading Takes a Hit from Online Scanning and Skimming, Researchers Say." *Washington Post*, April 6, 2014.

Saricks, Joyce. 2015. "At Leisure with Joyce Saricks: Story People." *The Booklist* 111, no. 1 (March 1): 19.

Stedman, Lawrence C. and Carl F. Kaestle. 1991. "Literacy and Reading Performance in the United States from 1880 to the Present." In *Literacy in the United States: Readers and Reading since 1880*. 75–128. Edited by Carl F. Kaestle, Helen Damon-Moore, Lawrence C. Stedman, Katherine Tinsley, and William Vance Trollinger, Jr. New Haven and London: Yale University Press.

Striphas, Ted. 2009. *The Late Age of Print: Everyday Book Culture from Consumerism to Control.* New York: Columbia UP.

Suskind, Dana. 2015. *Thirty Million Words: Building a Child's Brain.* New York: Dutton.

Turkle, Sherry. 2015. *Reclaiming Conversation: The Power of Talk in a Digital Age.* New York: Penguin Press.

Wolf, Maryanne. 2007. *Proust and the Squid: The Story and Science of the Reading Brain.* New York and London: Harper Perennial.

Wolf, Maryanne, and Mirit Barzillai. 2009. "The Importance of Deep Reading." *Educational Leadership* 66, no. 6 (March): 32–37. Available at: https://www

.mbaea.org/documents/resources/Educational_Leadership_Article_The__D87FE2B
C4E7AD.pdf.

Zickuhr, Kathryn, and Lee Rainie. 2014. *A Snapshot of Reading in America in 2013*. Pew
Research Center. Available at: http://www.pewinternet.org/2014/01/16/a-snapshot
-of-reading-in-america-in-2013/.

1.2 Myths about Reading

In the first edition of *Reading Matters*, we considered some myths about reading
such as:

> People don't read as *much* as they used to.
>
> Young people lack the reading skills of previous generations.
>
> Boys don't read.
>
> Men don't read but, if they do, they read mostly nonfiction.
>
> Book readers are introverted bookworms, who are antisocial and not very
> well-rounded.
>
> Real reading is a solitary affair.
>
> The quality of materials that people read is sinking. Where formerly
> people read Shakespeare, Milton, the King James Bible, and, of course,
> *Middlemarch*, now they are spending their time on best sellers, genre books,
> self-help books, and beach books recommended by media celebrities.
>
> It is the job of the librarian to help readers climb a reading ladder so that
> eventually they will read "only the best" and leave series books and
> genre books behind.

Providing evidence and citing studies, we said that *none* of these claims are
entirely true and the majority are just plain false. As noted in more detail in section
4.1, surveys of reading conducted over the past 50 years have repeatedly found
that 95 percent of people in nationwide North American surveys say that they read
something in the past week; 50 to 70 percent of the population reads books as a
chosen leisure activity; and 10 to 15 percent of the population are avid readers,
who borrow and buy the lion's share of books, magazines, newspapers, and other
media consumed.

Now, ten years later, we have some new myths that we consider in multiple
ways in various sections of the book:

- Print books are on the way out and will soon be reduced to a narrow
  market niche, following a pattern of obsolescence that has already
  happened to vinyl records. (See section 1.4.)

- Reading print is good because it engages the reader in an active process of filling in the gaps, thereby exercising the reader's power of
  the imagination. Other ways of getting stories (watching films, listening to audio books) are passive and therefore not as good—in
  fact, quite possibly bad. (See sections 1.4 and 2.4.)

- Popularity and quality are always inversely related. (See section 4.6 for a discussion of "quality" in the context of readers' experience.)

This section addresses in some detail one big myth that influences a lot of other things, such as the way people judge other people's reading choices and the way people recommend books to others. This is the myth:

- Accomplished readers reading the same text will have more or less similar experiences. Your best guide to another reader's experience with a book is your own experience. If you have read a masterpiece and found it amazingly wonderful, you should recommend it to others because a good book is a good book is a good book.

The Myth of the Equivalency of Reading Experiences; or, It's Not about You

It is easy to see how this misconception develops and why it persists. Because we can't know from observation what readers are actually experiencing and thinking as they read, we are apt to generalize from our own experience. If *we* find that a popular genre such as romance novels or first-person shooter video games seems boring, if not positively harmful, we may assume everyone else either does or *should* do so too. Cultural critics do this all the time when they attack some type of reading/viewing that they themselves don't enjoy and don't participate in: reading self-help books, romance novels, Oprah books, comics, or fanzines; playing video games; and so on. The false premise of the equivalency of experience is especially misleading when it comes to recommending books for others, as we shall see later. Readers' advisors, in particular, need to remind themselves, "It's not about you." (See section 4.6.)

So what makes me think that experienced readers use themselves as the measure of pleasure reading in general? Over the years, my students and I have conducted over 300 interviews with avid readers. In my graduate course on Genres of Fiction and Reading, one assignment requires each student to interview an avid reader, transcribe the interview, and make the anonymized interview available for the whole class to consider and discuss. Year after year, students say they were gobsmacked when they read the set of classmate's interviews. Each student knew how he or she personally engaged with pleasure reading; each had interviewed an avid reader; and most expected other readers to report similar experiences and preferences to their own. But no! Students were amazed at the variety of responses and how one reader's experience was flatly contradicted by another's experience.

Dimensions along which Readers Differ

When my students and I examined the transcripts, we found many dimensions along which avid readers differ one from another. Some reread favorite books, whereas others say there are so many new books out there that they don't have time to reread. Some read only fiction for pleasure, whereas others read only nonfiction. Some feel compelled to finish reading a book no matter how dull, whereas others have no compunction about abandoning a book they are not enjoying (see section 4.3 for more on dimensions of variation). But the most striking difference turned out to be the contrast between readers who try to read only "important books" and omnivores who read "indiscriminately" (Ross 2014, 83–91). In a nutshell, these two kinds of readers have distinctly different understandings of *what* materials to read and *how* to read them. Selective readers say that life is too short to waste time on an unimportant book. Nathan (professor of English, age 50) said, "I don't read popular literature that is not good literature. I always found the time for reading was precious—it had to be put to good use. If you wasted it, that's one fewer book that you could read at the end of your life." If pressed, these discriminating readers might say that there are certain books that they "should" read: more classics, more nonfiction, a better grade of fiction, books on "best 100" booklists, award-winning books—in short, books that are considered important in one way or another by cultural authorities.

Omnivores, on the other hand, say that they "read absolutely anything" they can get their hands on. Doreen (business consultant, age 38) said, "I will read anything. My panic is to be in the house without anything to read. That makes me just absolutely, totally panic-stricken." For these readers, a greedy voraciousness for reading materials of all kinds—"everything and anything"—often started in childhood and persisted. Robert (professor of English, age 57) said, "I know I began indiscriminately reading. It was never guided reading. . . . I read indiscriminately, always indiscriminately, and I still do. Things thrown in at the front door like that *Homemakers* magazine and the most convoluted post-structuralist criticism and recent novels I read indiscriminately." For these omnivores, the motivation is the experience itself at the time of reading, not the post-reading residue in increased intellectual capital—although they acknowledge that happens too. They enjoy books at all levels of prestige and difficulty, often reading several books at the same time. Patricia (teacher, age 48) said, "I'm too eclectic a reader [to read a book within the library's borrowing period]. I might read two chapters from a book and then not go back to it for another two months. I've been known to be reading twelve books all at the same time." The determining factor for which book is read at any given time is the reader's mood. Lorraine (elementary school teacher, age 27) said, "A lot of the time when you're reading, especially a book that's a little different from your favorite genre, you've got to be in the right mood. Maybe that's why I read two or three books at a time. I have to be in a certain mood to read a certain book."

Important Books and Selective Readers

Readers such as Neil (chemical technician, age 26) are never tempted by "unimportant books." He turned to Mortimer Adler's *How to Read a Book* as a guide in knowing which books to read and how to read them: "I only wanted important books. I hated novels. I didn't like novels, unless they were important in some respect, unless they were famous ... I read to gain knowledge—to gain the insights of the western world and what literature had to offer. I enjoy getting something out of reading. I think that's what it is. . . . I can never understand the people that say, 'Yeah, I read the book, but I can't remember it.' " Selective readers can't fathom why anyone would spend valuable time reading and then say later that they can't remember authors, titles, or key themes of the books they have just read.

For others, reading "important books" is aspirational. They push themselves to read challenging books that are just beyond their comfort zone. In some cases, the motivation for reading Dostoevsky or Dickens is to become the sort of person who would read and enjoy a universally recognized work of literature. David (student, age 26) said, "I maintain a distinction between books I like and books that are good." One summer after his first year of university, he decided to read "great literature": "I read Tolstoy, Chekhov, I read an entire book of Chekhov's short stories, three or four Thomas Hardy. . . . I still set aside time to read something that is supposed to be good for me." Dickens is often the go-to author for readers who decide to "read the classics." Nathan made an early start on Dickens and has been a lifelong reader of important books ever since. He said, "The first important book, really important book, that I read was a Dickens novel—I was about ten years old. It was *The Old Curiosity Shop*. I remember very, very clearly knowing it was a significant book." When asked, "What interested you about that book?" Nathan said: "The notion of reading a book that was for mature people. Reading a book that marked you as a serious person began to inspire me to read books that were beyond the children's section. I picked Dickens, because he was recommended to me by the librarian as being a serious work."

Selectivity is key for these readers—and one way to cope with the flood of material being published. Most of it can be ignored as not worth reading. David Shields in *How Literature Saved My Life* (2013, 140) quotes D. H. Lawrence as saying, "It's better to know a dozen books extraordinarily well than innumerable books passably." If you believe in investing a great deal of time in a single book through close reading and prolonged engagement, then it helps if you think there are only a very few books that really matter and are worth reading. Such readers often enjoy taking on the challenge of 1,000 page masterpieces such as William Gaddis's *The Recognitions*, Wallace's *Infinite Jest*, or Roberto Bolaño's *2666*. They are apt to say that the real question is not whether challenging books are worth the time spent but whether unchallenging books are worth the time wasted on them.

In "Bolaño Summer," Sven Birkerts (2015, 157–172) reports on his summer project reading Bolaño's 900-page novel, *2666*. While reading Bolaño, Birkerts thinks back to a time in his life when the experience of reading a novel seemed just as real as, or more real than, life itself, and he finds himself trying to analyze this sense of super-real intensity, "trying to figure out just how it is that a novel can come to possess a magic for the reader" (161). Halfway through, he has to draw on all his resolve to keep going: "I am determined to stick it through. Not just because I like to finish what I start and feel a sense of failure when I don't. . . . There is another reason I am staying the course, and this has to do with the dynamics of the reading process, with my sense of being engaged with something ongoing, of being *in relation*. . . . [This book] holds a certain kind of time—reflective, restorative,

durational time. Time that stands as a counter—and rebuttal—to the surface agita-
tion that governs so much of the rest of my life. I see the book, the fact of prolonged
immersion, as refuge" (163–164). Birkerts sees reading as recuperative—but it has
to be a special kind of close reading of "only the best."

Indiscriminate Reading

In comparison with these readers of important books, indiscriminate readers are
much less concerned with the "shoulds" of reading and much less deferential to
the reading hierarchies that are promoted by cultural authorities. Madeline (student, age 22) said, "I don't read for 'self-improvement.' I don't make an effort to
read in the interests of expanding my mind." Omnivores have their own version
of the Life's-Too-Short theme—life is too short to read a book that you are not
enjoying. They say: If you are not enjoying the book, put it down. You may enjoy
the book later, but it is the wrong book for you now. British novelist Nick Hornby
has documented a decade's worth of omnivorous reading in monthly columns
written for the magazine *The Believer*. Hornby (2006, 14) complains, "One of
the problems . . . is that we have got it into our heads that books should be hard
work, and that unless they're hard work, they're not doing us any good":

> And so we grind our way through serious, and sometimes seriously
> dull, novels, or enormous biographies of political figures, and
> every time we do so, books come to seem a little more like a
> duty. . . . Please, please, put it down.

Omnivores do put it down. They don't feel at all guilty about abandoning a
book that bores them. Every time they put down a dull book, they free up time
for another book they can read with gusto. Nancy Pearl, readers' advisor extraordinaire and originator of the One Book, One Community concept (see 4.7), has a
"Rule of 50," which was inscribed on Starbucks cups. "If you are 50 years old or
younger, read 50 pages before giving up on it; if you older than 50, the magic number is 100 minus your age" (Ross 2014, 247).

With the one proviso that the book must be enjoyable, omnivores say they
are willing to try almost anything. Phillip (student, age 20) insisted, "I'm not a
fussy, fussy reader. I can read just about everything." Asked to describe herself
as a reader, Daphne (student, age 29) said, "Voracious. I read a lot. I read a lot
and I really like variety too. I think some people get stuck on the one-author track,
but I really like to try and look for a huge variety in the fiction that I read." Victor
(actor, age 68) said, "I read just about anything from the comics to Shakespeare."
These readers celebrate the breadth and variety of their reading, from high to low,
from series books to George Eliot. They may sometimes describe their reading
choices "trash" or "schlock," but they are unapologetic, regarding variety as a
major strength. They may in fact read many of the same books as the selective
readers do, but they talk about their reading differently. Adam (librarian, age 24)
says:

> It's not just to better my mind—because I don't think of it in those
> terms. It's not like I sit down and go, "Oh, I'm going to better my

mind by reading this." But that's the result. I think that when you devote a lot of time to reading anything, you're presented with a number of new ideas you'd never thought of before and those ideas help you in your life—in handling all kinds of human situations.

For Adam and other omnivores, expanding their knowledge and ideas is an indirect by-product of the pleasurable reading experience, not the main goal.

A Cautionary Tale

Occasionally, a book appears in which dramatic differences in reading styles and expectations are sharply etched. One such book is Mikita Brottman's well-reviewed *The Maximum Security Book Club* (2016). Brottman, who is a professor at the Maryland Institute College of Art and psychoanalyst, has run a book club for prisoners at Maryland's Jessup Correctional Institution (JCI). The book describes a two-year period in which book club participants discussed 10 books that Brottman herself chose because she loved the books and found their dark themes personally compelling. The books were Conrad's *Heart of Darkness*, Melville's "Bartleby, the Scrivener," Bukowsky's *Ham on Rye*, Burrough's *Junkie*, Malcolm Braly's *On the Yard*, Shakespeare's *Macbeth*, Stevenson's *Dr. Jekyll and Mr. Hyde*, Poe's "The Black Cat," Kafka's *The Metamorphosis*, and Nabokov's *Lolita*. *The Maximum Security Book Club* narrates, book by book, the prisoners' struggles wrestling with these difficult books.

The ten books selected might seem like surprising choices, but Brottman has written a previous book, *The Solitary Vice: Against Reading* (2008), that outlines her view of what people *should* read. She quotes Kafka: "A book must be the ax for the frozen sea within us. That is what I believe." She wonders why, as a society, we seem to assume that reading—any reading—is a good thing. If anything, she thinks, we read too much and are not sufficiently selective. Reading shouldn't be fun, nor should it be hyped as fun on library posters ("Get Caught Reading!"). Reading should be hard work. In her academic teaching, Brottman guides college students through courses entitled "Understanding Suicide" and "Apocalypse Culture," featuring texts that are not "fun" but are valuable, all the same, for the way they engage with hard-hitting and profound ideas about "evil, consciousness, inhumanity" (205). Brottman says what we really should be paying attention to "in a marketplace stuffed and glutted with books, isn't the death of reading, but the death of discrimination. It's easy enough to get into the habit of reading; what's much more difficult is learning to become a conscious, discerning reader" (8). So, when it comes to recommending how and what other people should read, Brottman is on the side of selectivity, important books, and serious literature.

But she wasn't always this kind of reader herself. She is a late convert and perhaps, for that reason, a zealot for selectivity. She started out very much like those flashlight-under-the-covers readers who read voraciously, obsessively, and indiscriminately at all levels of quality. The first chapter of *The Solitary Vice*, "In the Attic," describes adolescent years where Brottman seemed to do little else *but* read, despite being urged by parents to get fresh air and a social life. Her chapter on attic reading will appeal to anyone interested in an account of the reading experience itself in all of its intensities (see section 4.3). Brottman read scary fairy stories, horror stories, *Macbeth*, Poe, *Dr. Jekyll and Mr. Hyde*, gothic novels, H. P. Lovecraft's *Lady Vampire*, "Tales from the Crypt," and comics that were "all the better if they included rats, ghouls, voodoo, vampires, and bodies chopped up and hidden under the floor." For Brottman, these scary stories were "the gateway to a fabulous landscape of fear" (2008, 25). "I didn't want to FIND myself in books—God forbid!—but to get away from myself, to disappear entirely" (2008, 27). In her adolescence, Brottman was selective not in terms of choosing only "important books" but in terms of picking books that transported her to worlds more real, dark, intense, and dangerous than her own everyday life. In retrospect she wonders if time in the attic with Jack the Ripper, Mephisto, Catherine and Heathcliff, Jane Eyre and Mr. Rochester, Count Dracula, Miss Havisham, Madeleine Usher, Melmoth the Wanderer, and the Crypt Keeper unfitted her for real life (25–37). But she acknowledges, "Books ... have given me more consistent, undiluted pleasure than almost anything else in my life" (2008, 19). And despite having written a book with the subtitle *Against Reading*, Brottman confesses in *The Maximum Security Book Club* (2016, xi) that "all that time spent reading paid off: I won a scholarship to study literature at Oxford."

When Brottman decided, as a sabbatical project, to start a prison book club, she picked books that she herself has loved (see section 4.8 for a contrasting approach to choosing books in prison book clubs). They are all "books that don't flinch from showing the isolation of the human struggle, the pain of conflict, and the price that must be paid in consequence" (xxv). When she herself had first read these books as an undergraduate, she found them tough-going and painful, because they made her "confront difficult subjects: the inevitability of death, our ultimate aloneness, and the absence of any obvious meaning to life" (xxvii). Nevertheless, she hoped that the prisoners would be ready for the workout required and would gain insight into their own situations. For the book club's inaugural read, Brottman chose a book by Conrad that she herself had read as a student at Oxford. In that first encounter, she had trouble getting past the first six or seven pages—"There was nothing to grab on to" and she would feel herself falling, "unable to focus, losing my place." "Looking back, I wasn't ready for *Heart of Darkness*" (3), she acknowledges, but after multiple readings as a classroom teacher, the novella spoke to her deeply because she is "fascinated by dark places and their inhabitants" (2016, xii). The prisoners, though familiar with dark places, said that the book was "monotonous and depressing," rendered impenetrable by "long words and endless sentences" (12). Some admitted that they were skipping "the boring parts." The oldest member in the group, Charles, who had spent most of his life in prison, complained, "This guy still hasn't got to the point after twenty-seven pages. There were forty-four words that I had to look up in the dictionary" (12). Brottman does everything possible to try to get the men in prison to experience the book in the same richness, complexity, and depth that she herself had achieved after "many rereadings." She sums up her failure: "I hadn't been able to get across my own experience of *Heart of Darkness*, and now it was too late" (26). "I'd give it a three out of ten. . . . And that's generous," said Charles (27).

In chapter after chapter, Brottman repeatedly makes the same discovery: the book club members' version of the Great Book under discussion is not at all the same as her version. With Melville's short story "Bartleby the Scrivener," she anticipated that the archaic vocabulary could be a stumbling block, but she didn't expect "their problems to begin with the title," which they couldn't get and didn't try to pronounce (33). In this work, the narrator, an elderly lawyer, tells the story of a clerk he hired to copy legal documents, who shows up for work the first day "pallidly neat, pitiably respectable, incurably forlorn! It was Bartleby." After doing "an extraordinary quantity of writing" in the first two days, Bartleby surprised and vexed his employer by declining in "a singularly mild, firm voice" all further requests to perform duties by saying, "I would prefer not to." As Bartleby continues to refuse to explain his "passive resistance," the narrator reflects on Bartleby's empty life: "What miserable friendlessness and loneliness are here revealed!" Bartleby's preference "not to" spreads to everything in his life and finally to life itself. He gives up copying; he spends a lot of time just staring at a brick wall; he refuses to be fired or to leave the law office, where he has taken up full-time residence. Eventually he is jailed, where he "prefers not to" dine, and dies of starvation. Finding Bartleby to be an unappealing character, the prisoners said that the story was "full of loose ends" and "didn't add up," and that anyway nothing happened. Brottman represents herself as surprised to find that the men expected literature to have "a clever point, an enlightening lesson, a key 'takeaway' " and that they had "little tolerance for indirection, oblique connections, arbitrary sidetracks" (47).

Brottman begins to realize that a reason for her liking to be at the jail was escapist: that "the prison absorbed me in the same way I'd get absorbed in a book. Deep in the world of the prisoners, I'd be temporarily out of touch with my own life" (70). Nevertheless, she continues to think that if prisoners live in six-by-seven-foot prison cells, they would want to double down on dark experience in their reading, rather than use reading as an escape from their own lives (see section 4.2 on reading for escape). Brottman chose the fourth book, *Junkie*, because she thought prisoners would be "curious about Burroughs's realistic, unflinching description of the addict's underworld," and she wondered if they would recognize themselves among the represented characters (67). The men found *Junkie* "depressing." Brottman explained that being depressing is "what makes it so powerful. If you concentrate, you can get curious about what makes it depressing, and that's really interesting" (79). Reading *Junkie* was supposed to engender empathy for struggling lives that grow in the dark, but instead of recognizing the claims to kinship of these fellow victims, "the prisoners saw [the characters] as unworthy of their time" (84).

A failure of empathy turns out to be even more of a problem when the men read *Lolita*. Having immense sympathy for Humbert Humbert herself, Brottman had "never thought of *Lolita* as a story about pedophilia. To me, it was a love story and a story about language" (201). The men, however, despised Humbert Humbert and were angered by the language, which they saw as a smokescreen "to make the vile lusts of a pedophile seem high-minded" (201). J. D., serving a 50-year sentence for murder, said, "It's all a cover-up. I know what he wants to do to her" (200). Sig said, "When I was first locked up, my daughters were aged five and six. For a long time, I really worried about them meeting somebody like Humbert Humbert and me being stuck in prison and not being able to do anything about it" (204–205).

The *Maximum Security Book Club* is a brave, honest, and revealing book. It provides insight into a number of interesting themes, including the everyday life of prisoners, lockdowns, prison food, drugs, and contraband—for example, a dead cat thrown over the fence stuffed with eight cell phones (163). But for anyone interested in the reading experience, it is an especially effective dramatization of the truth that an individual's encounter with a book is highly individual and unpredictable. Your version of the book is not the same version that another reader will construct, especially if that other reader is very different from you in terms of reading skills, past experience with literary structures, life experience, and so on. An experienced reader, after multiple readings of a favorite book, will have a wonderfully rich reading experience, but she can't give that same experience to other readers just by handing them the text. Readers' advisors, take note. When recommending books for others, the thing to focus on is not the quality of the text in itself but on the quality of the reading experience of the individual reader.

Case 2: "My Reading Was Always Indiscriminate."

Elizabeth (PhD candidate in English, 35) said that as a child, "I just read what I laid my hands on.... I read omnivorously." And she still does. She explicitly rejected the notion of a very refined palate for books:

> My own attitude [to reading] is grounded in my own experience, and that is that it's like eating food. I think the people who are the best judges of food are those who like a great variety of foods from very hearty, peasant kinds of various cultures to quite highly refined meals. Those who say they only like *haute cuisine* I have my doubts about. And I feel that way about books. For example, I remember reading a translation of Chaucer's *Canterbury Tales*, a Neville Coghill Penguin edition, when I was twelve, and loving it.... "The Miller's Tale," for example, I was quite horrified by and kind of thrilled by. And I think that that reaction to Chaucer is not a bad underpinning before going on to consider the refinements of the irony and so on. And I'm doubtful of people who don't get that sort of hearty excitement from reading.... I could quite easily read, say, a Harlequin Romance and *War and Peace* and a complicated history of the Wars of the Roses at the same time and not feel that there was anything particularly jarring about that juxtaposition. They're just books—stories.... I think in fact reading is a kind of sensual pleasure as eating is. So the metaphors work quite well. I am naturally very greedy and that's why I use those images so emphatically. It is an addiction with me—reading.

Comments

Indiscriminate readers often choose metaphors of eating to characterize their reading. They read with "gusto" (from *gustus*, Latin—taste) or with relish. They say they are "omnivorous," "voracious" (from *vorare*, Latin—to swallow), "avid" (from *avere*, Latin—to crave), "greedy," or "hungry" or "gluttons" (from *gluttire*, Latin—to gulp down) for books. They are looking forward to getting their teeth into a book. The Reading Is Eating metaphor draws on a particularly rich domain of common everyday experience, capable of considerable elaboration: there are different kinds of foods, various cooking styles, and many kinds of eaters and ways of eating. Some readers—the selective readers of important books—have refined, discriminating palates. In contrast, indiscriminate readers describe themselves as having a robust appetite—they are not picky eaters or readers (Ross 1987).

What Libraries Can Do

1. Watch out for attitudes and practices that value only one type of reading at the expense of others. Use what you know about the differences between selective readers and omnivorous readers to support both types of readers with displays and booklists, targeted to each group. Omnivorous readers often seek ways to increase the variety of what they read, sometimes relying on serendipity or some arbitrary system. They could be tempted by a display of unusual books of different types, perhaps with quirky titles, and a notice such as: "In a reading rut and looking for something new?"
2. Provide help to readers who want to read "the classics" or "important books" or "significant nonfiction" by providing displays or lists of books that have a track record of appeal. A reader who wants to start reading "classic books" should probably not begin with *Ulysses* or *The Sound and the Fury*, but *The Great Gatsby* could be a good bet.

To Read More

If you are curious about which books have been considered important (and how many of them you yourself have already read), check out one of the many lists of Best Books or Books You Should Read Before You Die, such as:

> Modern Library. 1998. "100 Best Novels." Available at: http://www.modern library.com/top-100/100-best-novels/.

The top six on the Modern Library Board's List of 100 best novels are, in descending order: *Ulysses* by James Joyce, *The Great Gatsby* by F. Scott Fitzgerald, *A Portrait of the Artist as a Young Man* by James Joyce, *Lolita* by Vladimir Nabokov, *Brave New World* by Aldous Huxley, and *The Sound and the Fury* by William Faulkner.

References

Adler, Mortimer Jerome. 1940. *How to Read a Book*. New York: Simon and Schuster.

Birkerts, Sven. 2015. "Bolaño Summer: A Reading Journal." In *Changing the Subject: Art and Attention in the Internet Age*, 157–172. Minneapolis, MN: Graywolf Press.

Brottman, Mikita. 2008. *The Solitary Vice: Against Reading*. Berkeley, CA: Counterpoint Press.

Brottman, Mikita. 2016. *The Maximum Security Book Club: Reading Literature in a Men's Prison*. New York: HarperCollins.

Ross, Catherine Sheldrick. 1987. "Metaphors of Reading." *The Journal of Library History, Philosophy, and Comparative Librarianship* 22, no. 2: 147–163.

Ross, Catherine Sheldrick. 2014. "Important Books vs. Indiscriminate Reading." In *The Pleasures of Reading: A Booklover's Alphabet*, 83–91. Santa Barbara, CA: Libraries Unlimited.

Shields, David. 2013. *How Literature Saved My Life*. New York: Alfred A. Knopf.

1.3 Histories of Reading

Robert Darnton (1990, 187), historian of the book and of reading, has remarked, "Reading has a history. It was not always and everywhere the same." A reader at the end of the twentieth century may have regarded reading as quintessentially an encounter of a solitary reader with a book made of paper. And more recently many readers have begun to think of books as downloadable files to be read on screens or to be listened to while working out or commuting. But readers in ancient Greece read from scrolls made of papyrus (the dried and split stems of a reed-like plant). The codex books read by the Romans were made of parchment (animal skins). In short, the physical format of the text in all its materiality makes a big difference to the experience of readers and to their understanding of what reading is, whether they are breathing in the pungent smell of vellum (calf skin) or watching ephemeral letters dance on a screen. Clearly, literacy practices change as societies change. Readers are embodied, and reading is contextualized in a particular time and place. As Roger Chartier (1994, 8) points out, "Reading is not uniquely an abstract operation of the intellect: it brings the body into play, it is inscribed in a space and a relationship with oneself or with others." There is a large and growing body of research on the history of the book and reading, much of it focusing primarily on the formats for reading—scroll or codex or screen—and the evolution and affordances of each. More recently researchers have studied reading practices and experiences, including those of "common" or ordinary readers. And Leah Price (2012) has written a brilliant book on all the things that Victorian readers did with books that did *not* involve reading them.

Technologies for Reading: Scrolls, Codex, and Digital

A number of excellent histories of books and reading spell out the varieties of reading forms and practices and reading technologies from cuneiform tablets to hypertext. One thing is clear: reading is an activity that is deeply connected to its historical period and to the material and social conditions in which the reading occurs. Most such studies are really histories of the format—scroll, manuscript codex, printed codex, digital—rather than histories of the reading experience, although something of the experience can be inferred from the affordances of the medium. Stephen Roger Fischer's *A History of Reading* (2003), for example, includes a chapter entitled "The Papyrus Tongue," which describes the way that the papyrus scroll demanded to be read aloud. With no separation between words, no punctuation, and no distinction between upper and lower case, the physical act of reading aloud gives "meaning to the tongue where no meaning is evident to the eye" (Fischer 2003, 47).

Although we may now think of reading as a silent and solitary activity, reading out loud and reading to an audience was the norm for centuries and continued after the codex book had replaced the papyrus scroll. Alberto Manguel's *A History of Reading* (1996) spends a chapter on "The Silent Readers," in which he tells the story of Father Ambrose, reader *extraordinaire* in the fourth century AD. Father Ambrose was the first recorded instance of a silent reader. We know about him because Saint Augustine found his practice of silent reading so remarkable that he described the phenomenon in his *Confessions*. According to Augustine, "When he read, his eyes scanned the page and his heart sought out the meaning, but his voice was silent and his tongue was still . . . [O]ften when we came to visit him, we found him reading like this in silence, for he never read aloud." Eyes scanning the page and tongue held still—as Manguel points out, this is exactly how we would describe a reader today, and yet this manner of silent reading did not become usual in the West until the tenth century (Manguel 1996, 43). Chartier (1994, 8–9) says, "A history of reading must not limit itself to the genealogy of our own contemporary manner of reading, in silence and using only our eyes; it must also (and perhaps above all) take on the task of retracing the forgotten gestures and habits that have not existed for some time."

With each new technology from the introduction of the alphabet on, elegiac voices have idealized the older technology and warned of dangers and losses attendant on the new (see section 1.1 on the loss of "deep reading" and section 1.4 on digital reading). The classic case is Socrates, whom James O'Donnell (1998, 18) has described as standing "on the boundary between the worlds of spoken and written discourse." In the *Phaedrus*, Socrates is represented as deeply critical of writing. In the dialogue as written by Plato, Socrates tells the young man Phaedrus that written words, when queried, maintain the same majestic silence as a painting. Written words seem to talk to you as though they are intelligent, but if you want to know more, they give you the same answer over and over again and they make no distinction between suitable and unsuitable readers. And Socrates has a second criticism of writing: it destroys memory. He tells Phaedrus the parable of the king of Egypt and the god Throth, who was the inventor of writing, geometry, writing, and dice. Presenting to the Egyptian king each one of his inventions in turn, Throth says about the art of writing that this wonderful invention is a recipe for memory and wisdom. Not so, says the king of Egypt. In fact relying on the written word will implant forgetfulness, since people will cease to exercise memory but will rely instead on external marks. "What you have discovered is a recipe not for memory, but for reminder," said the king of Egypt. The very things that Socrates objected to—the objectivity and externality of writing—are the qualities that we now value. And it is only because the Socratic dialogues were recorded by his disciple Plato that we can know about them 2,400 years later.

Ilkka Makinen (2014, 14) describes two contrasting reading practices—the scholastic way of reading and the monastic way of reading—that occurred in the late Middle Ages, when every book was written by hand. Scholars and students in scholastic universities read compilations and abridgments—"collections of text snippets from the church fathers, Aristotle and other authoritative authors"—not whole texts from beginning to end. "There was no need for a love of reading," says Makinen, because the important thing was to analyze the text to find bits that they could use in oral discussions. Makinen (17) explains:

> A preliminary step was restructuring the text of the Bible, the basis of knowledge, in order to better manage the important information. The typography was refined and the text was organised in a more efficient way. The text was divided into more comprehensible and controllable sequences, paragraphs and verses, which were marked with numbers; chapters were given titles; concordances, tables of contents and alphabetical indexes were compiled.

These strategies helped the scholastic reader save time by reading as little as possible. The love of reading existed not in the scholastic universities but in the monasteries, where monks read books in their entirety and had a "close and rather physical" relation to the text. Monks "were engrossed in the reading of the Bible, the writings of the church fathers, and other spiritual books. They chewed, swallowed, digested, and recited the texts. They had an emotional relationship with the texts, and they had a love of reading" (Makinen 2014, 18).

It was a very long process to turn the codex book into the easily navigable technology we know today (Saenger 1997). By the thirteenth century, manuscripts were provided with pagination, indices, and concordances, all of which supported access and discontinuous reading (Hillesund 2010). Gutenberg's invention of moveable type in the fifteenth century sped up the rate of change both in book production and in reading practices. With the first Bible printed with movable metal type in Mainz, Germany, in 1456, readers realized at once its advantages: speed of production, relative cheapness, and the uniformity of the texts. Lucien Febvre and Henri-Jean Martin (1976) provide some astonishing details about the explosion of printed texts in Europe from 1450, when there was only one printing press operating in the whole of Europe, to 1500, by which time more than 15,000 different titles had been published and around 20 million books had been printed. The story of the transformative effect of Gutenberg's invention has been told many times. Various accounts make a connection between advancing print culture and the fundamental changes that were going on in Europe at the same time: transformations in habits of thought, the secularization of society, the increasing authority of science, the expansion of universities as centers of learning, the rise of the nation-state, the expansion of printing in vernacular languages, the decline of

Latin, and the loss of the Roman Catholic Church's monopolistic power over salvation. For example, Marshall McLuhan and Walter Ong have examined the transition from an oral world dominated by the ear to a world of printed texts dominated by the eye (McLuhan 1962; Ong 1982). Elizabeth Eisenstein (1979) argued that it was not the capacity to read and write alone that transformed Western Europe but the capacity of the printing press for mechanical reproduction that made possible widespread circulation of texts, the rise of modern criticism, and the emergence of the celebrity author.

Gutenberg's printed Bible was an attempt to imitate the handmade manuscript bibles of the time, with its vellum pages and typefaces designed to look like scribal letter shapes. But the logic of speed, cheapness, and reproducibility almost immediately required a shift from vellum and parchment to paper. Large folio Bibles, each one made from the skins of 200 slaughtered calves, gave way to lighter bibles in quarto or octavo format made of the much cheaper paper. Within 50 years of the invention of the printing press, most of the typographic features that we expect in a book had been introduced: pages made of paper, readable type faces with spaces between words and spaces between paragraphs, the introduction of upper and lower cases of type, the use of chapters and running heads, pagination, and smaller sized formats suitable for the hand rather than the lectern. Because of these changes, notes Fischer (2003, 212), "reading ceased being a painful process of decipherment, and became an act of pure pleasure."

With this we are well on our way to the modern reader who reads for pleasure and who has access to a satisfyingly large stock of reading materials. German historian Rolf Engelsing has identified a *Leserevolution*, or reading revolution, in the second half of the eighteenth century. A new breed of avid reader emerged. According to Engelsing, from the Middle Ages until some time toward the end of the eighteenth century, people had just a few books such as the Bible and read them "intensively," over and over again, memorizing them, reciting them aloud, and transmitting them to the next generation (Chartier 1995, 17). Then there was a shift to "extensive" reading, as the presses produced an enormously expanded range and number of publications, especially periodicals and newspapers as well as novels. The proliferation of reading materials gave rise to skimming and skipping, brief immersion, and wholesale discarding. In short, this was the beginning of the fall into the so-called superficial reading that Birkerts (2015) and Carr (2010) lamented (see section 1.1). Or could it be said that readers were developing an expanded repertoire—new strategies to deal with the enormous expansion of available materials and at the same time gaining a new "love of reading" or *gout de la lecture*.

A number of mutually supporting factors converged to produce this proliferation of reading materials: the enormous increase in printing, the drop in costs, the growth of reading societies, and the creation of lending libraries. In his landmark study, *The English Common Reader* (1957, 301), Richard Altick described the expansion of print in Britain in the 1850s:

> No longer was it possible for people to avoid reading matter; everywhere they went it was displayed—weekly papers at a penny or

twopence, complete books, enticing in their bright picture covers, at a shilling, and all fresh and crisp from the press. No wonder that the fifties, which saw the spread of Smith's stall to almost every principal railway line in the country, were also the period when the sale of books and periodicals reached unprecedented levels.

In the first decades of the nineteenth century in the United States and Canada, a similar transformation in reading went hand in hand with changes in the technology of printing and distribution. The power-driven cylinder press and new paper-making machinery dramatically lowered the cost of printed material and made it affordable to a much wider class of readers. Whereas reading in seventeenth- and eighteenth-century New England had largely been limited to a few religious and devotional texts, now readers had access to a wide selection of fiction and works of instruction in newspaper, magazine, and book formats. In the United States, in the period between 1840 and the 1890s, three formats developed to make fiction available cheaply to a large readership: the story paper, the dime novel, and the cheap library.

In Rolf Engelsing's account, "extensive" reading came at a high cost. According to Engelsing, in their pursuit of commodified amusement, people began to read a text only once before racing on to the latest work. They also read more critically as texts lost their privileged status of sacredness and authority. In Engelsing's anxiety about the expansion of extensive reading and the desacralization of the printed word, we can see some familiar oppositional pairs that reappear in other contexts: deep reading versus superficial reading and active engagement with a central canonical text versus passive consumption of a stream of ephemeral materials whose apparent novelty conceals the fact that they are essentially the same commodified and repeated product (e.g., newspapers, magazines, dime novels, series books, genre books such as romances or detective fiction, best sellers, web pages). There are, it seems, many accounts of the decline of reading from some golden age of the past when reading was deep, intensive, whole, and life-affirming. Recently Sven Birkerts (2015) and Nicholas Carr (2010) blamed the global reach of the Internet and the introduction of hypertext that invites clicking and surfing, not attentive reading. As we saw in section 1.1, in this version of the fall, the agent is neuroplasticity: skimming and surfing digital texts allegedly undermine the development of the brain circuitry needed for "deep reading."

Whatever the gains and losses of technological change, the digitizing of texts represents a shift similar to what happened with the introduction of the codex book in the fourth century AD. As Chartier has pointed out, the material form of the book—whether papyrus scroll or codex in folded pages or digital hypertext—has its own logic and encourages its own particular relationship between readers and books. When the codex book superseded the scroll as the bearer of culture, a new rapport was established between readers and their books. In particular, the invention of the page and the introduction of pagination and indexes allowed readers to mark and refer to particular passages, which could then be cited in new texts—a requirement for the development of the footnote and the scholarly article.

So far the codex book has been holding its own because of its very real advantages and at the present time readers read both print and digital. Nevertheless, reading on screens has opened up new relationships to the text, new ways of reading, and new ways of telling stories.

In the early days of digital texts, these new possibilities were explored by pioneers such as Jay Bolter (1991), George Landow (1992, 2006), Richard Lanham (1993), and Janet Murray (1998, 2011). There was a consensus that the digital media introduced a transformative shift in reading and in the ways in which cultural products are produced, disseminated, and received. These theorists saw exciting new potentials for cultural expression and for education, as the electronic environment opened up new spaces for reading and for writing. For example, Janet Murray's *Hamlet on the Holodeck* (1998) sketched out the aesthetics of a new type of narrative that can now be seen in the work of video game designers, computer programmers, and web page designers. She looked forward to cyber story-tellers' discovering new modes of representation by taking full advantage of the technology's strengths: its interactivity, nonlinearity, ability to create immersive three-dimensional landscapes and machine-based fictional characters such as chatterbots and the convergence of text and images, audio, and video. As her title suggests, Murray saw in the immersive electronic environment a powerful tech-nology of sensory illusion that is "continuous with the larger human traditions of storytelling stretching from the heroic bards through the nineteenth-century nov-elists" (Murray 1998, 26). Not surprisingly, Murray's work has been very influen-tial with game designers. By the turn of the twenty-first century, the discourse had shifted away from a preoccupation with the hyperlink as the main characterizing feature of digital writing. In *Inventing the Medium* (2011), Murray examines four key resources or "affordances" available for use by designers in digital environ-ments: computational procedures, user participation, navigable space, and ency-clopedic capacity. Lev Manovich (1999) claims that the "Computer's post-Internet identity [is] a distribution machine for older, i.e. already established media forms and content." What is new, he says, are the new computer-based tech-niques of media access (e.g., storage and retrieval from huge databases), media analysis (e.g., data mining and visualization), and media generation and manipu-lation (e.g., 3-D computer graphics). As Katherine Hales (2010, 78) puts it in her conclusion to her essay, "How We Read: Close, Hyper, Machine": "Reading has always been constituted through complex and diverse practices. Now it is time to rethink what reading is and how it works in the rich mixtures of words and images, sounds and animations, graphics and letters that constitute the environ-ments of twenty-first century literacies." (For more on this topic, see sections 1.4, 2.4, and 3.4.)

Searching for the Real Readers

One way to sort out research on reading is to distinguish between the studies that focus on real readers and the ones that don't. The history of reading has been a flourishing area of study, but actual living-and-breathing readers of the past have been hard to recover. (For discussions of research on contemporary readers using laboratory experiments, national surveys, qualitative interviews, and ethnography, see sections 1.5, 3.1, 4.1, and 4.2.) The stumbling block has been gaps in evidence about past readers. Reading is often a private act engaged in alone. Unless readers choose to write about their reading experiences, these acts go unrecorded. And when reading experiences *are* recorded in letters and diaries, those doing the recording are apt to be elite readers, not servants and factory workers. Historical research therefore tended initially to focus on aspects of reading that left more evidentiary traces: the history of the technologies of printing and distribution; studies of authorship, publishers, and publishing; studies of the distribution of reading materials by bookstores and libraries; the educational institutions that support the spread of literacy and reading; and the regulatory environment within which books are written and read, such as church and government censorship and copyright regimes (Darnton 1982). The approach to studying the readers themselves was initially indirect. Literary critics talked about "implied readers," "inscribed readers," "intended readers," or "ideal readers," whose hypothetical responses could be inferred by examining the texts. To find out what readers had access to and *might* have read, researchers studied publishers lists, catalogs of library holdings and booksellers' offerings, advertisements for books, best-seller lists, and so on.

When researchers began to study real readers, initially the focus was on elite readers, particularly reading by canonical authors to uncover "influences." Literary historians examined writers' published work for evidence of literary borrowings and verbal echoes, and they tracked down the books held in authors' personal libraries in the hope of finding underlinings of significant passages and marginalia indicating reader response. Marginalia has also proved an unexpectedly rich resource for investigating the reading of authors and everyday readers alike. The challenge for reading historians is that the commonplace and the everyday experiences are most often left unrecorded. Cathy Davidson's account of readers of nineteenth-century American novels was based, among other sources, on the marginalia inscribed in copies of early American novels.

About well-used books, Davidson (1986, 79) notes, "Broken boards, turned-down pages, and abounding marginalia . . . reveal patterns of reading, patterns of use, the surviving traces of an interpretive community long-since gone" through which "some of the early readers remain surprisingly vivid even after nearly two centuries." The undisputed expert on marginalia is English professor Heather Jackson (2001, 2005). Jackson has been a seeker-out of marginalia of all kinds—both those produced by exceptional, celebrated readers and those produced by common, anonymous readers. An editor of the Coleridge project, she confesses, "Coleridge's marginalia converted me to writing in books" (Jackson 2001, 234). In *Marginalia*, she examined some 3,000 books annotated in English by various readers from 1700 to 2000. Jackson (51) notes continuities over time in the way that readers mark books:

> Readers continue to this day to do what readers did in the Middle
> Ages, besides doing much more in the way of recording individual

impressions. They mark up their books as a way of learning and remembering what they contain, and improve them by correcting errors and adding useful relevant information.

The burgeoning field of history of the book, or *histoire du livre*, has expanded our understanding of the reading practices and experiences of ordinary readers from various historical periods and geographical areas. But, as Christine Pawley (2006) observed in her introduction to a theme issue in *Library Quarterly* on retrieving the reading experiences of ordinary readers by means of library records: "Still, some readers are more difficult to recover than others. Especially hard to access are the reading choices and practices of millions of 'common readers,' those with relatively anonymous lives and whom archival collections tend to ignore." Using census records, library catalogs and circulation records, subscription lists, estate inventories, advertisements, printing and transportation records, autobiographies, diaries, letters, and other traces, book historians have tried to recreate a detailed picture of the what and how of reading of people in various different times and places. A notable pioneering example is William Gilmore's *Reading Becomes a Necessity of Life* (1989), which examined transformations in reading in rural New England from 1780 to 1835, as reading materials in the home grew from a Bible and Farmers' Almanac to an expanded mix of newspapers, periodicals, and books, including fiction. Readers' fan letters to authors and to publishers have also proved a fruitful source of evidence of reading experience and reception. For example, Robert Darnton (1984) reconstructed the Rousseauistic reading of Jean Ranson, an eighteenth-century provincial French merchant, by examining his letters to the Société Typographique de Neuchâtel, a Swiss publisher of French books.

In an impressive literature review of the history of reading, Leah Price (2004) observes that "studies of reading take a variety of forms: some are organized around a particular reading public (Kate Flint's *The Woman Reader*, Jonathan Rose's *The Intellectual Life of the British Working Classes*, and Jacqueline Pearson's *Women Reading in Britain, 1750–1835*), others around a category of book (Radway's *Reading the Romance*), still others around a particular form of evidence (H. J. Jackson's *Marginalia: Readers Writing in Books*)." Studies of "common readers" are almost always national or regional, but are usually qualified still further by the time period and often by materials read (Jane Austen, *Uncle Tom's Cabin*, penny dreadfuls, newspapers, religious tracts) and sometimes by the places where reading takes place (monasteries, railway stations, coffee houses, barracks, behind bars, on convict ships). Through many individual case studies, the history of reading is coming together, piece by piece. In these case studies, the researchers often pay as much attention to epistemological problems of interpreting the evidence and to the strengths and gaps of their sources as they do to their conclusions. Taken together, these individual studies of particular readers at very specific times and places demonstrate the complex interrelationships between reading and other factors such as geography; economics; the gender, age, social status, and religious/political affiliation of the reader; the marketplace and what was available to read; and the context for reading within a broader community. Some readers represented themselves as reading for socially sanctioned reasons of spiritual exercise, self-improvement, and the gaining of knowledge, but others read to be captivated and enthralled.

With the volume of reading materials burgeoning in the nineteenth century to include dime novels, penny dreadfuls, and an explosion of fiction, authorities tried to regulate reading. Clergy, librarians, book reviewers, and other authorities offered readers advice on *what* to read (spiritual texts and nonfiction, especially biography), what *not* to read (dime novels and fiction, especially unrealistic romances of housemaids marrying Dukes and stories that glamorize highway-men), and *how* to read (slowly, moderately, rationally, and reflectively). Readers' accounts are full of examples of unruly readers who sometimes accepted (but often avoided) guidance, reading unsanctioned materials at times of day and in places where reading was discouraged or forbidden. As Katie Halsey and W. R. Owens (2011, 3) say in their Introduction to *The History of Reading*, vol. 2: "The approach of examining specific groups of real readers "reveals the extent to which a history of reading differs from traditional literary history in attempting to discover the texts which were actually read as opposed to those which were (or are) considered to be of literary importance and merit."

All methods of inquiry have gaps and shortcomings. Autobiographies, dia-ries, letters, and to some extent even marginalia are composed with an audience in mind of future readers by whom the writer hopes to be viewed in a favorable light. Library holdings lists, circulation records, sales records from publishers and booksellers, and even possession of a book do not provide watertight evidence that the book was actually read. As historian Simon Eliot (n.d.) remarked: "To own, buy, borrow or steal a book is no proof of wishing to read it, let alone proof of having read it." An impulse to gather and provide access to evidence of actual reading lay behind the development by Simon Eliot and W. R. Owens in the 1990s of the Reading Experience Database. Currently the UK Reading Experience Database (UK RED) is an open access database and research project housed in the English Department of the Open University. Its goal is to provide systematic evidence that can be used as the basis for studies of the practices of past readers. The hope is that if a sufficiently large collection of individual reading accounts were found and made accessible, broader patterns and trends would emerge. Eliot (n.d.) explained the rationale for the development of a systemati-cally designed database:

> [T]he evidence for reading is obscure, hidden, scattered and frag-mentary. Its discovery is often a matter of serendipity. Again and again some of the best evidence for the history of reading tends to be the by-product of other research: one stumbles over an extensively glossed book, a diary entry reveals a day devoted to specific reading with comments attached, a public library report refers to the odd reading habits of a counting-house clerk, and so on.

With the help of hundreds of volunteers, the UK RED database now contains over 30,000 searchable records of the reading experiences of people in Britain from 1450 to 1945. In addition, Canada, New Zealand, Australia, and the

Netherlands have started their own national RED projects. But what counts as a "reading experience"? To be included, there must be "a recorded engagement with a written or printed text—beyond the mere fact of possession." Sources of evidence, both published and unpublished, include diaries, letters, memoirs, marginalia, commonplace books, sociological surveys, criminal court and prison records, parliamentary reports, the Mass Observation Archives, newspaper accounts, and published books. Moreover, the RED collects records of reading of all kinds of materials from books, almanacs, magazines, and newspapers to posters, advertisements, and playbills. Kate Halsey (2012) describes the richness of detail that these categories are intended to capture:

> RED records, for example, not just the title of the text read, but anything that is known about the physical details of the artifact—was it print or manuscript? What sort of text was it—book, magazine, broadsheet, poster, ticket, handbill, advertisement, even cereal packet? Was it read as serialised instalments, three-decker Victorian novel, or an abridged illustrated children's version? Who published it? Where did the reader get hold of the text—from a circulating library, a bookseller, a friend? Did the reader just find it, or read it surreptitiously in a bookshop? We record details too, of the reader, and the circumstances of the reading experience, including the reader's name, date of birth, socio-economic group, occupation, religion and nationality ... And we also, of course, record the reader's responses to what he or she read.

The three-volume *History of Reading* (2001), coedited in various pairings by Rosalind Crone, Katie Halsey, W. R. Owens, and Shafquat Towheed, demonstrates the value of the RED records that recover everyday, commonplace experiences with reading.

Case 3: The Reading Experience Database

The best way to check out the RED is to search for an author or a book or an aspect of reading that interests you. With the advanced search function, you can use different fields to narrow your search to, say, nineteenth-century readers of science or reading experiences with books borrowed from circulating libraries. When I did a keyword search in the UK RED on "read aloud," I retrieved 265 records. For example, here's an account recorded by Dorothy Wordsworth in her journal on February 2, 1802:

> After tea I read aloud the eleventh book of *Paradise Lost*. We were much impressed, and also melted into tears.

There are 68 records of the reading of *Jane Eyre*, including this one by William Thackeray in a letter written to William Smith Williams on October 23, 1847:

I wish you had not sent me *Jane Eyre*. It interested me so much that I have lost (or won if you like) a whole day in reading it ... Some of the love passages made me cry, to the astonishment of John who came in with the coals ... Give my respect and thanks to the author, whose novel is the first English one (and the French are only romances now) that I've been able to read for many a day.

Of the 146 records of children's reading between 1850 and 1899, here is a description by one Henrietta Litchfield of Kent being read to as a child by a very protective adult reader:

Lovely books she read to us ... *The Wide Wide World*, with all the religion and deaths from consumption left out, and all the farm life and good country food left in; *Masterman Ready*, with that ass Mr Seagrave mitigated, and dear old Ready not killed by the savages; *Settlers at Home*, with the baby not allowed to die; *The Little Duke* with horrid little Carloman spared to grow more virtuous still; *The Children of the New Forest*; *The Runaway*; *The Princess and the Goblin*, and many more.

Comments

Even in this small selection of accounts, some interesting features appear: emotional responses to the text as readers melt into tears and the desire to protect children from distressing episodes that might engender tears.

What Libraries Can Do

1. Have a generous and inclusive view of what counts as a reader. Readers in history have read silently and read aloud; they have read intensively and they read extensively. The shape of books has varied from a set of three-inch square clay tablet kept in a pouch in early Mesopotamia to the contemporary paperback to a file on an eBook reader. Librarians are familiar with a range of different formats, have watched formats come and go, and have the perspective to be able to avoid fetishizing a particular format. It is all reading.

To Read More on the History of Books and Reading

Altick, Richard D. 1998. *The English Common Reader: A Social History of the Mass Reading Public 1800–1900*, 2nd ed. Columbus: Ohio State University Press.
This groundbreaking book on the development of mass literacy in England, originally published by the University of Chicago Press in 1957, has been reissued with a new foreword by Jonathan Rose. To mark the 50th anniversary of the publication

of Altick's book, a symposium was held in 2007. For a collection of essays from the conference, check out Beth Palmer and Adelene Buckland's *A Return to the Common Reader* (2011).

Darnton, Robert. 1982. "What Is the History of Books?" *Daedalus* (Summer): 65–83.

In order to map the terrain of research on reading, Darnton provides a model of the Communications Circuit, which shows the progression of a text from author to publisher to shipper to bookseller to reader. "The reader completes the circuit, because he influences the author both before and after the act of composition" (67).

Harvard University Library. "Reading: Harvard Views of Readers, Readership, and Reading History." Available at: http://ocp.hul.harvard.edu/reading/.

This website provides digital access to more than 250,000 pages from 1,200 individual items that are source materials for investigating the history of reading. You can search the catalog or do a full-text search for topics of personal interest. Or you can browse preselected topics such as Learning to Read (Historical Textbooks, Missions to Native North Americans), Reading Collectively (Choosing Books, Book Clubs, Using Libraries), and Reading on One's Own (Commonplace Books, Marginalia).

References

Birkerts, Sven. 2015. *Changing the Subject: Art and Attention in the Internet Age.* Minneapolis, MN: Graywolf Press.

Bolter, Jay. 1991/2001. *Writing Space: The Computer, Hypertext, and the Remediation of Print*, 2nd ed. Mahwah, NJ: Lawrence Erlbaum.

Carr, Nicholas. 2010. *The Shallows: What the Internet Is Doing to Our Brains.* New York: W.W. Norton.

Chartier, Roger. 1994. *The Order of Books: Readers, Authors, and Libraries in Europe between the Fourteenth and Eighteenth Centuries.* Translated by Lydia G. Cochrane. Stanford, CA: Stanford University Press.

Chartier, Roger. 1995. *Forms and Meanings: Texts, Performances, and Audiences from Codex to Computer.* Philadelphia: University of Pennsylvania Press.

Crone, Rosalind, and Shafquat Towheed. 2011. *The History of Reading. Vol. 3, Methods, Strategies, Tactics.* Basingstoke, England: Palgrave Macmillan.

Darnton, Robert. 1982. "What Is the History of Books?" *Daedalus* 111, no. 3: 65–83.

Darnton, Robert. 1984. "Readers Respond to Rousseau: The Fabrication of Romantic Sensitivity." In *The Great Cat Massacre and Other Episodes in French Cultural History*, 209–249. New York: Penguin.

Darnton, Robert. 1990. "First Steps toward a History of Reading." In *The Kiss of Lamourette: Reflections in Cultural History.* London: Faber & Faber.

Davidson, Cathy N. 1986. *Revolution and the Word: The Rise of the Novel in America.* New York and Oxford: Oxford University Press.

Eisenstein, Elizabeth L. 1979. *The Printing Press as an Agent of Change: Communications and Cultural Transformations in Early Modern Europe.* 2 vols. Cambridge: Cambridge University Press.

Eliot, Simon. n.d. "The Reading Experience Database; or, What Are We to Do about the History of Reading?" In *Reading Experience Database.* Available at: http://www.open.ac.uk/Arts/RED/redback.htm.

Fischer, Steven Roger. 2003. *A History of Reading*. London: Reaktion Books.

Febvre, Lucien, and Henri-Jean Martin. 1958/1976. *The Coming of the Book: The Impact of Printing, 1450–1800*. Translated by David Gerard. London: NLB.

Gilmore, William. 1989. *Reading Becomes a Necessity of Life: Material and Cultural Life in Rural New England, 1790–1835*. Knoxville, TN: University of Tennessee Press.

Hales, N. Katherine. 2010. "How We Read: Close, Hyper, Machine." *ADE Bulletin* 150: 62–78. Available at: https://www.scribd.com/document/126406312/How-We-Read-Close-Hyper-Machine-N-Katherine-Hayles#.

Halsey, Katie, and W. R. Owens, eds. 2011. *The History of Reading, Volume 2: Evidence from the British Isles, c. 1750–1950*. Basingstoke, England: Palgrave Macmillan.

Halsey, Katie. 2012. "Working-Class Readers in the Nineteenth Century: An Introduction to the 'Reading Experience Database, 1450–1945' (RED)." In *Educating the People through Reading Material in the 18th and 19th Centuries*, 49–66. Edited by Reinhart Siegert. Bremen, Germany: Edition Lumiere. Available at: http://dspace.stir.ac.uk/bitstream/1893/9280/1/04-Halsey-Sonderdruck.pdf.

Hillesund, Terje. 2010. "Digital Reading Spaces: How Expert Readers Handle Books, the Web and Electronic Paper." *First Monday* 15, no. 4 (April 5). Available at: http://uncommonculture.org/ojs/index.php/fm/article/view/2762/2504.

Jackson, Heather J. 2001. *Marginalia: Readers Writing in Books*. New Haven, CT: Yale University Press.

Jackson, Heather J. 2005. *Romantic Readers: The Evidence of Marginalia*. New Haven, CT: Yale University Press.

Landow, George P. 1992. *Hypertext: The Convergence of Technology and Contemporary Critical Theory*. Baltimore: Johns Hopkins University Press.

Landow, George. 2006. *Hypertext 3.0: Critical Theory and New Media in the Era of Globalization*. Baltimore: Johns Hopkins University Press.

Lanham, Richard. 1993. *The Electronic Word: Technology, Democracy, and the Arts*. Chicago, IL: University of Chicago Press.

Makinen, Ilkka. 2014. "Reading Like Monks: The Death or Survival of the Love of Reading?" In *Reading in Changing Society. Studies in Reading and Book Culture 2*, 13–27. Edited by Marju Lauristin and Peeter Vihalemm. Tartu, Estonia: University of Tartu Press.

Manguel, Alberto. 1996. *A History of Reading*. New York: Viking.

Manovich, Lev. 1999. "Avant-garde as Software." Available at: http://manovich.net/content/04-projects/027-avant-garde-as-software/24_article_1999.pdf.

McLuhan, Marshall. 1962. *The Gutenberg Galaxy: The Making of Typographic Man*. Toronto: The University of Toronto Press.

Murray, Janet H. 1998. *Hamlet on the Holodeck: The Future of Narrative in Cyberspace*. Boston, MA: MIT Press.

Murray, Janet H. 2011. *Inventing the Medium: Principles of Interaction Design as a Cultural Practice*. Cambridge, MA: MIT Press.

O'Donnell, James J. 1998. *Avatars of the Word: From Papyrus to Cyberspace*. Cambridge, MA: Harvard University Press.

Ong, Walter J. 1982. *Orality and Literacy: The Technologizing of the Word*. London and New York: Methuen.

Palmer, Beth, and Adelene Buckland, eds. 2011. *A Return to the Common Reader: Print Culture and the Novel, 1850–1900*. Farnham, Surrey, and Burlington, VT: Ashgate Publishing.

Pawley, Christine. 2006. "Retrieving Readers: Library Experiences." *Library Quarterly* 76, no. 4: 379–387.

Price, Leah. 2004. "Reading: The State of the Discipline." *Book History* 7: 303–320.
    Available at: http://muse.jhu.edu/article/174092.
Price, Leah. 2012. *How to Do Things with Books in Victorian England*. Princeton and
    Oxford: Oxford University Press.
Saenger, Paul. 1997. *Space between Words: The Origins of Silent Reading*. Stanford, CA:
    Stanford University Press.
Steinberg, Sigfrid Henry. 1974. *Five Hundred Years of Printing*. Harmondsworth, England,
    and Baltimore: Penguin Books.
Stock, Brian. 1983. *The Implications of Literacy: Written Language and Models of
    Interpretation in the Eleventh and Twelfth Centuries*. Princeton, NJ: Princeton
    University Press.
Towheed, Shafquat, and W. R. Owens, eds. 2011. *The History of Reading, Volume 1,
    International Perspectives, c.1500–1990*. Basingstoke, England: Palgrave
    Macmillan.

1.4 Reading in the Digital Age

In academic discourse about screens versus paper, a repertoire for talking about reading has emerged. Some formats are "static" and "inert," while others are "interactive" and "dynamic." Some invite energetic engagement of the active reader, while others encourage passivity. Some are "sensuous," while others are flat. Some are "deep," while others are "shallow" (see section 1.1). In *Gutenberg's Fingerprint*, Merilyn Simonds (2017) says, "A printed book is a world I can hold in my hands. . . . Print books encourage depth; digital encourage breadth." Here is Keith Houston (2016, xvi) in his Introduction, inviting readers to pick up a big, heavy hardback in their hands: "Open it and hear the rustle of paper and crackle of glue. Smell it! Flip through the pages and feel the breeze on your face. An eBook imprisoned behind the glass of a tablet or computer screen is an inert thing by comparison." On the other hand, David Reinking (2001, 202–203), writing as a media expert within the discipline of education, says that the experience of reading conventional print is "static, silent, introspective, and typically serious" in contrast to reading in digital environments, which are "more sensuous, interactive, and playful." Printed texts, he says, are "static and inert," throwing the whole burden of keeping interested on the unsupported reader. Conversely, digital texts "require or encourage an active orientation to reading" because the lack of a "single linear and hierarchical structure" turns readers into writers as they "choose their own paths through linked textual nodes."

In some cases, the very same feature can be singled out by one observer as evidence of active engagement and by another as evidence of passivity. Consider sparseness of sensory inputs. Remember Maryanne Wolf in section 1.1, who argued that when readers are actively filling in gaps in a sparse text, their intellectual energies are aroused: "Little is given to the reader outside the text. For that reason, readers must engage in an active construction of meaning, in which they grapple with the text." The opposite is the case, claims Reinking: digital texts do a better job of engaging readers because they can integrate pictures, animations, and sound. But wait! Here's author Tim Parks (2015, 18) explaining that the eBook (to be distinguished from hypertext) is superior to traditional print because it is more austere:

> The e-book, by eliminating all variations in the appearance and weight of the material object we hold in our hand and by discouraging anything but our focus on where we are in the sequence of words (the page once read disappears, the page to come has yet to appear) would seem to bring us closer than the paper book to the essence of the literary experience. Certainly it offers a more austere, direct engagement with the words appearing before us and disappearing behind us than the tradition paper book offers. . . . It is as if one had been freed from everything extraneous and distracting surrounding the text to focus on the pleasure of the words themselves.

In these discussions, the active repertoire is always used to describe the favored technology, with the passive repertoire being reserved for the other guy. The use of these terms has the effect of turning the discussion into a moral argument. Framed this way, it is not just a question of difference and change; it is framed as a question of decline and the loss of what most properly constitutes human nature at its best. But what lies behind this hand-wringing?

What Are We Afraid Of?

Lynne Coady (2016), an award-winning Canadian novelist, started off her Kreisel Lecture on reading in the digital age by invoking a Sesame Street book about Grover called *The Monster at the End of This Book*. In this children's classic, Grover reads the title page, learns about the existence of the scary monster, and tries everything he can think of to prevent the reader from getting to the dreaded last page. It turns out, in a self-referential turn, that the monster is really Grover himself. Similarly, suggests Coady, the monster at the end of the horror story of digital reading is us: ordinary people who enjoy popular culture and who seek out entertainment of all kinds on the Internet. When new and expanding audiences arise for any new medium—dime novels and penny dreadfuls in the nineteenth century, television in the 1950s, video games in the 1970s, and most recently the Internet—the worry always is that people will read/view/engage with the wrong stuff: sex, violence, and sensationalism. "Internet culture," Coady says, "is our latest lowbrow bogeyman—the thing 'serious' writers feel an indirect pressure to eschew" (11). Hence the laments that people are skimming and clicking through discontinuous text in a crab-like sideways movement but not drilling down into serious works, usually literary novels. While it is true that all of Henry James and Charles Dickens and 40,000 other books can be downloaded free from the Gutenberg site, these serious works are not read by the majority, as critics point out. Instead people are reading and viewing blogs, unfiltered websites, self-published books, reviews on Amazon and Goodreads written by nonprofessionals, trashy entertainment, cat videos, and pornography. But the monster is us and always has been: there *never* has been a time when the reading of demanding literary texts has been a majority activity. As Margaret Atwood has pointed out, "We imagine a past about things being better, but we've forgotten a lot of stuff. Out of the Gutenberg printing presses poured lots of pornography, which we decided to forget. The classics are just the part of the iceberg that is still visible" (Lacy 2012).

Margaret Atwood (2012) addresses the whole highbrow/lowbrow issue in a more playful way in her *Guardian* article, "Why Wattpad Works," which begins as follows:

> "But Margaret," you can hear [people] whispering. "You're a literary icon at the height of your powers; it says so on your book covers. Why are you sneaking out with an online story-sharing site heavy on romance, vampires and werewolves? You should be endorsing Literature, capital L. Get back up on that pedestal! Strike a serious pose! Turn to stone!"

In 2012, Atwood joined the Toronto-based, social reading site Wattpad, which started in 2006 as a space where writers post their work and readers read for free. Writers share their work chapter by chapter, so that feedback from readers can help shape story development. Atwood notes, "This is nothing new. [It's] simply being reinvented by the internet ... *The Pickwick Papers* was published serially and people would respond to the chapters by letter. That's why Sam Weller became such a big part of the book" (Flood 2012). On Wattpad, two million writers post 100,000 stories and poems a day—fanfiction, mystery, romance, science fiction, werewolves, and vampires—in 25 languages for 20 million readers (Streitfeld 2014; see also section 3.4). Atwood herself posted a serial novel on Wattpad that, with feedback from readers, turned into her dystopian novel, *The Heart Goes Last* (2015).

Atwood (2012) says that she supports Wattpad because she supports literacy: "I got into trouble a while ago for saying that I thought the internet led to increased literacy—people scolded me about the shocking grammar to be found online—but I was talking about fundamentals: quite simply, you can't use the net unless you can read. Reading and writing, like everything else, improve with practice." To illustrate her point about the expansion of literacy, Atwood says that Allen Lau, cofounder of Wattpad, got a thank-you letter "from an old man in a village in Africa":

> The village had no school, no library, no landline, and no books. But it had a mobile phone, and on that they could read and share the Wattpad stories.... So that's why I'm judging the Wattpad poetry contest. Wattpad opens the doors and enlarges the view in places where the doors are closed and the view is restricted. And somewhere out there in Wattpadland, a new generation is testing its wings.

Managing Attention

The 100,000 stories and poems posted each day on Wattpad and the 700,000 books self-published each year may be an encouraging sign that more people are practicing their reading and writing skills, but they also signal the challenge of "overload" and "glut." Our scarce resource now is time and attention. Richard A. Lanham (2006) wrote *The Economics of Attention* to address what he calls the shift from solid "stuff" to "fluff" and our corresponding sense of "drowning," being "overwhelmed," and "inundated." He asks, "What happens to our expressive space when it moves from the stuff of the book to the volatile fluff of the computer screen? What kind of attention economy prevails there?" (21). But as early as the sixteenth-century people were already feeling overwhelmed by the "multitude of books." Ann Blair (2003) begins her article on "Reading Strategies for Coping with Information Overload ca. 1550–1700" with the case of Conrad Gesner, whose dream was to create a universal bibliography of all known books. In the preface to his *Bibliotheca univeralis* (1545), Gesner complained of that "confusing and harmful abundance of books." So a key skill that readers need is how to *avoid* reading (see the description of scholastic reading in section 1.3). Ann Blair (2003) remarks, "Many of the methods for managing an abundance of texts have remained identifiable in one form or another from antiquity to the present day: they typically involve selecting, sorting, and storing, carried out in various combinations and with various motives and technologies." Ann Blair's splendid book, *Too Much to Know* (2010), is an authoritative guide to strategies developed by scholars in early Modern Europe to cope with information overload.

In an economy of abundance, web writers and designers have developed tactics to help readers avoid reading. Readers want to be able to make shortcuts, find things quickly, and zero in on just those few passages that they want to read with close attention. As Naomi Baron (2015, xiii) points out, "If reading habits change, so do the ways authors tend to write." In her definitive guide to using typography, *Thinking with Type* (2010, 87), graphic designer Ellen Lupton explains:

> Designers provide ways into—and out of—the flood of words by breaking up text into pieces and offering shortcuts and alternate routes through masses of information. . . . Typography helps readers navigate the flow of content. The user could be searching for a specific piece of data or struggling to quickly process a volume of content in order to extract element for immediate use. Although many books define the purpose of typography as enhancing the readability of the written word, one of design's most humane functions is, in actuality, to help readers avoid reading.

In *Type on Screen* (2014), Lupton has written a companion guide about using typographic elements for screen-based applications. Her point is that reading is not one kind of thing but many and that different media support the process of reading in different ways. Similarly, Jakob Nielsen (2000), who has used eye-tracking equipment to record what readers look at when they read web pages, makes the case that good writing varies, depending on the medium and the reader's purpose: "Web users don't like to read. . . . They want to keep moving and clicking." Therefore, web writers should create pages that are easily scannable. They should break up blocks of text into smaller units, using typographic devices such as highlighted keywords, spacing, subheadings, bullets, and boxes.

Web users don't want an immersive, "deep" experience; they are searching, scanning, and mining. Anything that slows them down—ambiguous icons, confusing navigation bars, stretching information out over multiple pages, too many levels to click through—is a hindrance. In short, the stylistic features that enhance reading speed, so deplored by Nicholas Carr (2010) and Sven Birkerts (2015) (see section 1.1), are responses to the needs of readers, who have different expectations of different kinds of text.

Lupton (2010, 98) asks why readers of websites are less patient than readers of print. She says, "It is a common assumption that digital displays are inherently more difficult to read than ink on paper. Yet HCI studies conducted in the late 1980s proved that crisp black text on a white background can be read just as efficiently from a screen as from a printed page." Web users are impatient, Lupton says, not because of the essential character of display technologies but because these web readers have different expectations than do print readers. "They expect to be in search mode, not processing mode. Users also expect to be disappointed, distracted, and delayed by false leads. The cultural habits of the screen are driving changes in design for print, while at the same time affirming print's role as a place where extended reading can still occur."

Materiality

The fact of digital text throws the spotlight on something that was not noticed when the codex book was the only game in town: the physical experience of reading. Reading is a process not only of brains but also of eyes and hands and whole bodies. As Thomas McLaughlin (2015, 1) puts it in *Reading and the Body*, we think of reading as "an act of consciousness": "But reading is undeniably a bodily act. Eyes scan the page, hands hold the book, body postures align the entire musculoskeletal frame, adapting to the materiality of the book and to the physical space the reading body inhabits." Our bodies engage differently with text depending on whether we are reading a hardcover book, a paperback, a large computer screen, a dedicated e-reading device, a tablet, or a smartphone. In each case, there is a different engagement of hand and the material form of the text, a different posture of the body. After summarizing key studies on how users respond to new reading technologies, Terje Hillesund (2010) notes that "at some point all reading technologies have been new, and for coming generations it takes years of practice to internalise the use of dominant reading technologies in society, whether they be clay tablets, scrolls, manuscripts, printed books or computers."

The embodied nature of reading has always been the case, of course, but digital reading on screens provides what Marshall McLuhan has called an antienvironment, making the taken-for-granted an object of notice. I discovered the pull of screens-as-antienvironment when, as part of my long-standing project of interviewing avid readers (see section 1.6 for details), I added a question in 2011 on eBook reading. This timing captured readers just when eBook reading devices were moving from the domain of early adopters into a wider market. The question, "How do you feel about reading eBooks?" prompted, from the 22 interviewees, brief discussions of the pros and cons of digital reading followed by an enthusiastic account of what they loved about the physical book. For many like Chloe (nurse instructor, age 49), reading has always been "a very sensuous experience." She says, "I like feeling the page—I like the smell of the book." Noah (student, age 28) likes pages made of paper: "I like writing my funny comments on the side." Nadia (librarian, age 29) remembers where particular passages are located on the physical page: "I'm quite conscious of the shape of the words on the page. I'm conscious of not just where the words *are* on the page, but the spaces, the margins . . . If I want to try and find something, I'll know whether it's on the right or left hand side, part way down, end of a paragraph, beginning of a paragraph or whatever." Two themes cropped up repeatedly when avid readers considered the physical book. First, there is the sensuality of the experience of engaging with the book, which, beyond the visual appeal of book covers and fonts, involves the heft of the book in hand, the smell of binding and paper, and the rustle of turned pages. Second, there is the intimacy of the reading experience, which these avid print book readers fear will be lost in the digital environment, where the habitual ways of engaging with a text are changing. Kjell (student, age 25), who calls himself "a book snob," mentioned "the intrinsic quality of holding a book in your hand and just being absorbed in that text. I don't expect to get that same sort of intimacy with an eBook."

Lynne Coady (2016, 40) had a similar experience when, in preparation for her Kreisel Lecture on digital reading, she asked her 5,000 Twitter followers to describe what quality exactly they enjoyed about the experience of reading a book. She expected to hear about communion with the writer's mind, immersion in imaginary worlds, and absorption in language. She got that, but was surprised to get as much, if not more, "rhapsodizing on qualities like smell. The texture of pages beneath the fingers. The creak of a fresh binding being broken." Coady reported that these Twitter followers often mentioned the physical pleasures connected with reading a book, including special beverages, the "weight of a new stack in a bag, being carried home from the bookstore," and the satisfaction of seeing books "lined up on a shelf." She said, "The physical activity of 'curling up' with a book was evoked multiple times. . . . I now understand that readers' enthusiasm for the physicality of books isn't about romance, it's about pleasure itself."

In short, for many current readers, the printed book still represents the aura of bookishness, which goes beyond reading itself to include such elements as the book as an object of collection and display, the rituals of reading in a particular chair with beverage in hand, and the book as a generational link between grandparents, parents, and children. Andrew Piper (2012, ix) points out that, because the codex book got there first, "we cannot think about our electronic future without contending with its antecedent, the bookish past":

> Books and screens are now bound up with one another whether we like it or not. Only in patiently working through this entanglement will we be able to understand how new technologies will, or will not, change how we read. I can imagine a world without [print] books. I cannot imagine one without reading.

Screens and Paper

Many predictions and statements get made about the future of reading, the issue of reading print versus reading screens, and the relation between digital reading and other media. But what is the evidence? Can various claims be generalized, or are they simply statements of individual anxiety and personal preference during a time of technological change? We all know people who say they always have to print out something if they really want to read and understand it. And we know others who say they are perfectly happy reading on screens with no loss of pleasure, retention, or feeling of intimacy. So does it all come down to individual preference? Here are some of these predictions and claims:

- *Reading on screens leads to the death of reading.*

  The most committed readers read in many formats—printed books, screens on smartphones, tablets, and laptops—and at the same time they are consumers of other media including radio, television, streaming video, films, and video-games. In a summary of the 2012 survey, the Pew Research Center described the early adopters of eBooks as unusually bookish, standing out "in almost every way from other kinds of readers." According to the summary of findings of the Pew (2012) study, "Foremost, they are relatively avid readers of books in all formats: 88 percent of those who read eBooks in the past 12 months also read printed books. Compared with other book readers, they read more books. They read more frequently for a host of reasons: for pleasure, for research, for current events, and for work or school. They are also more likely than others to have bought their most recent book, rather than borrowed it, and they are more likely than others to say they prefer to purchase books in general, often starting their search online."

- *Young people are most at risk of becoming nonreaders because they are early adopters of screens.*

  A larger proportion of younger, compared to older, people have in fact taken to reading digital texts on screens—newspapers, websites, blogs, eBooks. The Pew Research Center found that in 2016 some 35 percent of 18- to 29-year-olds reported having read an eBook in the past year as compared with 19 percent of people 65 and over. But younger readers haven't stopped reading print books. Here is a summary from the same study: "These young adults are more likely than their elders to read books in various digital formats, but are also more likely to read print books as well: 72% have read a print book in the last year, compared with 61% of seniors" (Pew 2016).

- *Print books will disappear or become, like vinyl records, a small niche market.*

  The printed book has considerable staying power. In 2010, Amazon announced that for the first time it was selling more digital books than hardcovers (Tweney 2010). The Pew Research Center (2014) reported in January 2014 that, following the gift-giving season, half of Americans own either a tablet or an e-reader and 55 percent have a smartphone. Some people have predicted a relentless process of displacement of print by screens, but then in 2015 sales of eBooks leveled out. Since 2011, the Pew Research Center has tracked American reading of print books, eBooks, and audio books. The proportion of Americans who said that in the past year they had read an eBook increased from percent in 2011 to 28 percent in 2014 and then remained flat at 28 percent in their most recent survey in 2016. During this period, 65 to 70 percent, give or take, said that they had read a print book in the past year. In 2016, one-quarter of Americans said they had read *no* books in any format, and another quarter said they read books in multiple formats. Only 6 percent said they read digital books but not print books (Pew 2016). It turns out that many people read in a variety of formats, their choice depending on factors such as purpose and type of reading, convenience, and access to the desired text. Readers of the denigrated romance genre have been the strongest adopters of digital books, citing accessibility to desired titles and privacy, which protects them from other people's judgments about their reading choices. It seems likely that print and screens will eventually reach an equilibrium, where both play an important role in the ecology of reading.

- *Print books are better than eBooks when it comes to speed and accuracy of the reading and to retention of what is read.*

From the 1980s on, researchers in psychology, computer science, and library and information science have compared print to screens as a medium for reading, the goal being to improve e-reading technologies. Typically such studies use a laboratory experiment to measure and compare the speed and accuracy with which randomized subjects complete an assigned task on screens and in print. Until the mid-1990s, paper beat screens. Then screen technology got better, and studies began to report findings of "no significant difference" (Jabr 2013). Franziska Kretzschmar and colleagues (2013) used an experimental design to test whether reading from screens requires more cognitive effort than reading paper: "Young and elderly adults read short texts on three different reading devices: a paper page, an e-reader and a tablet computer and answered comprehension questions about them while their eye movements and EEG were recorded." Participants strongly preferred paper, but for young adults there was no difference in fixation durations or EEG activity across the three media tested. For older adults reading on a tablet required shorter fixations and lower EEG activity, suggesting an advantage for online reading, perhaps because screens offer "a higher degree of visual discriminability." There were no differences across media in "comprehension accuracy" in either the young adult group or the elderly group. In short, people perceive screen-reading as taking more effort, but they may well be wrong.

- *Print books are better than eBooks when readers want the experience of "deep" reading, absorption, intimacy, and being "lost in a book."*

When the Kindle was first released in 2009, Jeff Bezos, founder and CEO of Amazon.com, said, "Our top design objective was for Kindle to disappear in your hands—to get out of the way—so you can enjoy your reading. We hope you'll quickly forget you're reading on an advanced wireless device and instead be transported into that mental realm readers love, where the outside world dissolves, leaving only the author's stories, words and ideas" (Brown 2009). So far, a majority of studies indicate that readers pick digital reading when they are looking for something quick, but prefer print for prolonged immersion in a long form such as a novel or nonfiction book read for pleasure. That effortless experience of reading where the screen drops out of awareness probably requires some practice and familiarity with the new technology. The choice between print or screens seems to be a case of individual preference: people who enjoy reading novels on screens say that they have the "lost in a book" experience with eBooks; those who don't, don't. Quite possibly these preferences are generational. When Åse Kristine Tveit and Anne Mangen (2014) asked 143 15-year-old students in Norway to read Lars Christensen's novel *The Joker* in one format for 15 minutes and then switch to the other format, they found that overall most students preferred reading on the Sony e-reader to reading on paper. This preference was particularly marked among boys and reluctant readers, whereas the most avid readers preferred paper. On the question, "Most comfortable for my eyes," 54 percent preferred the e-reader, 29 percent preferred paper, and 17 percent said there was no difference. On the question, "Easiest to immerse into the story," 33 percent picked the e-reader, 29 percent said paper, and 38 percent said no difference. The biggest gap between the e-reading and paper experience related to the physical experience. The eBook was rated "Best to hold on to" by 71 percent and "Most comfortable in turning over the pages" by 75 percent of the teen participants.

How Do Real Readers Read Digital Text?

Laboratory experiments based on timed reading tasks may not be generalizable to voluntary reading in everyday settings. Surveys tell us about broad trends but don't tell us much about people's practices, motivations, and experiences. Therefore, we need more fine-grained studies to shed light on the actual, everyday, embodied experience of real readers reading in the contexts in which reading naturally occurs. A small body of empirical research is emerging, the findings of which are suggestive and sometimes surprising. For example, Terje Hillesund (2010) interviewed 10 academic "expert readers" to find out how they handled print and digital texts in the performance of their scholarly reading of articles and books. Hillesund found that his group of academic readers engaged in sustained, discontinuous reading, which, he says, "seems to be characteristic of scholarly expert reading"—that is, they read for a long, uninterrupted period but not in linear order from beginning to end. Instead they jumped back and forth within a text or between different texts. Relevance to their current scholarly project was the litmus test these expert readers used to decide what is interesting and what is not: Will this text be usable for the scholar's own future writing? When one interviewee, Adam, searches for full-text articles in journal portals, he looks at a lot of potentially useful articles, "skimming abstracts, looking at keywords, studying reference lists and reading introductory parts of articles." According to Hillelsund (2010), many articles are weeded out as not worth consideration, some are downloaded and stored, and a few of these are printed out on paper to be carefully read either immediately or later. Hillesund remarks that Adam's reading may look "superficial, but his skimming provides him with a broader picture and is actually the first move in an exhaustive in-depth reading of selected articles."

To turn to everyday readers, Anika Hupfeld and her colleagues (2013) in the United Kingdom used a photo diary method together with intensive interviews to investigate how 16 participants read digital eBooks for pleasure. Hupfeld and colleagues recruited nine male and seven female eBook-reading participants with a view to achieving a mix of gender, age, and device use (e-reader, smartphone, tablet, laptop). To find out how eBook reading fits into readers' everyday lives, they asked participants to keep a photo diary, using a digital camera to capture episodes of reading. The researchers followed up with an interview to ask questions about each picture. In the photo diaries, which were kept for an average of 10 days, participants were asked to record "all instances of book and e-book reading, as well as any behaviors relating to book and e-book use, such as acquisition, annotation, organization, sharing" (2013, 5). Participants were also asked to record any other reading, such as reading news, magazines, or work documents, done on the same devices used for eBook reading. Three readers also decided to keep written diaries.

The rich data provided by the 16 participants allowed Hupfeld and colleagues to explore a wide range of facets within the ecology of e-reading, starting with motivations for acquiring an e-reader in the first place and proceeding to how readers experimented, learning what their device did, and did not do, well. Hupfeld et al. (2013, 6) summarize, "This [initial] phase of use was often marked by a period of 'playing around' during which assumptions were tested, unexpected uses discovered and users came to an understanding of which kinds of reading the devices supported very well, and which kinds they did not." A section on managing the e-reading process focuses on how people acquired, used, organized, deleted, and retained digital content, "sometimes in contrast to these same, more ingrained practices with print books" (7). For example, P1 (male, 50+) said he bought print books rather than eBooks on occasions when he expected to reread the book, share it, give it as a gift, or read it in the bath. P9 (female, 50+) distinguished between her eBook library, which she regards as a "short-term and functional" collection that she will "read and discard," and her physical books, some of which she has kept since she was seven and to which she feels emotionally attached: "I can't imagine having my e-reader collection when I was seven and keeping them until I was 55, it's just not the same" (9). Many said that they felt that, with the option of eBooks, they read more because, if they wanted a particular book, they could download it almost instantly and they could read opportunistically on their device during waiting time.

After a settling-in period of becoming familiar with the reading device, participants wove their eBook reading into the routines of their life, reading at home and on the go—alongside, and in combination with, reading printed books. Hupfeld and colleagues report, "People were as inclined to curl up with an e-reader as they would have been with a traditional paper book" (9). P2 (female, 50+) read on her Kindle at breakfast, keeping her hands free for coffee and cutlery, and she also found the Kindle good for reading outside, drink in hand, without the pages fluttering in the wind. A smartphone loaded with eBooks allowed for opportunistic reading as well as choice to suit a reading mood. A new father P16 (male, 18–29) said that having books on his iPhone meant that "when I do have a moment to quickly read I can do so; it's not like having to make sure that you've got a paperback book with you all the time.... If I wasn't reading an e-reader I wouldn't be reading anywhere near as much as I used to [before becoming a father]." Hupfeld and colleagues conclude that eBooks "support both ad hoc and routine reading practices in new ways": because of lightweight e-readers, always-present smartphones, and access to downloadable new content, "e-reading can be tailored to suit many new situations."

With eBooks and audio books becoming widely available, many avid readers are like Regna (proof reader, age 29) from my study, who says, "I like them all because they all have different purposes":

> I like hard cover. I like it for collecting's sake—all my *Harry Potters* are hard covers, and I like to hear the crack of the spine when you open it. And they just last longer, which is nice. Paperbacks are definitely my favorites, just because they fit in my bag. Audio books I can see for long drives, or if your eyes are too tired to read, or if you want to listen to *Harry Potter* and get all those little things you never noticed before. EBooks I like, but it's not for me. I like having a collection. I like having a different book in my bag every week. I like appreciating the physical design and typesetting of the book. But I do like them for the people who read tons and tons of mass market paperbacks, and they just can't have that many physical books. Or for travelling. And then there is the anonymity and storage that are advantages of eBooks.

Case 4: It Is All Storytelling

Kathleen Schreurs, a recent doctoral graduate at Western, has contributed this excerpt from her case study of Dean, whom she interviewed as part of her doctoral research on the implications of digital and electronic culture on reading and writing.

Dean is an award-winning author of short stories and novels. Like many authors, he publishes his works in print and online as eBooks and posts on websites and blogs. He is also an avid reader and works part-time at a university library. During an interview, Dean remarked on the current trend to use "e" before words such as writing, reading, and book in order to convey the digital and electronic ways stories are written and read.

> I: Do you feel that the term *e-writing* is appropriate to describe electronic trends in writing today?

Dean: I would always default back to just writing and story—a narrative, you know. Putting a label on it like "e" sounds kind of like an awareness that's right now. Long term, I think it's just gonna be always called *writing*.

I: Do you think *e-reading* will go back to being *reading*?

Dean: I think so. People won't be as aware of [the format]. It will be *reading*. Story has always been story; books have always been books. Yeah, that's a good one, though. Books are interesting because: will they call them books forever? Reading and story—I think they'll always be those things by themselves. It's kind of like a hyper-awareness right now—the digital revolution is happening and people are like, "Right, there's a difference between electronic and not." But I don't know that that will always be the case. That doesn't mean that there won't always be a distinction between the two, but just terminology might evolve so that it's all kind of the one thing.

Comments

This passage illustrates the varying and shifting terminology of reading and writing in the digital age. This era marked by the development of new media is one in which transitory language has been adopted to describe new (electronic and digital) ways of reading and writing. One way this is accomplished is through the use of prefixes like "e," "i," and "cyber." Like other terms in society's newly adopted "e" lexicon, such as "e-commerce," "e-health," "e-business," "e-zine," "e-card," "e-dating," and so on, we have embraced such terms as "eBook" and "e-reading." Through interviews with authors, we see that these terms variously describe works that are digitally born, composed, and read on a computer or other electronic device; texts that are online; and works that make use of the language, style, and formats of e-culture such as blogs, social media, and fanfiction sites. However, Dean sees, as others do, consistency in readership and authorship. That constancy is the dedication to story. While other aspects of the craft of writing may change, story remains. Other authors in this study remarked, "I still think storytelling is the same no matter how you're getting it down on the page... There's different tools at your disposal and how you use it is up to you but it's still storytelling" and "The primary commitment of creative writing is to tell story regardless of the form." Authors recognize story as an element of their work that will stand the test of time. While terminology may change to reflect the digital revolution, the soul of authorship remains constant for authors: the dedication to sharing stories with readers.

To Read More on Screens and Paper

Bracken, James K. 2014. "Reading Screens vs. Reading Paper: New Literacies?" *ALA Choice* (December). Available at: http://ala-choice.libguides.com/c.php? g=407670&p=2776670.

James K. Bracken, dean and professor, University Libraries, at Kent State University, offers a thread through the labyrinth of materials on the contentious question, "Which is better for reading—print books or screen?" He reviews some 100 English-language books published since 2000, providing succinct one- to three-sentence summaries of the highlights of each. This literature review is divided into five sections: Reference Literature, Textbooks, Histories, Critical Studies, and Attention and Engagement. A sidebar for Works Cited provides, for each book, a thumbnail cover illustration; information on author, title, ISBN, and publication date; and a hyperlink to OCLC's WorldCat, this latter feature demonstrating one of the advantages of reading screens.

Piper, Andrew. 2012. *Book Was There: Reading in Electronic Times*. Chicago: The University of Chicago Press.

An engaging, balanced, and personal exploration of the reading experience, both what it has been and what it is becoming. "Each of the chapters is organized around something that we *do* when we read: how we touch books and screens, how we look at them, how we share them with each other, how we take notes with them or navigate our way through them, where we use them, or even how we play with them. I am interested in understanding how we relate to reading in a deeply embodied way" (xiii).

References

Atwood, Margaret. 2012. "Why Wattpad Works." *The Guardian*, July 6. Available at: https://www.theguardian.com/books/2012/jul/06/margaret-atwood-wattpad-online-writing.

Baron, Naomi S. 2015. *Words Onscreen: The Fate of Reading in an Online World*. Oxford: Oxford University Press.

Blair, Ann M. 2003. "Reading Strategies for Coping with Information Overload ca. 1550–1700." *Journal of the History of Ideas* 64, no. 1: 11–28. Available at: http://nrs.harvard.edu/urn-3:HUL.InstRepos:3228379.

Blair, Ann M. 2010. *Too Much to Know: Managing Scholarly Information Before the Modern Age*. New Haven, CT and London: Yale University Press.

Brown, Ian. 2009. "Not Exactly Kindling His Passion." *The Globe and Mail*, November 21. Available at: http://www.theglobeandmail.com/arts/not-exactly-kindling-his-passion/article4295695/.

Coady, Lynne. 2016. *Who Needs Books? Reading in the Digital Age*. Edmonton: The University of Alberta Press.

Flood, Alison. 2012. "Margaret Atwood Joins Story-Sharing Website Wattpad." *The Guardian*, June 25. Available at: https://www.theguardian.com/books/2012/jun/25/margaret-atwood-joins-wattpad.

Hillesund, Terje. 2010. "Digital Reading Spaces: How Expert Readers Handle Books, the Web and Electronic Paper." *First Monday* 15, no. 4 (April 5). Available at: http://uncommonculture.org/ojs/index.php/fm/article/view/2762/2504.

Houston, Keith. 2016. *The Book*. New York and London: W. W. Norton & Company.

Hupfeld, Annika, Abigail Sellen, Kenton O'Hara, and Tom Rodden. 2013. "Leisure-Based Reading and the Place of E-Books in Everyday Life." In *Human-Computer Interaction* – INTERACT Part II. Lecture Notes in Computer Science vol. 8118, 1–18. Edited by P. Kotzé, G. Marsden, G. Lindgaard, J. Wesson, and M. Winckler. Berlin and Heidelberg: Springer.

Jabr, Ferris. 2013. "The Reading Brain in the Digital Age: The Science of Paper versus Screens." *Scientific American*, April 11. Available at: https://www.scientific american.com/article/reading-paper-screens/.

Kretzschmar, Franziska, Dominique Pleimling, Jana Hosemann, Stephan Füssel, Ina Bornkessel-Schlesewsky, and Matthias Schlesewsky. 2013. "Subjective Impressions Do Not Mirror Online Reading Effort: Concurrent EEG-Eyetracking Evidence from the Reading of Books and Digital Media." *PLoS* 8, no. 2. Available at: http://journals.plos.org/plosone/article?id=10.1371/journal.pone.0056178

Lacy, Sarah. 2012. "'Every Time Technology Changes, It Changes What People in the Plot Can Do.' An Interview with Margaret Atwood." *Pando*, August 30. Available at: https://pando.com/2012/08/30/every-time-technology-changes-it-changes-what -people-in-the-plot-can-do-an-interview-with-margaret-atwood/.

Lanham, Richard A. 2006. *The Economics of Attention: Style and Substance in the Age of Information*. Chicago: University of Chicago Press.

Lupton, Ellen. 2010. *Thinking with Type: A Critical Guide for Designers, Writers, Editors, and Students*, rev. 2nd ed. New York: Princeton Architectural Press.

Lupton, Ellen. 2014. *Type on Screen: A Guide for Designers, Developers, Writers, and Students*. New York: Princeton Architectural Press.

McLaughlin, Thomas. 2015. *Reading and the Body: The Physical Practice of Reading*. New York: Palgrave Mcmillan.

Nielsen, Jakob. 2000. *Designing Web Usability*. Indianapolis, IN: New Riders.

Parks, Tim. 2015. "E-books Are for Grown-ups." In *Where I'm Reading From: The Changing World of Books*, 15–18. New York: New York Review Books Collections.

Pew Research Center. 2012. "The Rise of E-reading." April 4. Available at: http://libraries.pewinternet.org/2012/04/04/the-rise-of-e-reading/.

Pew Research Center. 2014. "E-Reading Rises as Device Ownership Increases." January 16. Available at: http://www.pewinternet.org/files/old-media/Files/Reports/2014/PIP_E-reading_011614.pdf.

Pew Research Center. 2016. "Book Reading 2016." September 1. Available at: http://www.pewinternet.org/2016/09/01/book-reading-2016/.

Piper, Andrew. 2012. *Book Was There: Reading in Electronic Times*. Chicago, IL: The University of Chicago Press.

Reinking, David. 2001. "Multimedia and Engaged Reading in a Digital World." In *Literacy and Motivation: Reading Engagement in Individuals and Groups*, 195–221. Edited by Ludo Verhoeven and Catherine E. Snow. Mahwah, NJ: Erlbaum.

Simonds, Merilyn. 2017. *Gutenberg's Fingerprint: Paper, Pixels and the Lasting Impression of Books*. Toronto: ECW Press.

Streitfeld, David. 2014. "Web Fiction, Serialized and Social." *New York Times*, March 23. Available at: https://www.nytimes.com/2014/03/24/technology/web-fiction-serialized -and-social.html?_r=1.

Tveit, Åse Kristine, and Anne Mangen. 2014. "A Joker in the Class: Teenage Readers' Attitudes and Preferences to Reading on Different Devices." *Library and Information Science* Research 36, no. 3–4: 179–184.

Tweney, Dylan. 2010. "Amazon Sells More E-Books Than Hardcovers." *Wired*, July 19. Available at: http://www.wired.com/2010/07/amazon-more-e-books-than -hardcovers/.

1.5 Introduction to Reading Research

More than a decade ago at an academic luncheon, a mutual friend introduced me to a professor in educational psychology, remarking that we would have a lot in common since we are both interested in reading. The conversation was developing along familiar lines when she said: "The most important distinguishing feature that separates good readers from readers in trouble is." Anticipating her answer, I thought to myself: It's the knowledge of how stories work. But she continued, "the ability to read correctly single words on a word recognition test." Good readers can quickly identify words out of context, she said, explaining this idea with reference to the movement of the eye traveling over the page, saccades, laboratory experiments, and so on. More recently, Stanislas Dehaene's *Reading in the Brain* (2009, 239) confirmed the diagnostic value of the ability to read not just single words but pseudowords: "One of the revealing tests used to tease dyslexics apart from normal readers requires reading meaningless pseudowords like 'cochar' or 'litmagon.' " This experience of talking to the psychologist at lunch reminded me again of the fact that reading looks different, depending upon which disciplinary lens you look through. Reading researchers themselves come from a great variety of disciplines, including education, psychology, sociology, history, library and information science, literary and cultural studies, and recently neuroscience. And sometimes it can seem that disciplinary boundaries have created research traditions that are hermetically sealed. An assumption taken for granted in one discipline is challenged in another. Findings that are foundational within one discipline are little regarded in another.

Which aspects of reading have received the most attention? Perhaps the largest body of research has been done by educational psychologists, focusing on questions relating to the acquisition of literacy. Debates about reading are so heated because, as Andrew Piper (2012, xiii) says, "they ultimately, always come back to 'the kids.' " Educational psychologists ask: What do children need to know in order to become good readers? What risk factors set up a child for reading failure? What are the pathologies that stand in the way of fluent reading? What is known about reading that should drive educational policy and practice? Other disciplines have focused on aspects of reading that vary from individual factors such as reading interests and preferences to social and economic factors such as advertising, censorship, and the relation of reading to power structures. Psychologists, who have been studying reading since the days of Edmund Burke Huey a century ago, have researched reading as the outcome of complex cognitive processes within individuals. Linguists have studied competencies that enable us to generate sentences and understand them when we hear or read them. Psycholinguistic research has looked at discrete variables such as the role of short-term memory, phonemic awareness, and miscue analysis. Going beyond the individual to social patterns, demographic research has investigated the correlation of reading with such factors as the gender, age, level of income, level of education, and geographic location of the reader. This body of demographic research, reported in more detail in section 4.1, is often conducted in the service of the book industry or of public policy to find out who reads, how much they read, and what they read. In the library field, researchers have studied both the circulation and use of library books and the nature of the users who do the using.

Some disciplines study reading by focusing on texts as autonomous objects. Within literature departments, literary critics have studied the rhetorical resources of the text itself, examining texts as sources of evidence about literary genres, about the readers implied by the texts, and about gaps in the text that invite interpretive activity from readers. Sociologists, historians, and cultural studies scholars, on the other hand, are less interested in the individual reader than in the social practices and power relations that accompany reading. They have examined the political economy of the production, distribution, and consumption of reading materials and more generally have studied the roles played by publishing houses, libraries, and booksellers. In the work of researchers such as Brian Street (1995), literacy research becomes a branch of cultural studies, where the researcher lays bare the power relations that pervade literacy practices. As we saw in section 1.3, historians have studied the book as an agent of social or intellectual change and book reading as part of the history of taste. They have examined census records, library catalogs, subscription lists, and estate inventories to discover which books have been available to readers from different economic classes and during different historical periods. Responding to technological change in the production, distribution, and consumption of books, cultural studies researchers have written about the "late age of print" (Striphas 2009) and the challenges to cultural authority when "literary culture became popular culture" (Collins 2010).

By and large, historians and literary scholars have tended to focus attention on texts and deduce from the texts what they imagine the readers must experience. So one way to sort out research on reading is to distinguish between the studies that focus on real living-and-breathing readers and the ones that don't. Empiric studies of real readers can be further sorted by the setting in which the study is conducted: the laboratory or the natural setting in which reading typically occurs. Only a small number of book-length studies take an ethnographic approach to studying contemporary reading and readers. Some of the best of these studies have examined how children become readers (Clark 1976; Heath 1983; Cochran-Smith 1984), sometimes focusing on the case study of a single child (Bissex 1980; Butler 1975; Clay 1991; Crago and Crago 1983).

Although we know that a key factor in reading for pleasure is that the reader is in control and can make choices, few reading studies focus on materials chosen by the reader, preferring instead to ask readers to respond to pre-selected texts. Among the most interesting book-length studies that focus on voluntary reading or reading of personal significance are: Donald Fry's *Children Talk about Books* (1985), which reports case studies of individual children's reading; Janice Radway's *Reading the Romance* (1984), which used a combination of individual and group interviews and questionnaires to understand readers' experience of romantic fiction; Wendy Simonds's *Women and Self-Help Culture* (1992), which is based in part on open-ended interviews with 30 readers of self-help books; Elizabeth Long's *Book Clubs* (2003), an ethnographic study of 77 contemporary women's reading groups in Houston Texas; and Ian Collinson's *Everyday Readers* (2009), which used semistructured interviews with 21 readers in order to explore everyday book reading culture. The growing visibility of social reading, book clubs, and mass reading events has prompted such studies as *Reading Communities: From Salons to Cyberspace*, edited by DeNel Rehberg Sedo (2011), and Danielle Fuller and DeNel Rehberg Sedo's *Reading Beyond the Book* (2013), discussed in section 4.7. *Plotting the Reading Experience*, a collection of papers delivered at an international conference in Oslo and edited by Rothbauer and colleagues (2016), includes a variety of interesting articles based on empirical data with real readers, including recorded accounts of four-year-olds visiting libraries, online postings on fan sites, amateur reviews of works of social melodrama such as Kathryn Stockett's *The Help* posted on a Norwegian website for readers, and observational studies of voluntary school reading groups and therapeutic shared reading programs.

Sometimes it seems not that there is too little information about reading but that there is *too much*. Nevertheless, we have the sense of a growing body of work that is achieving an increasingly nuanced understanding. The questions asked by the research are at varying levels of specificity from the legibility of type faces on paper and screens to what happens in the brain during reading to the role of reading in the reader's quest for identity. Here is a sampling of some of the research questions asked and emerging findings.

- *What factors of type, line spacing, and line width make reading easier?*

  Miles A. Tinker conducted a long series of careful pioneering studies of the factors that affect the readability of type, including the typeface used, illumination, surface quality, and spacing. He found that typefaces in common use are all equally legible. Readers dislike very short and very long lines as well as material set solid, that is, set with no leading, or extra space, between the lines.

  Tinker, Miles A. 1963. *Legibility of Print*. Ames: Iowa State University Press.

- *How is the readability of texts measured?*

  Most of the work on readability has been directed toward developing a formula for counting some easily identifiable characteristics of a sample text. The impetus for this work has been the recognition that readers, especially beginning readers, need text that can be understood with ease. There are now hundreds of readability formulae. Most calculate the average number of words per sentence or the ratio of polysyllabic words to one-syllable words or the ratio of rare words to frequently used words. The Fog Index combines both average number of words per sentence and the number of words of three or more syllables to produce a readability score usually expressed as a grade level. Because some common polysyllabic words such as "watermelon" are easier to read than short, rare words such as "weald," some formulae take word frequency into account. However measures based on sentence length, word length, and word frequency can't deal with such factors as the grammatical complexity of sentence structure, the difficulty and abstraction of the concepts involved, or the coherence and organization of the text. The cloze procedure, which is better at accommodating these complex factors, works by measuring the predictability or redundancy of a passage. In the cloze procedure, subjects are asked to read a passage from which words have been deleted at fixed intervals such as every fifth word. The more successful readers are at filling in the missing words, the more readable the passage is judged to be. My Microsoft Word software rates this paragraph you are now reading at a grade level of 12.0 on the Flesch-Kincaid readability scale, which is based on word length and sentence length.

Klare, George R. 1984. "Readability." In *Handbook of Reading Research*, vol. 1. Edited by P. David Pearson and Rebecca Barr. New York: Longmans.

• *What do our eyes do as they scan a page or screen?*

Psychology Professor Keith Rayner has reviewed the major findings of 25 years of research on eye movements in reading. He argues that understanding eye movements is crucial for understanding the reading process itself. During reading, our eyes do not move smoothly along the line of letters. Because only the fovea, at the center of the retina, has a resolution fine enough to allow us to recognize small print, our gaze moves along a line of print in a series of jumps and stops. During the jumps or saccades, which are typically of six to nine letter spaces, the eye moves very fast. The jump is followed by fixations, when the eye is relatively still and all the intake of visual information occurs. About 10 to 15 percent of the time, readers regress to look back at material already read. "As text difficulty increases, fixation durations increase, saccade lengths decrease, and regression frequency increases."

The perceptual span, or area of effective vision during reading, extends 14 to 15 characters to the right of fixation but only three to four letter spaces to the left of fixation. Reading skill influences the size of the span, with beginning readers and adult dyslexic readers having smaller spans than skilled readers. Readers differ a lot, one from another, in fixation times and saccade length. A large body of research has demonstrated that this variability is related to "cognitive processes associated with comprehension."

Rayner, Keith. 1997. "Understanding Eye Movements in Reading." *Scientific Studies of Reading* 1, no. 4: 317–339.

• *What happens in the brain when we read?*

The alphabet is only some 4,000 years old. Stanislaus Dehaene argues that our brains didn't evolve to read—we haven't had time. Instead humans have co-opted for purposes of reading the brain circuitry that developed during primate evolution for other uses. According to Dehaene, all writing systems use the same set of basic shapes—shapes that are already a part of the visual system in all primates. So what happens when we read? Functional magnetic resonance imaging fMRI is a breakthrough technology that lets researchers see which parts of the brain are engaged during reading. An area of the left occipital-temporal region of the brain that Dehaene calls "the brain's letterbox" responds to written words. This visual word form area extracts the identity of a string of letters, and transmits this information to two other areas of the brain, the left temporal lobe that decodes letters into sounds and the frontal lobe that decodes meaning. As Dehaene describes it, "Whenever our eyes stop, we only recognize one or two words. Each of them is then split up into myriad fragments by retinal neurons and must be put back together before it can be recognized. Our visual system progressively extracts graphemes, syllables, prefixes, suffices, and word roots. Two major parallel processing routes eventually come into play: the phonological route, which converts letters into speech sounds, and the lexical route, which gives access to a mental dictionary of word meanings" (11). In a manner that is still unknown, various areas of the brain have to work together to make sense of ambiguous statements such as these newspaper headlines noted by Dehaene: "Milk Drinkers are Turning to Powder" and "Include your Children When Baking Cookies" (111).

Dehaene, Stanislas. 2009. *Reading in the Brain: The Science and Evolution of a Human Invention*. New York: Viking.

- *How do people read web pages?*

Jakob Nielsen used eye-tracking equipment to record what the eyes were doing when 232 readers looked at thousands of web pages. He found that that people read very, very fast, following an F-shaped pattern. Web readers first read in a horizontal sweep across the screen, usually in the upper part of the content area—that is, the top bar of the F. Then moving down a bit, they read across the page in a shorter sweep. Then they scan down through the text, focusing on the content's left side. Nielsen warns web writers that readers of web pages do not read "in a word-by-word manner" but rapidly skim, looking for relevant information.

Nielsen, Jakob. 2006. Nielsen Norman Group. "F-Shaped Pattern for Reading Web Content." April 17. Available at: https://www.nngroup.com/articles/f-shaped -pattern-reading-web-content/.

- *What methods work best at teaching children initially how to read?*

Jeanne Chall's synthesis of 50 years of research suggests that teachers of beginning reading should present well-designed phonics instruction.

Chall, Jeanne S. 1983. *Learning to Read: The Great Debate*, 2nd ed. New York: McGraw-Hill.

- *What distinguishes a skillful reader?*

The single most striking characteristic of skillful readers is that they speed through stretches of text with apparent effortlessness (Adams 1990, 19).

Adams, Marilyn J. 1990. *Beginning to Read: Thinking and Learning about Print. A Summary.* Center for the Study of Reading. University of Illinois at Urbana, Champagne.

- *What is the most important factor in the making of readers?*

In 1983 a national commission in the United States called the Commission on Reading was organized by the National Academy of Education and the National Institute of Education. The Commission spent two years winnowing some 10,000 research reports and concluded: "The single most important activity for building the knowledge required for eventual success in reading is reading aloud to children." (Anderson et al. 1985, 23)

Anderson, Richard C., Elfrieda. H. Hiebert, Judith A. Scott, and Ian A. G. Wilkinson. 1985. *Becoming a Nation of Readers: The Report of the Commission on Reading.* Washington, DC: US Department of Education, National Institute of Education.

- *What is the relation between early reading proficiency and later literacy achievement?*

A pioneering and still highly regarded article by Keith E. Stanovich (1986) explained how, in developing readers, the rich get richer and the poor get poorer. Frequent readers encounter more words and build a larger vocabulary; a larger vocabulary makes it easier to understand what is read; better reading comprehension makes reading easier, more efficient, and more fun, which leads to more reading. As Stanovich (1986, 380) puts it, "The critical mediating variable that turns this relationship into a strong bootstrapping mechanism that causes major individual differences in the development of reading skill is the volume of reading experience." The upshot? In a related study, Cunningham and Stanovich (1997) found that a child's facility in reading in the first grade usually is a good indicator of how well that person will read ten years later in the 11th grade.

Stanovich, Keith E. 1986. "Matthew Effects in Reading: Some Consequences of Individual Differences in the Acquisition of Literacy." *Reading Research Quarterly* 21, no. 4 (Fall): 360–407.

Cunningham, Anne E., and Keith E. Stanovich. 1997. "Early Reading Acquisition and Its Relation of Reading Experience and Ability 10 Years Later." *Developmental Psychology* 33, no. 6: 934–945. Available at: https://static1 .squarespace.com/static/5731ee0840261d67c7155483/t/576c4c4cb8a79bcb10f e8251/1466715218324/Cunningham+and+Stanovich_Early+reading+acquisition +and+its+relation+to+reading+experience+and+ability+10+years+later_1998 .pdf.

- *Do children need books in their home?*

Sociologists consider books in the home to be a marker for a family culture that supports learning and enjoys reading. When Evans and colleagues (2010) compared international achievement data across 27 countries, they concluded that a home library is as important as parental education and twice as important as the father's occupation in predicting educational outcomes. For children of the least well-educated parents, the presence of books makes the biggest impact: "It is at the bottom, where books are rare, that each additional book matters most" (Evans et al. 2010, 187). With the achievement gap between rich and poor in the United States now 30 to 40 percent greater than it was several decades ago, researchers are looking at the best ways to get books into the hands of low-income children, especially during summer holidays when disadvantaged children lose ground. McGill-Franzen, Ward, and Cahill (2016) summarize some promising research on summer reading programs that give out free books that the readers themselves choose for pleasure reading.

Evans, M., J. Kelley, J. Sikora, and D. Treiman. 2010. "Family Scholarly Culture and Educational Success: Books and Schooling in 27 Nations." *Research in Social Stratification and Mobility* 28, no. 2: 171–197.

McGill-Franzen, Anne, Natalia Ward, and Maria Cahill. 2016. "Summers: Some Are Reading, Some Are Not! It Matters." *The Reading Teacher* 69, no. 6: 585–596.

- *Why do children from professional families do better in school than children from working-class or welfare families?*

Betty Hart and Todd Risley tape-recorded and coded samples of time in the homes of 42 children from differing socioeconomic groups over a longitudinal period from age 7 to 9 months to 36 months. They discovered that that by age three there was already a 30 million word gap between the number of words heard by children in welfare families and the number of words heard by children in professional families. "By the time the children were 3 years old, trends in amount of talk, vocabulary growth, and style of interaction were well established and clearly suggested widening gaps to come. Even patterns of parenting were already observable among the children. When we listened to the children, we seemed to hear their parents speaking; when we watched the children play at parenting their dolls, we seemed to see the futures of their own children." During the period studied, welfare children had received half as much language experience (616 words heard on average per hour) as working-class children (1,251 words per hour) and less than one third as much language experience as the children of professionals (2,153 words per hour). Another key difference was in the quality of language experience: on average welfare children heard 5 encouragements and 11 prohibitions per hour whereas the professional child heard 32 encouragements and 5 prohibitions per hour. Extrapolated, this data suggests that in the first four years a child from a professional home would have heard 560,000 more instances of encouragements than discouragements, whereas a child from a family on welfare would have heard 125,000 more prohibitions than encouragements.

Hart, Betty, and Todd R. Risley. 1996. *Meaningful Differences in the Everyday Experience of Young American Children*. Baltimore, MD: Brookes.

Hart, Betty, and Todd R. Risley. 2003. "The Early Catastrophe: the 30 Million Word Gap by Age 3." *American Educator* (Spring). Available at: http://www.aft.org/pubs-reports/american_educator/spring2003/catastrophe.html.

- *What is the relationship between the various kinds of literacies and social well-being?*

When the Organisation for Economic Cooperation and Development (OECD) tested adult skills within its 22 high-income member countries and two partner countries, they found that people with greater proficiency in literacy, numeracy, and problem solving were more likely to be employed and to be paid more. The 2013 report concluded, "In all countries, individuals who score at lower levels of proficiency in literacy are more likely than those with higher proficiency to report poor health, believe that they have little impact on the political process, and not participate in associative or volunteer activities."

OECD. 2013. *OECD Skills Outlook 2013: First Results from the Survey of Adult Skills*. OECD Publishing. Available at: http://dx.doi.org/10.1787/9789264204256-en.

- *Where does meaning lie—in the text or in the reader?*

Reader-response theorists and cognitive psychologists are converging on the view that reading is a transaction between reader and text in which an active reader constructs meaning from a text on the basis of the reader's previous experience with language, with the way that stories get told, and with the way the world works. Hence, when reading Dehaene's example of the newspaper headline, "Include your Children When Baking Cookies," the reader uses her knowledge of lifestyle newspaper stories to dismiss the interpretation that this could be a gruesome *Titus Andronicus* situation. The view of the reader as an active meaning-maker contrasts with a previous model of reading in which meaning resided in the text and where the reader's job, like Little Jack Thumb, was to pull out the meaning that was already right there.

- *How do people feel about books as objects?*

When asked, "What are the things in your home which are special to you?" 22 percent mentioned books (36 percent mentioned furniture, 26 percent mentioned visual art, 23 percent photographs, 21 percent the television set, and 15 percent plants) (Csikszentmihalyi and Rochberg-Halton 1981, 58). The authors sum up the value of books that makes them special: "books, more than any other kind of objects, are special to people because they serve to embody ideals and to express religious and professional values" (71).

Csikszentmihalyi, Mihaly, and Eugene Rochberg-Halton. 1981. *The Meaning of Things: Domestic Symbols and the Self.* Cambridge: Cambridge University Press.

With so many studies on reading being published each year, reading is obviously a complex field. However, there are a number of core findings that should be emphasized as significant for library professionals, parents, and community members:

- Although we speak of readers and nonreaders, in modern societies the ability to read is not a binary variable. It is *not* the case that either you can read or you can't. In fact almost everyone in modern societies *can* read at a very basic level. The problem is that many can't read well enough to cope with the increasing literacy demands of an information society. Reading is a skill with many gradations of proficiency from being able to read a STOP sign to reading and understanding a poem by Emily Dickinson.

- Reading is an acquired skill. People learn to read well by doing lots and lots of reading. Large amounts of reading are crucial for developing reading fluency, whether in a first or in a second language.

- Pleasure is the spur that motivates beginning readers to spend the thousands and thousands of hours reading that it takes to read well. Readers who become proficient are those who enjoy reading and who do a lot of it by choice in their leisure time. Such readers give themselves lessons in reading that are never learned by children who dislike and avoid reading. A key way to maximize the likelihood that the reading experience will be pleasurable is to give the reader choice.

- Beginners are more likely to choose an activity when they feel they are succeeding and when they get pleasure from it right from the start. This is why reading aloud is such a winning strategy in the making of readers. The novice reader experiences the pleasure of stories in a risk-free environment where it is impossible to fail or appear incompetent.

- When young readers begin to read independently, the ideal book is one that they will love, whatever its literary qualities. An enjoyable book hits the Goldilocks standard of being neither too easy (and therefore boring) nor too hard (and therefore frustrating). Research indicates that the greatest improvement in reading happens when young readers are engaged with books that they can read with at least 95 percent accuracy. For struggling readers who have avoided voluntary reading, problems snowball because at school they increasingly are faced with texts that are too hard for them. With each year, the proficiency gap grows between children who read for pleasure and struggling readers who don't.

- The experience of confident and successful readers is beneficent circle: (1) an initial experience with texts and stories that is pleasurable; (2) an acquired knowledge about reading that comes from exposure to texts and stories; (3) a desire to repeat the pleasurable experience at first by hearing more stories and later by reading on one's own; (4) achievement of competency in reading acquired through lots of practice listening to and reading texts; (5) the reader's sense of himself/ herself as a skilled and successful reader who is good at reading and therefore who want to engage in more of it.

To Read More on Reading Research

Kamil, Michael L., P. David Pearson, Elizabeth Birr Moje, and Peter P. Afflerbach, eds. 2011. *Handbook of Reading Research.* Vol. IV. New York and Abingdon, Oxon, UK: Routledge.

This massive fourth volume edited by Michael Kamil and colleagues continues a series that began in 1984 to summarize key patterns and findings in reading research conducted in the field of educational psychology. Volume four examines reading studies published since 2000 when the third volume was published. Contributed authoritative essays survey research, especially randomized experimental trials and large-scale national evaluations that can inform educational policy and practice. The editors note that since the third volume there has been a shift in emphasis from the primary grades to grades four and up.

References

Bissex, Glenda L. 1980. *GNYS AT WRK: A Child Learns to Write and Read.* Cambridge, MA: Harvard University Press.

Butler, Dorothy. 1975. *Cushla and Her Books.* Boston: The Horn Book.

Clark, Margaret. 1976. *Young Fluent Readers.* London: Heinemann Educational Books.

Clay, Marie M. 1991. *Becoming Literate: The Construction of Inner Control.* Portsmouth, NH: Heinemann.

Cochran-Smith, Marilyn. 1984. *The Making of a Reader.* Norwood, NJ: Ablex.

Collins, Jim. 2010. *Bring on the Books for Everybody: How Literary Culture Became Popular Culture.* Durham, NC: Duke University Press.

Collinson, Ian. 2009. *Everyday Readers: Reading and Popular Culture.* Sheffield, UK: Equinox Publishing.

Crago, Maureen, and Hugh Crago. 1983. *Prelude to Literacy: A Preschool Child's Encounter with Picture and Story.* Carbondale and Edwardsville: Southern Illinois University Press.

Dehaene, Stanislas. 2009. *Reading in the Brain: The Science and Evolution of a Human Invention.* New York: Viking.

Fry, Donald. 1985. *Children Talk about Books: Seeing Themselves as Readers.* London: Open University Press.

Fuller, Danielle, and DeNel Rehberg Sedo. 2013. *Reading beyond the Book: The Social Practices of Contemporary Literary Culture.* New York: Routledge.

Heath, Shirley Brice. 1983. *Ways with Words: Language, Life and Work in Communities and Classrooms*. New York: Cambridge University Press.

Long, Elizabeth. 2003. *Book Clubs: Women and the Uses of Reading in Everyday Life*. Chicago and London: The University of Chicago Press.

Piper, Andrew. 2012. *Book Was There: Reading in Electronic Times*. Chicago: The University of Chicago Press.

Radway, Janice. 1984. *Reading the Romance: Women, Patriarchy and Popular Literature*. Chapel Hill: University of North Carolina Press.

Rehberg Sedo, DeNel, ed. 2011. *Reading Communities from Salons to Cyberspace*. Houndmills, UK: Palgrave Macmillan.

Rothbauer, Paulette M., Kjell Ivar Skjerdingstad, Lynne (E. F.) McKechnie, and Knut Oterholm, eds. 2016. *Plotting the Reading Experience: Theory, Practice, Politics*. Waterloo, ON: Wilfrid Laurier University Press.

Simonds, Wendy. 1992. *Women and Self-Help Culture: Reading between the Lines*. Piscataway, NJ: Rutgers University Press.

Street, Brian. 1995. *Social Literacies: Critical Approaches to Literacy in Development, Ethnography and Education*. London: Longman.

Striphas, Ted. 2009. *The Late Age of Print: Everyday Book Culture from Consumerism to Control*. New York: Columbia UP.

1.6 Reflecting on Reading

One good way to think about the role of the reader is to begin with your own experiences and reflect upon your own reading history. Were you read to as a child? Who read to you? What can you remember about the first stages of reading on your own? Did you have a favorite book that you read and reread and maybe still have to this day safely somewhere in a cupboard or bookcase? Did you come from a reading family or did you discover reading on your own later, perhaps with the help of a teacher? Aidan Chambers in *The Reading Environment* says that he was born into a house where there was little reading of any kind but a lot of oral storytelling, and he was read to every day by a primary school teacher (1991, 87). When you recall the experience of being read to, does your memory include a physical experience —being held on a parent's lap or bounced to the rhythm of a nursery rhyme or seated side-by-side with a sibling. Growing up, did you think of reading as something you excelled at? Or did you dread being called upon to read aloud in class and think of reading as a source of humiliation and frustration? Can you remember being spellbound by a story read aloud by a teacher or librarian? What was your first experience of going to the library? Can you remember particular childhood books that were special favorites? Eloisa James (2012, 5), Shakespearean scholar and author of bestselling romance novels, reports that she collected novels compulsively from the age of seven on, "cataloging them and keeping my favorites close to the door in case of fire. My boxed set of *The Chronicles of Narnia* bore a large sign instructing my parents not to forget it as they carried my (presumably unconscious) body through the door, just before the ceiling fell in."

To develop a reading autobiography, a good place to start is with the question that initiates almost all the interviews in my study of avid readers who read for pleasure: "What's the first thing that you can remember about reading?" I now have 302 open-ended, qualitative interviews conducted by me and by Masters of Library and Information Science students in my course on Genres of Fiction and Reading at Western. To capture the individual reader's unique history and experience of pleasure reading (see section 4.3), interviewers asked the following questions:

- What is the first book that you can remember either having read to you as a child or reading yourself?

  What can you remember about it?

  Can you think of a book/story that really stands out in your memory?

  What was special about it?

  Can you explain what you mean by X?

- What do you remember reading next? Next? After that?
- Was there anything in your childhood experience that you would say fostered reading? Discouraged reading?
- When you were a child, did you think of yourself as a reader? (Probe: If not, then when did you start to think of yourself as reader? What made the difference?)
- How, if at all, did your reading interests change as you reached adolescence?
- How do you choose a book to read?
- Where do you get the books that you read?
- Are there types of books that you do *not* enjoy and would not choose?
- Has there ever been a book that has made a big difference to your life in one way or another? (Probe: What kind of a difference? How did it help you?)
- What would it be like for you if for one reason or other you *couldn't* read?
- If you could get an author to write for the "Perfect Book," what would it be like? What elements would it include?
- How do you feel about different formats for reading—for example, audio books or eBooks?
- What would you say is the role of reading in your life?

Whether your early childhood was rich in books or whether you read reluctantly as a child and came to book reading later in life, you will probably be able to remember the feelings, positive or negative, associated with childhood reading. As Margaret Meek says in *How Texts Teach What Readers Learn* about a similar exercise in constructing an autobiography of reading: "Summon up your best recollections and you will probably remember two things above all others—the difficulties and successes you had on your way, and the important turning points in your understanding of what reading was all about" (Meek 1988, 4). In a *New York Times* article, "What's Your Reading History?" Amanda Christy Brown and Katherine Schulten (2010) provide a framework of questions that teachers can use to help students recreate their reading lives. The reader is asked to pick a single memory of a positive experience with reading and then ask these questions:

> What book is being read? What does it look like? Feel like? Are the pages thick or thin? Are there pictures? What colors and images stand out? What does it smell like? Where did this book come from? How did you happen upon it? Did someone give it to you? Did you borrow it from the library? If you chose it, what attracted you to it? . . .
>
> Where are you? Indoors? Outdoors? Cuddled up on a couch or lying in the grass? . . .
>
> Who is reading? A parent? Grandparent? Sibling? Try to remember the voice. . . . What characters do you meet as you become immersed in the world of the book? Are they like you or different?

Joe Queenan's *One for the Books* (2012) is a whole book of reflection on one reader's lifelong obsession with reading. He reports that for him the presence of the books themselves are an *aide-memoire*, which is one of many reasons why he prefers paper to screens. In each room of his house, he is surrounded by real, hold-in-your-hand books whose physical presence reminds him of particular times and places in his life when he bought or read the book. Because he almost always writes on the book's inside flap his name and the date and city of purchase, he says, "In some sense, all my books are memorabilia" and all come "with a backstory": "Books I bought in Chicago. . . . Books I bought in Paris . . . books given to me by friends, ex-friends, colleagues, relatives, or my wife" (231–233).

To recall their reading, many serious readers keep lists—lists of books trusted friends have recommended, books they have bought, books they have read, books that they haven't read yet but plan to read sometime. Some are straight lists recorded in a notebook or on Goodreads or LibraryThing. Others are annotated with the date and place of reading and brief impressions of the book and sometimes are enriched with quotations from the book considered especially apt. In fact, a list can easily turn into a reading diary or journal, similar to the one described by Daphne (student, age 29), who identifies herself as a "voracious reader":

> I have a book journal. So every time I finish a book I have to keep track of everything. I write the author, how many pages it was, first person or third person, the plot line, all the characters, and what I thought about it. I also include who recommended the book to me—if somebody recommended it to me because, you know, friends are a big part—and any comparisons to other books.

A reading diary is an ideal medium for personal reflection. In *A Reading Diary* (2004), Alberto Manguel uses the rereading of a favorite books as the starting point for exploring the connection between his own reading and events—both current and remembered—in the everyday world. The resulting book records reflections on friends, travel, and public and private events—all as elicited by his reading. December's reading is Kenneth Grahame's *The Wind in the Willows*, in which Mole's losing of his familiar home triggers Manguel's elegiac reflection on the recent death of a friend and the unwanted nature of change: "I want my friends to be there always. . . . I want the places I like to stay the same. . . . I don't want to keep missing voices, faces, names." In a life that has included travel from a childhood in Buenos Aires, Argentina, to residences in Italy, England, Tahiti, Canada, and France, the books in Manguel's library are the home that can be transported everywhere.

Reflecting on reading can often happen most felicitously in the context of rereading, as Wendy Lesser discovers in her book *Nothing Remains the Same* (2002). In her 40s, Lesser reread books that had meant a lot to her when she first read them 20 or 30 years earlier. Revisiting *Don Quixote*, Wordsworth's "Immortality Ode," *Education of Henry Adams*, *Middlemarch*, *Anna Karenina*, George Orwell's *The Road to Wigan Pier*, *The Winter's Tale*, Ian McEwen's *The Child in Time*, and *Huckleberry Finn*, among others, she juxtaposes two readings performed by the older and younger reading selves. She says, "You know there are two of you because you can feel them responding differently to the book. Differently, but not entirely differently: there is a core of experience shared by your two selves" (Lesser 2002, 4). Rereading two of her favorite books from adolescence Kingsley Amis's *Lucky Jim* and Dodie Smith's *I Capture the Castle*, Lesser finds that she can no longer respond to the core emotions—resentment, withheld fury, embarrassment, and righteous vindication—that she now sees at the heart of *Lucky Jim*. The opposite happens when Lesser rereads Dodie Smith's novel about two English sisters, Rose and Cassandra Mortmain, who fall in love with two American brothers and whose experiences are captured in Cassandra's journal entries. Lesser is startled by how similar her own views of life and her own beliefs and preferences have become to Cassandra's and wonders, "Did I, at thirteen, absorb the book so fully that it shaped my habits and superstitions as I grew older? Or was I drawn to Cassandra's personality precisely because it mirrored my own gradually emerging character?" (Lesser 2002, 35).

Similarly, Patricia Meyer Spacks reports in *Rereading* (2011) on her year-long project of rereading dozens of novels: childhood favorites, old standbys, canonical works that she had never really liked, guilty pleasures, books she had read often because she taught them in her courses. In *Rereading*, Spacks says that the distance between the remembered reading and the present reading is "a way to evoke memories . . . of one's life and of past selves" (2). Reflecting on *Gone with the Wind*, a book that enthralled her as a ten-year-old but turned out to be unreadable later, she remarked, "I believe firmly in a magical theory about reading—that one mysteriously discovers, at every stage of life, just the book that one really needs at that moment. *Gone with the Wind* belonged to the ten-year-old moment when I was beginning to wonder about the relations of men and women and how they might come about" (2011, 151).

With the goal of reading a book a week and recording the experience, Sara Nelson similarly ends up reflecting on the intersection of the reading and the personal life. Senior contributing editor of *Glamour*, mother of three, wife, daughter of a Jewish mother, younger sister of a writer of literary fiction, best friend of another avid reader, Nelson says, "What I am doing, I think, is trying to get down on paper what I've been doing for years in my mind: matching up the reading experience with the personal one and watching where they intersect—or don't" (7). In *So Many Books, So Little Time* (2004), Sara Nelson starts the year with a list of books that she wants to read (*The Autobiography of Malcolm X, Cakes and Ale, The House of Mirth, A Tale of Two Cities, In Cold Blood, Empire Falls*, etc.) but the plan falls apart within the first week when she can't get into Ted Heller's *Funnymen*. She concludes, "I don't always choose the books. . . . Sometimes the books choose me" (14).

In the growing subgenre of reading memoir, readers describe their engagement with pleasure reading, often reporting on a year-long challenge during which they read books according to some arbitrary category (Ross 2014). This reading memoir subgenre usually combines autobiography and literary criticism but can also be inflected by elements of self-help (Beha 2009; Sankovitch 2011), opinionated curmudgeonliness (Queenan 2012), or some version of an "extreme reading" adventure (Rose 2014; Morgan 2015). Joe Queenan (2012, 75–76) describes his various reading challenges (many of which got derailed): a year reading only short books; a year reading books that he always thought he would hate; a year reading books picked randomly from library shelves with his eyes closed; a year reading authors such as F. Scott Fitzgerald and Harper Lee, who burned out early; a year reading all 138 books in his own collection that he had started reading but never finished. A thoroughly successful reading challenge began when he picked up a novella by Mario Bellatin called *Beauty Salon* about a gay, cross-dressing Mexico City hairdresser, only because the blurb on the back cover by Francisco Goldman said that Mario Bellatin's books were like "gifts from the future." In "an aleatory daisy chain" in which a blurb on the back of the current novel leads to the next, Queenan (150–152) read Goldman's *The Ordinary Seaman*, followed by a chain of a dozen linked authors, each one wonderful, until he reached the perfection of *The House of Paper* by the Uruguayan novelist Carlos Maria Dominguez. And then he stopped. Novelist Susan Hill spent a year reading nothing but books already on her shelves. In *Howards End Is on the Landing* (2010), she explained, "I wanted to repossess my books, to explore what I had accumulated over a lifetime of reading, and to map this house of many volumes" (2).

Christopher Beha (2009) and Nina Sankovitch (2011) took up their year-long reading projects as a way of reading their way out of a personal crisis. For Christopher Beha, the challenge was to read all 50 volumes of the Harvard Classics, selected in 1910 by Dr. Charles W. Eliot, then president of Harvard. Reflecting on his year of reading, Beha says, "[T]hese books have helped me to find meaning in events—illness and loss as well as moments of great joy—that didn't make any sense to me. At the same time, life helped me to make sense of these books" (249). For Nina Sankovitch, the challenge was to read one book a day and write about it for 365 days "as an escape back to life. I wanted to engulf myself in books and come up whole again." She says, "The rules for my year were simple: no author could be read more than once; I couldn't reread any books I'd already read; and I had to write about every book I read. I would read new books and new authors, and read old books from favorite writers" (28).

In the "extreme reading" category, Ann Morgan (2015) decided that she would spend 2012 reading a book translated into English from each of the world's 195 UN-recognized countries, in order to embrace a "global community of stories." Phyllis Rose (2014), author of popular biographies of Virginia Woolf and Josephine Baker, opted for serendipity. She more or less randomly picked a fiction shelf at the New York Society Library and read her way through it. Her book on this "Off-Road or Extreme Reading," she says, records "the history of an experiment": "So I would read my way into the unknown—into the pathless wastes, into thin air, with no reviews, no best-seller lists, no college curricula, no National Book Awards or Pulitzer Prizes, no ads, no publicity, not even word of mouth to guide me." Her rules for picking the shelf: it had to include several authors, only one of whom could have more than five books on the shelf; it had to have a mix of contemporary and older works; and one book had to be a classic that she had not previously read. Having picked her shelf—LEQ-LES—she began her experiment by reading *One for the Devil* written by the South African novelist, Etienne Leroux, and translated into English from Afrikaans. Problems arise almost immediately. At first Rose thought that she was reading a country house mystery, but Leroux had no interest in narrative, and even after Rose had finished the book, she was "unable even to guess what this book was about" (15). This experience with a mistaken genre identification leads Rose to some interesting observations on the difference between popular genres and serious fiction and also prompts her to reflect upon the sources of her pleasure in reading:

> We give the name "reading" to many activities, and the only one that matters to me is the one in which attention is fiercely focused, each word has weight, and each sentence makes me more aware of the world I am reading about than the one in which I actually live. In this sense every successful reading experience for me is escapist. (20)

Case 5: "A Jumbled Message"

When Allan (graduate student, age 31) heard that I was interviewing avid readers, he volunteered himself as an interviewee because he felt so strongly about reading. As a child, he was a nonreader before the term "dyslexia" was commonly understood. His parents were counseled to keep him in school "until the frustration mounted" and then to send him to trade school. Allan said, "I feel so strongly about this, because, if that advice had been taken, I would not be working on my fourth degree—my second graduate degree—and I would have been a different person."

Ross: What did a printed page or a word written on a page look like to you back then? Can you describe it?

Allan: That's an interesting question, because one of the problems with learning disabilities and reading disabilities is that one can never get inside someone else's head. With me, I was just reading the way everyone else reads. ... But it was comprehension that was lacking. I didn't realize this at the time, but I think that at two stages messages were being dropped. I had poor scanning skills for a written page. I'd track across a page, and then without me being consciously aware, I'd drop down a couple of lines, or even up a line. So I was inputting a jumbled message. I was also dropping words, pulling in words from above and below. There'd be occasional reversals—I still do reversals. ... So besides doing those physical problems, I also would jumble the message inside. I saw physical pages the way everybody else did. I read a physical page not quite like the way everybody else did. But then inside, the messages would get jumbled.

Comments

Allan told me that there were three phases to his reading life. During the first phase before he went to school, he and his younger brothers were read to for at least half an hour every night—"A. A. Milne, Winnie the Pooh stories"—and reading was sheer pleasure. "Then school started, and reading became something different in my mind— a confusion." But he came from a reading family and, "because of the influence of [his] eldest brother having all these books around," during the summer when he was 12, he picked up a book in the Edgar Rice Burroughs series, *John Carter on Mars*. Allan said, "This particular summer when I was twelve, my skills in reading had been increasing generally over the years. But I still had the stigma about reading— because it was such a challenge, and such a demanding thing, and had taken so much time."

The third phase began with the breakthrough book *John Carter on Mars*: "I was amazed by it—I think that's the best word. I got into it, and there was a whole series on the shelf. ... After I read the first one, I just looked at the rest and I knew it was going to be a good summer because I had all these stories to carry on with. It was a very new discovery. It was fun. Now I could start to associate reading with enjoyment and pleasure. Reading had been the means to learn before that, but it was not the means to enjoy."

To Read More

Rose, Phyllis. 2014. *The Shelf: From LEQ to LES*. New York: Ferrar, Straus and Giroux.
The serendipitously chosen books on the shelf become a jumping-off point for
Phyllis Rose to reflect wittily upon various facets of the reading experience: certain
novels that live on forever without actually being read (Gaston Leroux's *The
Phantom of the Opera*); women writers and privilege (only 3 of the 11 writers on
her shelf, or 27 percent were women); regionalism (Rose says it's a useful term that
a dominant literary culture uses to make it unnecessary to read some body of work);
gate-keeping processes of acquisition and weeding that determine the books to be
found on library shelves; the popularity of detective fiction; and the role of libraries
in promoting "random reading through their open stacks and that ultimately random
system of organization, alphabetical order."

References

Beha, Christopher R. 2009. *The Whole Five Feet: What the Great Books Taught Me About
Life, Death and Pretty Much Everything Else*. New York: Grove Press.

Brown, Amanda Christy, and Katherine Schulten. 2010. "What's Your Reading History?
Reflecting on the Self as Reader." *New York Times*, March 4. Available at: https://
learning.blogs.nytimes.com/2010/03/04/whats-your-reading-history-reflecting-on-
the-self-as-reader/?_r=1.

Chambers, Aidan. 1991. *The Reading Environment: How Adults Help Children Enjoy
Books*. South Woodchester, England: The Thimble Press.

Hill, Susan. 2010. *Howards End Is on the Landing*. London: Profile Books.

James, Eloisa. 2012. *Paris in Love*. New York: Random House.

Lesser, Wendy. 2002. *Nothing Remains the Same: Rereading and Remembering*. Boston
and New York: Houghton Mifflin Company.

Manguel, Alberto. 2004. *A Reading Diary*. New York: Farrar, Straus, and Giroux.

Meek, Margaret. 1988. *How Texts Teach What Readers Learn*. South Woodchester,
England: The Thimble Press.

Morgan, Ann. 2015. *World between Two Covers: Reading the Globe*. New York: W. W.
Norton & Company.

Nelson, Sara. 2004. *So Many Books, So Little Time: A Year of Passionate Reading*. New
York: Berkley Books.

Queenan, Joe. 2012. *One for the Books*. New York and London: Viking.

Rose, Phyllis. 2014. *The Shelf: From LEQ to LES*. New York: Ferrar, Straus and Giroux.

Ross, Catherine Sheldrick. 2014. "Year of Reading." *The Pleasures of Reading: A
Booklover's Alphabet*, 253–257. Santa Barbara, CA: Libraries Unlimited.

Sankovitch, Nina. 2011. *Tolstoy and the Purple Chair. My Year of Magical Reading*. New
York: Harper Collins.

Spacks, Patricia Meyer. 2011. *On Rereading*. Cambridge, MA: Harvard University Press.

Chapter 2

Becoming a Reader: Childhood Years

Lynne (E. F.) McKechnie

In *Voices of Readers: How We Come to Love Books*, Carlsen and Sherrill (1988) share excerpts from over 1,000 reading autobiographies completed by their students of education and librarianship. These reading accounts give us a vivid sense, from the perspective of readers themselves, of the complex task of learning to read, as in this example:

> My first recollection of reading was the wonderful experience of having stories read to me by my parents and older sister. My sister read to me from a primer so much that I memorized the books and by looking at the pictures I could recite it verbatim. Oh, the sheer joy of reading a book! Although I couldn't actually read, I think that this was the motivation I needed. I wanted to read more than anything else in the world. (Carlsen and Sherrill 1988, 30)

This chapter looks specifically at children and reading. It begins with a brief overview of what is known about children and reading—what surveys and other large studies tell us. It continues with a description of how children become readers. Two topics of current interest follow: the unsettling issue of readicide and the emergence of multimodal reading. The chapter concludes by looking at the relationship between children, public libraries, and reading.

2.1 What We Know about Children and Reading

Surveying Childhood Reading

Large-scale national surveys of children's and teen's reading are becoming more common. The questions tend to be very general and differ somewhat across constituencies. The following findings are typical:

- *United States*: For its sixth biannual study to explore family attitudes and behaviors around reading books for pleasure, Scholastic (2017a) surveyed 2,718 parents and children (birth to 17 years). The average family owned 104 children's books. Fifty-eight percent of children reported loving or liking reading books for fun. Three-quarters of parents said they started reading to their children before age one, an increase from 30 percent in 2014. On average, kids read 8 books over the summer with 62 percent agreeing that they enjoy summer reading. Kids' favorite books included the Harry Potter series, books by Dr. Seuss, *Diary of a Wimpy Kid, Magic Tree House*, and the Junie B. Jones series.

- *Canada*: Scholastic Canada's (2017b) survey of 1,931 English and French Canadian parents and children found that 86 percent of children were reading, or had just finished, a book. The average family owned 80 children's books, and 94 percent of children reported their favorite books were ones they had chosen themselves. Ninety percent of children said they had time to read in school. Seventy-six percent reported liking to read in the summer.

- *United Kingdom*: The National Literacy Trust's (Clark 2016) annual survey of 32,569 children and young people (8 to 18 years old) reports that 58 percent enjoyed reading either very much or quite a lot, with 41.4 percent stating they read daily. Reading for fun (31.6 percent) was more frequent than reading for information (17.9 percent). Children and young people spent more minutes reading online (average 100.4 minutes) than reading a book (42 minutes). *Diary of a Wimpy Kid* and Harry Potter books were the most frequently identified favorite titles.

- *International*: The Progress in International Literacy Reading Study (PIRLS), a large comparative study conducted in 2016 by the International Association for the Evaluation of Educational

Achievement, compared the reading literacy of grade four students across 50 countries. The Russian Federation and Hong Kong had the highest scores. In nearly all countries, girls outperformed boys. Since the first PIRLS study in 2001, the number of good readers internationally has continued to increase over time, with almost all students (95 percent) achieving basic literacy skills.

What the Experts Say

Much of what we know about children and their reading comes through the expert observation and reflection of skilled parents and practicing teachers and librarians as well as scholars who have been working in this area for a long while. Here are four experts who are wise observers of children reading. Margaret Meek is a parent, a teacher, and an internationally recognized reading expert. She states firmly that helping a child learn to read is fundamentally an uncomplicated task:

> To learn to read, children need the attention of one patient adult, or an older child, for long enough to read something that pleases them both. A book, a person, and shared enjoyment: these are the conditions of success. The process should begin at an early age and continue as a genuine collaborative activity until the child leaves school. Understanding the reading process may help, but there is nothing so special about it that any interested adult cannot easily grasp it by thinking about why he or she enjoys reading. (Meek 1982, 9)

For Donald Fry, a scholar of reading, the central issue in becoming a reader is to see oneself as a reader:

> Even before we can read, we behave like readers. Very young children borrow books from libraries, go to bookshops, and number books amongst their possessions. They pick up their comics at the newsagents, choose from catalogues, and begin to make out the differences between timetables and maps and recipes and other things that they see their parents using. They handle and arrange books, turning over the pages which they cannot yet read, but which they recognise. They play at reading, accompanying their turning of pages with their own version of the story: perhaps they read aloud to toys, to an imaginary playgroup or an invisible friend. They play at writing, too, making 'books', or seeing their own words made into writing by adults and being read. They already know about books, naming titles, recognising books and series of books. And, of course, they attend to stories that are read to them, at home and elsewhere, feeling themselves to be part of a community that reads, and coming into the sure possession of what story is and what a story does. They see themselves as readers, and we could say that unless they do so, and are encouraged to do so, they will not learn to read. (Fry 1985, 94)

Margaret Mackey, a professor and expert in young people's reading and their multimedia and digital literacies, recently completed an auto-ethnographic study of her own childhood reading during the 1950s and 1960s in St. John's, Newfoundland, Canada. Through careful reconstruction and reexamination of the books and other media along with the places that formed the infrastructure of her development as a reader, Mackey reveals the individual nature of becoming a reader and how it is intrinsically tied to the materiality of the texts, the places, and the times of reading:

> We learn to read in grounded, individual and local times and spaces. We learn to read with our minds and bodies and with the social understanding we develop out of our own locations and circumstances. (Mackey 2016, n.p.)

Roger Sutton, editor of *Horn Book* since 1996 and expert in children's literature, reminds us of the intrinsic value of reading for readers of all ages and warns about interfering with the process:

> Adults can be like this with children's books looking for utility or edification, and completely forgetting what drew them into reading in the first place. Given the chance kids will read the same way adults do: for themselves. Don't think of books for young people as tools: try instead to treat them as invitations into the reading life. (Sutton and Parravano 2010, xiv)

To Read More

Carlsen, G. Robert, and Anne Sherrill. 1988. *Voices of Readers: How We Come to Love Books*. Urbana, IL: National Council of Teachers of English.
"Using excerpts from over 1,000 reading autobiographies, the authors provide insight into a number of questions asked of their participants including: What did they remember about learning how to read? What books did they remember reading? Who, if anyone, had been important in developing their attitudes toward reading? When and where did they read?" (1988, x). A fascinating book in which the voices of readers are central to understanding childhood reading.
Mackey. Margaret. 2016. *One Child Reading: My Auto-Bibliography*. Edmonton: University of Alberta Press.
"Margaret Mackey draws together memory, textual criticism, social analysis, and reading theory in an extraordinary act of self-study. In *One Child Reading*, she makes a singular contribution to our understanding of reading and literacy development. Seeking a deeper sense of what happens when we read, Mackey revisited the texts she read, viewed, listened to, and wrote as she became literate in the 1950s and 1960s in St. John's, Newfoundland. This tremendous sweep of reading included school texts, knitting patterns, musical scores, and games, as well as hundreds of books. The result is not a memoir, but rather a deftly theorized exploration of how a reader is constructed" (Mackey 2016, n.p.).
An engaging and meaningful book for scholars, librarians, teachers and readers.

Meek, Margaret. 1982. *Learning to Read*. London: Bodley Head.

> Intended for parents, this book examines what happens as children learn to read and shows how parents can best help them at each stage. Meek (1982, 25) describes her book as follows:

>> An alternative viewpoint, that reading is too important to be left to experts, is presented in this book. Reading is whole-task learning, right from the start. From first to last the child should be invited to behave like a reader, and those who want to help him should assume that he can learn, and will learn, just as happened when he began to talk. Once a child knows that print has meaning and that he can make it mean something, he will learn to read. The adult's job is to read with him what both can enjoy, to let him see how the story goes, to help him observe what is there to be read, and to tell him what he needs to know when he finds it difficult. Learning to read in the early stages, like everything else a child has come to know, approximates adult behaviour with a genuine, meaningful function.

References

Carlsen, G. Robert, and Anne Sherrill. 1988. *Voices of Readers: How We Come to Love Books*. Urbana, IL: National Council of Teachers of English.

Clark, Christina. 2016. *Children's and Young Peoples' Reading in 2015: Findings from the National Trust's Annual Survey*. London: National Literacy Trust. Available at: http://www.literacytrust.org.uk/assets/0003/1643/Young_people_s_reading_2015_-_Final.pdf.

Fry, Donald. 1985. *Children Talk about Books: Seeing Themselves as Readers*. Milton Keynes, England: Open University Press.

International Association for the Evaluation of Educational Achievement. 2017. *PIRLS 2016 International Results in Reading*. Chestnut Hill, MA: TIMSS & PIRLS International Study Center, Lynch School of Education, Boston College. Available at: http://timssandpirls.bc.edu/pirls2016/international-results/.

Mackey, Margaret. 2016. *One Child Reading: My Auto-Bibliography*. Edmonton: University of Alberta Press.

Meek, Margaret. 1982. *Learning to Read*. London: Bodley Head.Scholastic. 2017a. *Kids and Family Reading Report*, 6th ed. Available at: http://www.scholastic.com/readingreport/key-findings.htm#top-nav-scroll.

Scholastic. 2017b. *Kids and Family Reading Report: Canadian Edition*. Available at: http://www.scholastic.ca/readingreport/files/KFRR_2017_Book_FINAL_CAN.pdf.

Sutton, Roger, and Martha V. Parravano. 2010. *A Family of Readers: The Book Lovers' Guide to Children's and Young Adult Literature*. Somerville, MA: Candlewick Press.

2.2 Becoming a Reader

With reading described as an essential skill for success throughout life and evidence that powerful literacy is not universal, the question of *how* one becomes a reader is clearly important. The roots of literacy are grounded in childhood. A number of early landmark studies have investigated how children become readers.

Dolores Durkin (1966) surveyed almost 10,000 children just as they began to attend school and found that only 229 (2.4 percent) could read 18 or more common words. She then interviewed a sample of parents from both the early reading and nonreading groups to find out how they differed. What distinguished the parents of the early readers was their involvement in activities with their children such as reading aloud to them; answering their questions; helping them with printing, spelling, and the sounds of letters; identifying words; and encouraging them to write. Durkin followed the early readers in a longitudinal study through to the end of grade six, discovering that they continued to do well academically.

Margaret Clark (1976) studied 32 children, all of whom could read before starting school, to explore the factors that contribute to children's progress in learning to read. While these precocious readers had varying backgrounds in terms of family income and education levels, all came from families where books were read and stories were told. Glenda Bissex (1980) in *GNYS AT WRK* presents a case study of her own young son, showing how he considered himself to be a writer (a "genius at work") and underscoring the intricate and dynamic interplay between writing and reading. What is common to these studies and others like them is a sense that becoming a reader is a process that is complex and is situated in early life experiences before the onset of formal education. The memories of childhood reading by the participants in Catherine Ross's study of avid adult readers confirm this.

Case 6: Cultivating Readers

Here is what the readers in Catherine Ross's study of avid adult readers said about the reading environments of their childhood that fostered a love of reading. The following is a sample drawn from many, many similar statements from readers:

Robert: I have read ever since I could do the alphabet. . . . Our house had a lot of books spread around. I know I began indiscriminately reading. It was never guided reading. Mother just left books around. So I never had any sense of censorship. Having books around is the most important thing, so far as I'm concerned, in a house. You can take your child to all sorts of organized visits to the library, and that's very good. But if the books aren't around in the house, I doubt very much that you will cultivate a reader. (Professor of English, 57)

Arthur: We were very poor even by the standards of that day and living in a very backwoods area. Rural, so there weren't any—there were very few books in our home. However, both my father and mother read magazines and read the newspaper. They were avid readers, and I suppose there was something in me that brought me to read, because, as I went to school, I found most of the reading interesting. And a lot of the reading, of course, came from the school books themselves. (Director of a men's mission, age 62)

Doreen: [Our family] had tons and tons of books. Any special event was always topped with a book. We had every kind of book you can imagine. Plus we lived at the library. Both of my brothers and me. My parents were avid readers. We had a cottage where we kept what we called our summertime books and they were reread every summer. ... I had an Aunt Jean and she was the one who started me and every year she gave me a Lucy Maud Montgomery book. And then my grandmother had kept all my mother's books and as she saw that I was at the age where I should have them, I got them. (Business consultant, age 38)

Aaron: My dad read to me every single night. We used to lie on his bed and he'd read to me. ... I looked forward to it, and he encouraged me to read too. He'd give me a chance to go ahead as well—he wouldn't just steal the show. (Master's student in English, age 23)

Anita: Both my parents are great readers. I don't remember either of them saying, "You should read" or "Reading is a wonderful thing." I think we all just did it by following their example. ... My mother was the sort who went to the library every week and got five books out and read them. And then, as soon as we were old enough, we had library cards and we would go with her. I just took [reading] for granted. I thought everybody did it. It didn't have to be sold to me. I just enjoyed it so much. And now, all of us are readers. (MLIS student, age 25)

Comments

Aidan Chambers says, "Readers are made, not born. No one comes into the world already disposed for or against print" (Chambers 1973, 16). Nevertheless, the early years tend to set the pattern for what follows. An overwhelming majority of the committed adult readers in Ross's study came from families that strongly supported reading in childhood. Financial security mattered less than a family sense of valuing books and reading.

What We Know about Early Reading

Research emphasizes an approach to learning to read called emergent literacy. According to Teale and Sulzby (1986), the emergent literacy paradigm places the onset of literacy acquisition at birth rather than at the introduction of formal reading instruction in school (see section 1.1 on the critical period from birth to age four for hearing language). Listening, speaking, reading, and writing are considered interrelated and develop concurrently. Literacy learning occurs in real-life settings where literacy has real functions. From the perspective of emergent literacy, children's literacy is often learned through social interaction and the role modeling of others.

One thing we know about early reading is the importance of hearing stories read aloud. *Becoming a Nation of Readers: The Report of the Commission on Reading* (Anderson et al. 1985), a major U.S. Department of Education study, flatly states: "The single most important activity for building the knowledge required for eventual success in reading is reading aloud to children" (Anderson et al. 1985, 28). This assertion is strongly supported in the results of Gordon Wells's study, *The Meaning Makers* (1986). Wells placed tape recorders in the homes of 128 children, half of whom were 15 months and the other half 39 months old at the beginning of the study. On one day every three months for two and one-half years, 18 ninety-second audio recordings were made at random intervals to capture the naturally occurring conversations in the children's homes. The best indicator of later success at school was the child's knowledge of literacy, particularly the number of stories read aloud to the child. Wells estimated that Jonathon, a star reader in later years at school, had heard more than 5,000 stories read aloud at home before he went to school. In contrast, Rosie had heard almost no stories and in school experienced great difficulty with both her language and her reading skills. Reading aloud to children has been described by many, including Aidan Chambers (1991), as being powerful for many reasons: it helps children learn how narratives work; it makes difficult materials accessible; it encourages children to read a text themselves; and it is a shared, social-bonding experience.

Margaret Meek provides a convincing argument for the importance of immersing children in stories and other texts. In *How Texts Teach What Readers Learn* (1988), Meek claims that the act of reading itself provides "private lessons in reading." She says that children who have been read to before school "can turn pages, tell a story from pictures, recognize advertisements on television and know that print is common in their world" (Meek 1988, 7). Reading aloud to children helps them see the relationship between print and speech. It gives them a sense of stories and how they work. Through being read to, children learn that book language differs from conversational language. "The most important single lesson that children learn from texts is the nature and variety of written discourse, the different ways that language lets a writer tell, and the many different ways a reader reads" (Meek 1988, 21). Joan Gibbons (1999, 20) agrees, stating, "Through hearing, reading and discussing stories, children begin to understand the nature of texts. Understanding different ways in which books are read and exploring the various ways in which meaning is expressed is a reading task that does not end with childhood; it continues for as long as the reader continues to tackle new kinds of reading experiences."

Although it is important to ensure that a parent or some other caring older person reads to children, there is some evidence to suggest that *how* parents read with their children may be just as important as whether or not they read to their children. Bergin, Lancy, and Draper (1994) videotaped 32 white, working-class parent-child pairs while the parent and child were sharing a picture book. They discovered that parents use widely variant approaches to this task and that specific behaviors were associated with positive and negative outcomes. Fluency and positive emotions associated with reading were found to be important in predicting success with reading. "[P]airs who view the child's reading as a source of fun, keep the story flowing without letting the child get bogged down in decoding (by using semantic-oriented rather than decoding-oriented correction tactics), encourage questions about the story, and express humor while reading have children who are more fluent and more positive about reading" (Bergin, Lancy, and Draper 1994, 72). They note that parents of successful readers tended to send the message that "Reading is fun!" while parents using negative behaviors broadcast a sense that "Reading is work."

Reading aloud to children varies across social class, with lower frequency of storybook-sharing in low-income homes (Teale 1986) and lower availability and use of reading and writing materials in low-income families (Anderson, Teale, and Estrada 1980). Interventions have been tried, and there is some evidence to indicate that they work. In a study whose purpose "was to test whether it was possible to enhance parent involvement in children's language and literacy development" (Svensson 1994, 84), 25 Swedish children received twice-yearly visits from 2.5 through 6.5 years of age. In each visit, the parents were given books and other educational materials as well as information about language and literacy development. These children were compared to a control group who received no intervention. Svensson found that the families in the experimental group read books, played with nursery rhymes, did finger plays, and sang songs more often than they had before the interventions and more than occurred in the control group.

In an overview of group intervention programs designed to increase the awareness and participation of parents in early literacy activities such as Running Start (funded by Chrysler in eight U.S. school districts) or Partnership for Family Reading (funded by Metropolitan Life in Newark, NJ), Lancy and Talley (1994) note that such efforts have been successful in at least creating a stronger and broader cultural awareness of the importance of early literacy activities. Carr (1994) found that encouraging parents to work with their children by assigning storybook reading and other daily literacy tasks to be completed at home, enriching the literacy environment of the classroom, and providing cross-age and peer tutors for children experiencing difficulty resulted in noticeable improvements in the literacy skills of an urban, low-income kindergarten class.

Factors That Foster Early Reading

The research has clearly established that particular contexts and activities are needed for children to become readers. As identified by many researchers, including Chambers (1991), Clark (1976), Clay (1966), Hall (1987), Heath (1982), Meek (1982), and Sulzby and Teale (1991), the following factors foster early reading:

- Hearing stories read aloud by a parent or another caring adult
- Having opportunities to do emergent story readings ("reading" on one's own)
- Having ready access to reading materials either at home, at school, or through a public library
- Having free choice of reading materials so that stories are enjoyed and the experience is pleasurable
- Having both the space and the time for shared and individual reading
- Being part of a "readerly" family where parents, siblings, and extended family act as role models
- Having opportunities to talk about reading both while being read to and in other contexts such as at the family dinner table
- Having a sense that reading is a valuable activity
- Having access to an enabling adult

Children and Adults Reading within the Zone of Proximal Development

The enabling adult turns up time and time again in studies of early reading acquisition. The work of Lev Vygotsky, particularly his concept of the zone of proximal development, is helpful in explaining why the presence of a more experienced reader is so important. Vygotsky (1978, 86) described the zone of proximal development as

> the distance between the actual developmental level as determined by independent problem solving and the level of potential development as determined through problem solving under adult guidance or in collaboration with more capable peers.

Vygotsky held that children learn new cognitive skills by practicing them in social interaction with a more experienced person until the skill is mastered and internalized and can be carried out independently. A number of studies have used the conceptual framework of Vygotsky's zone of proximal development as a way of understanding the joint adult-child collaboration in learning situations, including those involving stories and literacy. Tizard and Hughes (1984) compared the language experience of middle- and working-class four-year-old children at home and at nursery school by making audio recordings of their naturally occurring talk in both settings. They found that the home setting provided a very powerful environment for learning. The home setting had the advantage of its low adult-to-child ratio, the close emotional relationship between mother and child, the long-shared context, the wide range of activities engaged in, and the home setting's potential to embed learning in contexts meaningful to the individual child. Of special interest here, "The longest conversations tended to occur in the context of story-reading and joint adult-child play, and . . . the context which provoked the most questions from children was story-telling" (Tizard et al. 1980, 74).

Two other research studies are worth noting that look specifically at how literacy learning happens within the zone of proximal development. Shirley Brice Heath (1982) speaks directly of the role of adult scaffolding in children's literacy development. She notes how adults help the children make text-to-life connections, encourage children to talk around a story, converse with children as they read stories together, and employ tactics like pausing during reading to allow children to practice prediction. I conducted an observation study of 30 four-year-old girls and their mothers on an ordinary visit to their local public libraries (McKechnie 1996, 2000). One of the most important roles of the library, I discovered, was to support young children in their literacy development. The most frequently observed activity after the selection and checkout of library materials was shared reading of stories, with 21 (70 percent) of the girls being read to by their mothers or another adult while in the library. These story read-alouds were captured by the tape recorders the girls wore during their visits. The mothers proved themselves to be adept reading teachers, as they shared stories with their daughters.

As David Lancy and Susan Talley (1994, 3) point out, "Those who are expert in the uses of literacy—parents and older siblings as opposed to reading teachers—model and introduce these uses to children. They create situations—dinner table conversations, interactive bedtime story rituals—where children can flap their stubby little literacy wings without fear of crashing to the ground." They read with their children within the zone of proximal development.

Case 7: The Important Role of Adults in Bringing Children to Reading

Elissa (age four) was a participant in my study of preschoolers using public libraries (McKechnie 1996, 191). In the following excerpt from an audio recording of their visit to the library, Elissa and her mother were reading *The Very Hungry Caterpillar*, a classic picture book written and illustrated by Eric Carle.

Elissa: You know what?

Mother: What?

Elissa: This is it. This is the caterpillar one.

Mother: What happens to him?

Elissa: Gets big.

Mother: And then what?

Elissa: Then . . . he gets bigger.

Mother: Uh huh?

Elissa: And then he gets fat.

Mother: Right! And when he finishes eating and getting big and fat, what happens at the end?

Elissa: Butterfly!

Observation Note: Mother laughs joyfully.

Comments

Elissa's recognition of the book reveals her growing knowledge of children's literature. Through the content of the story, she seems to have learned something about the life cycle of butterflies. Her ability to retell the story in the proper sequence shows that she understands something about the structure and conventions of stories. Elissa's mother supports her daughter's reading by asking open questions ("And then what?") and affirming Elissa's retelling of the story by repeating it using Elissa's own words ("big" and "fat"). Elissa's mother provided room and time for her to "read" this story, providing clues and cues as needed, and reinforcing the competence Elissa brought to the task. Elissa and her mother were working together in Vygotsky's (1978) zone of proximal development.

What Libraries Can Do

1. Provide large, rich collections.
2. Run story time programs for babies, toddlers, and preschool children both in the library and through outreach to other community locations. These programs should include complementary activities such as crafts, songs, and finger plays that extend and reinforce the stories.
3. Facilitate access to reading materials through booklists and pathfinders, displays, and readers' advisory services.
4. Provide areas for reading, especially areas for young children and adults to read together.
5. Loan materials, either individual titles or specially prepared kits, and work cooperatively with other organizations such as nursery schools, daycare centers, "family literacy programs or other community-wide

programs that serve children in their homes or in community locations" (Teale 1995, 116).

6. "[E]ducate parents, preschool teachers, or child care professionals in what and how to read to preschoolers" (Teale 1995, 118).

What Parents Can Do

1. Read to your child.
2. Share a wide variety of books (fiction, nonfiction, poetry, picture books) in a wide variety of narrative genres with your child.
3. "Involve your child in the selection of books" (Bouchard 2001, 26).
4. Buy books for your child. "We like to possess copies of the books that mean most to us. Owning them allows us to reread them whenever we want, helps us to remember what is in them. Seeing them on our shelves and handling them now and then gives us pleasure ... " (Chambers 1991, 61).
5. Go to the library with your child—attend story time programs and borrow books.
6. Make books with your child.
7. Serve as a role model by reading yourself.
8. Provide time for reading. "Adults who care for children as readers must make sure that children have time for reading" (Chambers 1991, 36). It is equally important to provide quiet, comfortable spaces for reading.
9. Encourage early writing activities such as dictating stories for an adult to write down, making shopping lists, playing with magnetic fridge letters, scrapbook making, and play-dough letter modeling (Binkley 1988, 9–10).

To Read More about Becoming a Reader

Chambers, Aidan. 1991. *The Reading Environment: How Adults Help Children Enjoy Books*. Stroud, *Gloucestershire*: Thimble Press.
Chambers writes about the factors that contribute to a reading-friendly environment, including access to book stocks, displays, reading areas, reading time, storytelling, reading aloud, book owning, friends and peers, and the enabling adult. This book is full of practical suggestions for teachers, librarians, parents, and others who work with children and reading.

Immroth, Barbara Froling, and Viki Ash-Geisler, eds. 1995. *Achieving School Readiness: Public Libraries and National Education Goal No. 1*. Chicago: American Library Association.
With chapters on storytelling, play, social development, learning styles, oral and written language, and emergent literacy by leading scholars and practitioners, this book places the reading lives of young children within the larger context of their overall development. Drawing on the research literature, it includes suggestions for ensuring and enhancing healthy early literacy development.

Teale, William H., and Elizabeth Sulzby, eds. 1986. *Emergent Literacy: Reading and Writing*. Norwood, NJ: Ablex.
> Teale and Sulzby explore young children and their reading and writing, covering the period from birth through five or six years. With chapters contributed from leading researchers in the field, they provide an excellent overview of early literacy development as a continuing and changing process. A landmark work.

Three Great Books for Parents

Full of inspiring stories and practical tips and written in highly accessible language, any of these three titles would help parents interested in fostering the development of their children as readers. The author of *Cushla and Her Books* (1980) and *Babies Need Books* (1998), Dorothy Butler is widely acknowledged as the person most responsible for popularizing the importance of reading to babies. Marie Clay was the first to use the term "emergent literacy" in her doctoral research of 1966. Bernice Cullinan was a professor of Early Childhood and Education at New York University, where she taught reading for 30 years. Mem Fox is an award-winning, Australian children's author and a passionate advocate of reading to children.

Butler, Dorothy, and Marie Clay. 1987. *Reading Begins at Home: Preparing Children for Reading Before They Go to School*. Portsmouth, NH: Heinemann.

Cullinan, Bernice E. 2000. *Read to Me: Raising Kids Who Love to Read*. New York: Scholastic.

Fox, Mem. 2001. *Reading Magic: Why Reading Aloud to Our Children Will Change Their Lives Forever*. San Diego, CA: Harvest Original/Harcourt.

References

Anderson, Alonzo B., William H. Teale, and Elette Estrada. 1980. "Low-income Children's Preschool Literacy Experiences: Some Naturalistic Observations." *The Quarterly Newsletter of the Laboratory of Human Cognition* 2: 59–65.

Anderson, Richard C., Elfrieda H. Hiebert, J. A. Scott, and I. A. G. Wilkinson. 1985. *Becoming a Nation of Readers: The Report of the Commission on Reading*. Pittsburgh, PA: U.S. National Academy of Education.

Bergin, Chris, David F. Lancy, and Kelly D. Draper. 1994. "Parents' Interactions with Beginning Readers." In *Children's Emergent Literacy: From Research to Practice*, 53–77. Edited by David F. Lancy. Westport, CT: Praeger.

Binkley, Marilyn R. 1988. *Becoming a Nation of Readers: What Parents Can Do*. Indianapolis, IN: D.C. Heath with the U.S. Department of Education.

Bissex, Glenda. 1980. *GNYX AT WRK: A Child Learns to Read and Write*. Cambridge, MA: Harvard University Press.

Bouchard, David. 2001. *The Gift of Reading*. Victoria, BC: Orca Books.

Butler, Dorothy. 1980. *Cushla and Her Books*. Boston, MA: Horn Book.

Butler, Dorothy. 1998. *Babies Need Books: Sharing the Joy of Books with Your Child from Birth to Six*. Portsmouth, NH: Heinemann.

Carr, Eileen M. 1994. "It Takes a Whole Village to Raise a Child: Supplementing Instruction for 'At-Risk' Kindergarten Students." In *Children's Emergent Literacy: From Research to Practice*, 238–249. Edited by David F. Lancy. Westport, CT: Praeger.

Chambers, Aidan. 1973. *Introducing Books to Children*. London: Heinemann Educational Books.

Chambers, Aidan. 1991. *The Reading Environment: How Adults Help Children Enjoy Books*. Stroud, *Gloucestershire*: Thimble Press.

Clark, Margaret M. 1976. *Young Fluent Readers: What Can They Teach Us?* London: Heinemann.

Clay, Mary M. 1966. *Emergent Reading Behaviour*. PhD diss. University of Auckland, New Zealand.

Durkin, Dolores. 1966. *Children Who Read Early*. New York: Teachers College Press.

Gibbons, Joan. 1999. "Literature for Children." In *Learning to Read: Beyond Phonics and Whole language*, 195–214. Edited by G. Brian Thompson and Tom Nicholson. New York: Teachers College Press.

Hall, Nigel. 1987. *The Emergence of Literacy*. Portsmouth, NH: Heinemann.

Heath, Shirley B. 1982. "What No Bedtime Story Means: Narrative Skills at Home and School." *Language in Society* 11, no. 1: 49–76.

Lancy, David F., and Susan D. Talley. 1994. "The Conditions That Support Emergent Literacy." In *Children's Emergent Literacy: From Research to Practice*, 1–20. Edited by David F. Lancy. Westport, CT: Praeger

McKechnie, Lynne (E. F.). 1996. *Opening the "Preschoolers' Door to Learning": An Ethnographic Study of the Use of Public Libraries by Preschool Girls*. PhD diss. University of Western Ontario, London, Ontario, Canada.

McKechnie, Lynne (E. F.). 2000. "The Ethnographic Observation of Preschool Children." *LISR* 22, no. 1: 61–76.

Meek, Margaret. 1982. *Learning to Read*. London: Bodley Head.

Meek, Margaret. 1988. *How Texts Teach What Readers Learn*. Stroud, Gloucestershire: Thimble Press.

Sulzby, Elizabeth, and William H. Teale. 1991. "Emergent Literacy." In *Handbook of Reading Research*, Vol. 2, 727–758. Edited by Rebecca Barr, Michael L. Kamil, Peter Mosenthal, and P. David Pearson. White Plains, NY: Longman.

Svensson, Ann-Katrin. 1994. "Helping Parents Help Their Children: Early Language Stimulation in the Child's Home." In *Children's Emergent Literacy: From Research to Practice*, 79–92. Edited by David F. Lancy. Westport, CT: Praeger.

Teale, William H. 1986. "Home Background and Young Children's Literacy Development." In *Emergent Literacy: Writing and Reading*, 173–206. Edited by William H. Teale and Elizabeth Sulzby. Norwood, NJ: Ablex.

Teale, William H. 1995. "Public Libraries and Emergent Literacy: Helping Set the Foundation for School Success." In *Achieving School Readiness: Public Libraries and National Education Goal No. 1*, 113–133. Edited by Barbara Froling Immroth and Viki Ash-Geisler. Chicago: American Library Association.

Teale, William H., and Elizabeth Sulzby, eds. 1986. *Emergent Literacy: Writing and Reading*. Norwood, NJ: Ablex.

Tizard, Barbara, Helen Carmichael, Martin Hughes, and Gill Pinkerton. 1980. "Four Year Olds Talking to Mothers and Teachers." In *Language and Language Disorders in Childhood*. Edited by Lionel A. Hersov and M. Berger (a book supplement to the *Journal of Child Psychology and Psychiatry*, Vol. 2). Oxford, England: Pergamon Press.

Tizard, Barbara, and Martin Hughes. 1984. *Young Children Learning*. Cambridge, MA: Harvard University Press.

Vygotsky, Lev. 1978. *Mind in Society: The Development of Higher Psychological Processes*. Edited by Michael Cole, Vera John-Steiner, Sylvia Scribner, and Ellen Souberman. Cambridge, MA: Harvard University Press.

Wells, Gordon. 1986. *The Meaning Makers: Children Learning Language and Using Language to Learn*. Portsmouth, NH: Heinemann.

2.3 Readicide and Its Antidotes: Maintaining Childhood Reading

Kelly Gallagher, author of *Readicide: How Schools Are Killing Reading and What You Can Do about It* (2009), dedicates his book to "those educators who resist the political in favor of the authentic" (iii). He provides the following definition:

> Read-i-cide *n*: The systematic killing of the love of reading, often exacerbated by the inane, mind-numbing practices found in schools. (2009, 2)

Jennifer and Ponniah (2015, 1) note that "reading to score well on tests impedes the desire for reading [and] in fact it causes the fear of failure, and anxiety towards reading," and they suggest pleasure reading as an antidote to readicide. In an interview published in a thematic issue dedicated to readicide in *Knowledge Quest* (39, 4, March/April 2011), the journal of the American Association of School Librarians, Gallagher states, "There is no magic pill [to fix the problem of readicide]. What works is bringing kids back to interesting books and an array of reading materials including newspapers, comics, magazines, and blogs" (Clark 2011, 11).

Parents and librarians also participate in readicide. Three prominent practices illustrate the presence of readicide in literacy endeavors of today's schools, libraries, and parents: an overemphasis on particular skills, the promotion of dialogic reading, and the implementation of levelled reading.

Overemphasis on Particular Skills

Convened by the U.S. National Institute for Literacy and building on an earlier study by the National Institute of Child Health and Development (2000), the National Literacy Panel published *Developing Early Literacy: A Scientific Synthesis of Early Literacy Development and Implications for Intervention* (Lonigan and Shanahan 2008). The focus of this inquiry was "to establish which early skills or abilities could properly be said to be the precursors of later literacy achievement" (Lonigan and Shanahan 2008, vi). Emphasis was placed on traditional characteristics and tasks of literacy, including alphabet knowledge, phonological awareness, and print awareness. The findings of this report were integrated into many classroom and library contexts. The American Library Association's "Every Child Ready to Read" (2017) initiative is a prominent and ongoing example. A model program for workshops for parents, which incorporated six prereading skills (narrative skills, print motivation, vocabulary, phonological awareness, letter knowledge, and print awareness), was developed, field tested, and then presented as a formal kit for public libraries in 2002, with a second revised kit appearing in 2010. Project VIEWS2 (Valuable Initiatives in Early Learning That Work Successfully), a four-year study, demonstrated that storytimes that explicitly address these skills make a positive difference in children's early literacy skills (Campana et al. 2016). While admirable both in intent and in the rigor brought to the important issue of helping children become readers, the problem with programs like Every Child Ready to Read is that their focus on particular skills can cause us to ignore other aspects of emergent reading such as those enumerated under "Factors That Foster Early Reading" in section 2.2. Furthermore, some of the components and strategies offered by the program (e.g., the tip sheets with instructions for reading specific titles to a child) disrupt the natural reading of a story to focus on vocabulary building or letter recognition and turn the reading experience into work rather than pleasure.

Dialogic Reading

Dialogic reading was developed by Grover J. Whitehurst through his Stony Brook Reading and Language Project (2001). Whitehurst notes:

> When most adults share a book with a reader, they read and the child listens. In dialogic reading, the adult helps the child become the teller of the story. The adult becomes the listener, the questioner, the audience for the child. No one can learn to play the piano just by listening to someone else play. Likewise, no one can learn to read by listening to someone else read. Children learn most from books when they are actively involved. (1992, para. 7).

Dialogic reading involves the PEER sequence, an interaction between the adult and the child in which the adult

- prompts the child to say something about the book;
- evaluates the child's response;
- expands the child's response by rephrasing and adding information to it; and
- repeats the prompt to make sure the child has learned from the expansion (Whitehurst 1992, para. 8).

Some research suggests that dialogic reading is effective, especially for children from low-income families and those experiencing disabilities. Lonigan and Whitehurst (1998) studied the impact of shared reading through a field experiment with three- and four-year-old children from low-income families who attended subsidized child care. Parents and teachers were trained in dialogic reading, and the children experienced shared reading for six weeks. Compared to a control group who received no intervention, the children who experienced dialogic reading (especially at home) scored higher on standardized tests of oral language.

The problem with this study and many like it is that, whereas we know that reading is a complex and nuanced phenomenon, reading ability was operationalized by the constrained variables measured by standardized tests such as vocabulary size. Zevenbergen et al. (2016), in an interview study with parents participating in a home-based dialogic reading program, found that 40 percent of the lower-income parents reported difficulties implementing the program, including finding time to do it, "remembering the questions to ask," getting the child to focus, and getting "used to asking unfamiliar questions and that sort of thing" (9). Furthermore, the long-term effects of dialogic reading on conventional reading success have not yet been substantiated (Salinger 2001).

Case 8: Does Dialogic Reading Always Work?

A search for "dialogic reading" on YouTube, a popular site for sharing videos, yields some interesting examples. Reading Massachusetts is a not-for-profit organization dedicated to fostering early literacy. It posted several short videos. One of these, "Dialogic reading in action!" (2012, found at http://www.youtube.com/watch?v=62wDFYeGORk), is described as follows:

> Pheap and her son Kayden show us that Raising a Reader MA is about more than just reading a book, it's an engaging activity that promotes interaction between adults and children. Before Raising a Reader MA, Kayden's teacher said, "He has hardly said a word at school the entire year! He murmurs under his breath and often covers his mouth when speaking. He also tends to restrain himself from smiling or laughing." The addition of a simple reading can help open up children to the world of words and paves the way to academic success throughout a child's life.

In the scene presented in this video clip, Pheap and Kayden are sharing a picture book by Rosemary Wells, one of her award-winning titles about two little rabbits named Max and Ruby. While lively talk occurs between mother and child, what happens here appears more like an oral worksheet emphasizing traditional preschool academic skills as Kayden's mother asks him to point to and count objects and identify colors. There is little or no sense of story and narrative. There is no linking of the story to Kayden's own life. And Pheap is definitely the one controlling this "reading"—not once does Kayden ask a question or offer a comment of his own. This looks very different from the shared reading described in Case 7 between Elissa and her mother.

Comments

A major problem with dialogic reading, then, is that it can be implemented as a reading controlled by the adult rather than the child.

While interest may be high at first, it may quickly be experienced by the child as work. The success of dialogic reading depends on the skills of the adult involved and the relationship between the child and the adult. While the techniques can be taught, unless the adult is a reader herself or himself, it will be very difficult to implement them appropriately.

In an article for early childhood educators and parents about best practices for dialogic reading that draws on 20 years of research, Kiely (2014) concludes by reminding the reader, "We must bear in mind that unless the child is enjoying the story and the experience of interacting around the story, our struggle to improve oral language skills will be in vain" (25).

Levelled Reading

A practice that has become increasingly evident in the last 20 years is the implementation of levelled reading in both children's formal reading education and their pleasure reading. Brabham and Villaume (2002, 438) note that "in general, levelled text refers to reading materials that represent a progression from simple to more complex and challenging texts." Many schemes are used, including Fountas and Pinnell's text-level gradient and Lexile scores. Some of these measures have associated commercial programs for structuring, guiding, and measuring children's reading achievement, including the Lexile Framework for Reading and the Accelerated Reader program. More and more children's literature is being levelled. For example, the HarperCollins I Can Read series of beginning-to-read books for early elementary school-age children, which includes many classics of children's literature such as Caldecott medal award-winning *Frog and Toad Are Friends* (Lobel 1970), now includes not just a "level" on the front cover but also a description of the scheme and the characteristics of each of the levels on the back cover of each title in the series. NoveList K-8 Plus, the popular readers' advisory database, lists Lexile scores for all children's materials.

Teachers, parents, and librarians welcomed the labeling, as it helped them identify texts at a child's reading level. But problems quickly emerged. The pedagogical approaches and algorithms for assigning levels to texts use different criteria, so the same book might be levelled as appropriate for very different levels. There is evidence that even within one levelling scheme, results can vary widely. For example, both *The Poky Little Puppy* (Lowrey 1942) and Pulitzer Prize–winning *The Color Purple* (Walker 1982) have Accelerated Reader levels of 4.0, designated as being suitable for a reader in the first month of the fourth grade (Grigsby 2014). Pitcher and Fang's (2007) linguistic analysis of 20 levelled texts found that the algorithm used was neither consistently implemented across the texts nor a reliable indication of difficulty. Brabham and Villaume (2002, 438) point out that "some schools are caught up in 'levelling mania' ... [They] become so enamored with levelled text that they lose sight of other important aspects of effective reading instruction." Rather than allowing children to select texts that interest them, some teachers and parents restrict them to texts that are at their designated level. Any book that has not been levelled with the scheme in use at their school will not be allowed and will probably not be in the school's collection. Cregar (2011, 42) notes:

> Traditional unrestricted browsing behaviors are profoundly changed when [Accelerated Reader] selections are mandated by teachers . . . When book level number on the library book spine is an obvious number, students not only focus on that number as they browse, they often shun other books that do not fit their [Reading Level] criteria.

Warren and Maynard (2011) conducted a focus group study with children 11 to 13 years old to capture children's perceptions of "age banding," a British term related to levelled reading. The children reported feeling "that age banding is provided for adults and gives parents the ability to control what their children read." They also reported not wanting "to be associated with younger children or inferior readers by reading books banded at an age below theirs." Warren and Maynard (2011, 135) concluded that "age-banding neglects individualism by failing to take into account the diverse and ever-changing reader preferences of different children."

The American Association of School Librarians has issued a *Position Statement on Labeling Books with Reading Levels* (2011), which reiterates the concerns expressed by librarians and children and condemns the practice. It reminds us of the importance of a "minor's right to access resources freely and without restriction." Although most of the literature references practices in school libraries, many reports of public libraries also share the same concerns about the negative effects of levelling and age banding, having received requests from children, parents, and teachers for levelled texts (Parrott 2017).

Excerpts from data from my book ownership study (McKechnie 2004, 2007) show that children know about readicide. When asked if he liked to read, Rick (age 12) responded: "It depends. If someone goes and picks a book for me and tells me to read it and, if I don't like it, that's when I don't like reading. But if I pick a book that I think I'll like, that's when I like it. I'd rather read when I know I like it." Quiet Rebel (age 11) had a large set of children's literature classics like *Treasure Island* and *Robinson Crusoe* on his bookshelf. When asked if he had read all the titles, he responded, "Not one." When asked whether he planned to read then one day, his response was pointed and terse: "Maybe in 10 or 26 years." These boys were talking about "free voluntary reading," a strategy that is an effective antidote to readicide.

Antidotes to Readicide

Stephen Krashen (2004) developed the concept of Free Voluntary Reading (FVR) when he conducted a major review of the published literature about reading. He identified several trends and important variables in the literature, but none was more robust in predicting success in reading for children and teens than the opportunity to do FVR. Krashen defined FVR as follows:

> Free voluntary reading means reading because you want to. For school-age children, FVR means no book report, no questions at the end of the chapter, and no looking up every vocabulary word. FVR means putting down a book you don't like and choosing another one instead. It is the kind of reading highly literate people do all the time. (2004, x)

Unfortunately, overemphasis on particular skills, dialogic reading, and levelled reading do not involve much, if any, FVR. Fortunately, public libraries provide many services to enable children in their development as readers. Because section 2.2 focused on younger children, the examples discussed here will pertain to older, school-age children. Readers' advisory services, booktalking, book discussion groups for older children, mounting displays, and preparing recommended reading lists all support children as voluntary free readers. Two activities that have attracted increasing attention over the last 10 years are briefly described here: summer reading programs and reading aloud to older children.

- *Summer reading programs* have been offered by public libraries for many years. Children who participate are typically asked to read and report on books and earn small incentives and rewards as they do this. Research indicates that most summer reading programs are effective in supporting children as readers. Literature reviews (Cooper et al. 1996; Library and Archives Canada 2006) confirm the existence of the summer slip—the tendency for children, especially those from low-income families, to score more poorly on standard tests for reading and mathematics when they return to school in the fall. Studies of library summer reading programs, including evaluations of individual summer reading programs (e.g., Los Angeles County 2001), Roman and Fiore's national Dominican Study (2010), and a more recent study by Dynia et al. (2015), found that children, even those from lower income families, who participated in a public library summer reading program maintained reading levels. Perhaps more importantly, children and their parents reported enjoying the programs.
- In *Becoming a Nation of Readers*, the U.S. Department of Education's *Report on Reading* (Anderson et al. 1985), *reading aloud to children* was identified as the single most important activity for building the knowledge required for success in reading. Although reading aloud is normally associated primarily with preschool children, the report also recommended that it should continue through the grades. This is an especially powerful activity for parents and older children to do together. At the age of nine, Alice Ozma (2011) and her father committed to reading aloud together for 100 nights. They enjoyed it so much that their reading

streak continued for 3,281 days, ending on Alice's first day at college. Alice's book is a story of commitment to her father and to reading.

What Libraries Can Do

1. Do not overlook the well-established body of research that demonstrates the importance of voluntary free reading and reading for pleasure in the development of children as readers.
2. Offer programs and other services that support voluntary free reading. Readers' advisory, booktalking, displays, and reading lists help introduce titles to children that they might enjoy reading. Book discussion groups and summer reading programs provide opportunities for children to enjoy and share reading with others.
3. Collect resources to help parents read aloud and their older children identify good books for reading aloud together, such as Judy Freeman's *Books Kids Will Sit Still For 3: A Read-Aloud Guide* (Libraries Unlimited, 2006), Bob Reid's *Reid's Read-Alouds: Selections for Children and Teens* (ALA, 2009), and Jim Trealease's *Read-Aloud Handbook*, 7th ed. (Penguin, 2013).

What Parents Can Do

1. Read with your children (of all ages) as often as possible.
2. Take care to make the reading fun rather than work.
3. Make a wide variety of reading materials available to your children. Purchase books the child owns herself/himself, and regularly visit your local library to borrow materials.
4. Allow your children to select their own reading materials independently to ensure they are likely to have something that they will want to read.

To Read More about Preventing and Healing Readicide

Gallagher, Kelly. 2009. *Readicide: How Schools Are Killing Reading and What You Can Do about It*. Portland, ME: Stenhouse Publications.
  Gallagher begins by defining and describing readicide. The majority of his book focuses on potential solutions to the problem that teachers, librarians, and parents could implement to avoid readicide.

Krashen, Stephen. 2004. *The Power of Reading: Insights from the Research*, 2nd ed. Westport, CT: Libraries Unlimited.
  A review of the research literature on reading. Krashen identifies the ability to do FVR as the most important variable in becoming a reader.

Ozma, Alice. 2011. *The Reading Promise: My Father and the Books We Shared*. New York: Grand Central Publishing.

References

American Association of School Librarians (AASL). 2011. "Position Statement on Labeling Books with Reading Levels." *AASL*, American Library Association. Available at: http://www.ala.org?aasl/advocacy/resources/statements/labeling.

American Library Association (ALA). 2017. "Every Child Ready to Read @ Your Library." ALA. Available at: http://www.everychildreadytoread.org/.

Anderson, Richard C., Elfrieda H. Hiebert, Judith A. Scott, and Ian A. G. Wilkinson. 1985. *Becoming a Nation of Readers: The Report of the Commission on Reading.* Pittsburg: U.S. National Academy of Education.

Brabham, Edna G., and Susan K. Vallaume. 2002. "Leveled Text: The Good News and the Bad News." *The Reading Teacher* 55, no. 5: 438–441.

Campana, Kathleen, J. Elizabeth Mills, Saroj Ghoting, and Judy Nelson. 2016. "Supercharge your Storytimes: Using Intentionality, Interactivity, and Community." *Children and Libraries* 14, no. 1: 36-38.

Clark, Ruth Cox. 2011. "Reversing Readicide: An Interview with Author Kelly Gallagher." *Knowledge Quest* 39, no. 4: 10–11.

Cooper, Harris, Barbara Nye, Kelly Charlton, James Lindsay, and Scott Greathouse. 1996. "The Effects of Summer Vacation on Achievement Scores: A Narrative and a Meta-Analytic Review." *Review of Educational Research* 66, no. 3: 227–268.

Cregar, Elyse. 2011. "Browsing by Numbers and Reading for Points." *Knowledge Quest* 39, no. 4: 40–45.

"Dialogic Reading in Action." 2012. Raising a Reader Massachusetts. December 11. Available at: http://www.youtube.com/watch?v=62wDFYeGORk.

Dynia, Jaclyn M., Shayne B. Piasta, Laura M. Justice, and Columbus Metropolitan Library. 2015. "Impact of Library-Based Summer Reading Clubs on Primary-Grade Children's Literacy Activities and Achievement." *Library Quarterly* 85, no. 4: 386–405.

Gallagher, Kelly. 2009. *Readicide: How Schools Are Killing Reading and What You Can Do about It.* Portland: Stenhouse.

Grigsby, Susan K. S. 2014. "The Story Is More Important Than the Words: A Portrait of Reader-Focused Library Program." *Knowledge Quest* 43, no. 1: 22–28.

Jennifer, J. Mary, and R. Joseph Ponniah. 2015. "Pleasure Reading Cures Readicide and Facilitates Academic Reading." *Journal on English Language Teaching* 5, no. 4: 1–5.

Kiely, Joan. 2014. "All about Dialogic Reading." *Nursery World* 114, no. 3: 22–25.

Krashen, Stephen. 2004. *The Power of Reading: Insights from the Research*, 2nd ed. Westport, CT: Libraries Unlimited.

Library and Archives Canada. 2006. "Literature Review on the Impact of Summer Reading Clubs." Available at: http://www.collectionscanada.gc.ca/obj/009003/f2/009003-06-040-e.pdf.

Lobel, Arnold. 1970. *Frog and Toad Are Friends.* New York: Harper.

Lonigan, Christopher J., and Grover J. Whitehurst. 1998. "Relative Efficacy of Parent and Teacher Involvement in a Shared-Reading Intervention for Preschool Children from Low-Income Backgrounds." *Early Childhood Research Quarterly* 13, no. 2: 265–292.

Lonigan, Christopher, and Timothy Shanahan. 2008. *Developing Early Literacy: Report of the National Early Literacy Panel.* Washington, DC: National Early Literacy Panel. Available at: https://lincs.ed.gov/publications/pdf/NELPReport09.pdf.

Los Angeles County Public Library Foundation. 2001. "Evaluation of the Public Library Summer Reading Program: Books and Beyond … Take Me to Your Reader." Available at: http://www.colapublib.org/eDocuments/EvalSRP-2001.pdf.

Lowry, Janet. 1982. *The Poky Little Puppy.* New York: Simon and Schuster.

McKechnie, Lynne (E. F.). 2004. " 'I'll Keep Them for My Children' (Kevin, 9 years): Children's Personal Collections of Books and Other Materials." *Canadian Journal of Library & Information Science* 28, no. 4: 73–88.

McKechnie, Lynne (E. F.). 2007. " 'Spiderman Is Not for Babies' (Peter, 4 years): The Boys and Reading Problem from the Perspective of the Boys Themselves." *Canadian Journal of Library & Information Science* 32, no. 1/2: 57–67.

National Institute of Child Health and Human Development. 2000. *Report of the National Reading Panel: Teaching Children to Read: An Evidence-Based Assessment of the Scientific Research Literature on Reading and Its Implications for Reading Instruction.* Available at: http://www.dys-add.com/resources/SpecialEd/Teaching ChildrenToRead.pdf.

Ozma, Alice. 2011. *The Reading Promise: My Father and the Books We Shared.* New York: Grand Central Publishing.

Parrott, Kiera. 2017. "Thinking Outside the Bin: Why labeling Books by Reading Level Disempowers Young Readers." *School Library Journal* 63, no. 8: 42-45.

Pitcher, Brandy, and Zhihui Fang. 2007. "Can We Trust Levelled Texts? An Examination of Their Reliability and Quality from a Linguistic Perspective." *Literacy* 41: 43–51.

Roman, Susan, and Carole D. Fiore. 2010. "Do Public Library Summer Reading Programs Close the Achievement Gap? The Dominican Study." *Children and Libraries* 8, no. 3: 27–31.

Salinger, Terry. 2001. "Assessing the Literacy of Young Children: The Case for Multiple Forms of Evidence." In *Handbook of Early Literacy Research*, Vol. 2, 390–420. Edited by Susan B. Neuman and David K. Dickinson. New York: Guilford Press.

Walker, Alice. 1982. *The Color Purple.* New York: Harcourt, Brace, Jovanovich.

Warren, Claire, and Sally Maynard. 2011. "Age Banding and Its Impact on Children and Their Reading." *Journal of Librarianship and Information Science* 44, no. 2: 129–136.

Whitehurst, Grover J. 1992. "Dialogic Reading: An Effective Way to Read to Preschoolers." *Reading Rockets.* Available at: http://www.readingrockets.org/article/400.

Whitehurst, Grover J. 2001. "Emergent Literacy: Development from Prereaders to Readers." In *Handbook of Early Literacy Research*, Vol. 2, 11–29. Edited by Susan B. Neuman and David K. Dickinson. New York: Guilford Press.

Zevenbergen, Andrea A., Sydnee Worth, Delaney Dretto, and Kelsey Travers. 2016. "Parents' Experiences in a Home-Based Dialogic Reading Programme." *Early Childhood Development and Care*: 1–13. Available at: http://dx.doi.org/10.1080/03004430.2016.1241775.

2.4 Multimodal Reading

Recent research in education has broadened understandings and explorations of literacy. First introduced in 1996 by the New London Group, the concept of multi-literacies has been widely accepted to refer to "the multiplicity of communication channels and medias, and the increasing saliency of cultural and linguistic diversity" (NLG 1996, 61). We now see literacy as going far beyond the traditional emphases on the reading and writing of print texts to encompass all elements involved in meaning making, meaning expression, and meaning transfer (Kress 2000). Multimodal literacy includes written language, oral language, visual representation, audio representation, tactile representation, gestural representation, and spatial representation as ways of meaning making (Cope and Kalantzis 2009, 178–179). This book has as its focus one element of multiliteracies—the traditional practice of reading texts, especially reading for pleasure. Libraries have provided books and stories in a variety of formats, including print, recorded sound, film, and multimedia kits. Recently, they have begun to collect digital texts, including picture book apps, and eBooks for children, making them available for loan or for use in the library. This section on multimodal reading explores digital texts and their child readers.

What the Research Says about Children's Pleasure Reading of eBooks

Given the rapid development of digital technology and applications suitable for use by children and the way digital materials have penetrated into everyday and school lives, it is not surprising that the literature has expanded on the topic of digital materials for children. However, Schreurs's overview of the research, *Children's E-books Are Born: How E-Books for Children Are Leading E-book Development and Redefining the Reading Experience*, notes that most of the literature "focuses largely on literacy and education, . . . little attention has been paid to if and why children enjoy the e-reading experience, and . . . the majority of current research examines children e-reading from an adult perspective" (2013, 2). Although research on children's pleasure reading of digital texts is limited, a few studies do exist. Scholastic conducts biannual national surveys of children and teens reading. Now in its sixth edition, the latest report presents data collected in 2016 through a national American survey of 2,718 parents and children, of which 1,043 were children ages 6 to 17. When asked whether they preferred print or eBooks, 45 percent reported liking print books better, 38 percent had no preference, and only 16 percent preferred eBooks (Scholastic 2017, 15).

Maynard (2110) provided eBook readers and eBooks to three families, each with two children aged 7 to 12 years. Families were also given funds to purchase other titles. The parents and children were asked to e-read at least 20 minutes per day and keep diaries, which logged when and what they read. They were interviewed before and after the e-reading. Although little qualitative data were collected, some interesting results emerged. Everyone, even one of the children who described himself as a reluctant reader, enjoyed e-reading. Everyone learned how to use the provided devices quickly and easily. The children indicated that they especially enjoyed eBooks with interactive features such as puzzles. After their e-reading experience, all the adults stated they preferred traditional print books, whereas half the children preferred eBooks.

Howard and Wallace (2016) studied parental perceptions of apps for preschoolers. Fifty-three percent of the 133 participants in their online survey indicated that they provided children with access to picture book apps, usually on an iPad. However, most expressed a strong preference for print books, citing as drawbacks worries about too much screen time and fewer opportunities for adult-child bonding time.

What Children Tell Us about Their E-reading for Pleasure

Two recent studies have looked specifically at children's e-reading practices from the perspectives of the children themselves. McKechnie and Schreurs (2017) studied the e-reading practices of 20 children aged 2 to 12 years. The children were asked to read a book they had on their own family's iPad and then another on the iPad the researchers brought, while the researcher observed what they did and asked questions. Children too young to read independently usually participated in shared readings with a parent. The researchers made observation field notes and the sessions were audio recorded and transcribed. Seven major themes emerged from the data.

1. When asked which were his favorite picture book apps, Theo (age four) proclaimed, "Every single one is my favorite." The children all loved the eBooks.

2. However, all the children regarded their iPads primarily as gaming spaces. Suzanne (age eight) was delighted to discover interactive elements in the eBooks ("Wait a minute . . . eBooks also have games?").

3. The children, even the youngest, were all tech savvy, confidently operating their iPads and navigating the picture book apps and eBooks. Hero (age eight) informed the researcher, "My very first time I knew it. I knew it before I even learned it."

4. Kids become tech savvy in many ways, including learning from someone else, exploring on their own, and transferring skills learned while using other apps.

5. Traditional print books are still very important to children, and they can articulate the affordances of both eBooks and print books (see Case 9).

6. The kids understood that eBooks and book apps go beyond the traditional print book in several ways, largely in terms of their interactive features.

7. No matter what the format, for these children a "book" was a "book." Lydia (age six) conflated the two formats when she told the researcher, "I like reading paper books better on the iPad," and Wolfman (age eight), when asked if he preferred print or eBooks, simply replied, "I read practically the same."

To understand how e-reading fits within the full reading lives of children, I conducted an in-depth case study of Stella (age six), a child who had participated in my earlier study when she was three (McKechnie 2017). Stella's personal collection of reading materials and other media was inventoried and Stella and her mother were asked questions about her collection and her at-home reading practices. An interesting picture emerged. Stella had 200 items. However, both she and her mother noted that Stella's younger brother, Sam (age three), had a bookshelf full of materials in his room, many of which had belonged to Stella when she was younger and some of which were hers now but had made their way onto Sam's bookshelf. Sam had 221 items, and so together the two children owned 421 items. Stella's collection included materials in many formats: 67 picture books, 16 information books, 2 reference books, 19 series books, 24 beginning-to-read books, 14 toy books, 17 books related to popular culture, 6 magazines, 4 comic books, 30 films and TV shows on DVDs, 12 long play audio records, and 28 picture book apps on the family's iPad Mini. In addition, the children's playlist on Netflix included 12 shows. Stella's e-reading materials comprised 14 percent of her collection.

Shared reading of traditional print books is a daily event for Stella. She and her brother settle into the big red chair in Sam's room for bedtime stories with either their mother or father. After the shared bedtime stories, Stella usually "reads" independently in her own bed before falling asleep and occasionally at other times during the day. Stella's mother is reading aloud the *Enchanted Pony Academy* series to Stella; the books have a special place on her shelf, with a bookmark marking their place in volume being read. The children watch the DVDs and Netflix shows only on Saturdays and in the family's media room, where these materials are housed. eBook reading happens occasionally, most often in the car on "longish" road trips. Stella's collection and pleasure reading practices did not differ very much from those of the children I studied before the emergence of eBooks. Her reading included e-reading, which she said she enjoyed, but it did not yet have a very large role. One interesting phenomenon was evident in Stella's collection: the emergence of multiple linked formats of a single text. *Paw Patrols* emerged first as a television show on Nickelodeon in 2013 and quickly became available in many forms. *Paw Patrols* was on the children's Netflix playlist. Stella also had Paw Patrols books (series), sticker books, and DVDs of the television shows, and she went online to the *Paw Patrols* website, where she could play video games.

Case 9: Children's Understandings of the Affordances of Print and Digital Books

In McKechnie and Schreurs's (2017) study of the e-reading practices of children, the participants were able to talk about what they liked about print books and what they liked about eBooks.

When asked what they liked about print books:

Stella: [Pointing to *Pat the Bunny,* a touch-and-feel toy book for young children] "That one smells." (age 3)

Jake: [Demonstrating how you can use *Captain Underpants* as a mini flip book] "Like you can use your thumb and landscape through the pages and make it look like it's moving. You can't do that on an iPad." (age 12)

When asked what they liked about eBooks:

Hero: "It doesn't need electricity. It's better for the environment." (age 8)

Joel: "You don't have to read them. They read themselves." (age 8)

Theo: "You can press the animals and they say stuff." (age 4)

Jane: "I like eBooks because they light up." (age 6)

Elsa: "Because they can speak." (age 6)

Sarah: "Because you don't need a bookshelf." (age 11)

What Libraries Can Do

1. Children love e-reading for pleasure. Build collections of digital materials (eBooks and picture book apps) for children's pleasure reading.
2. Because not all materials are of the same quality, use collection development tools such as reviews and lists of recommended titles to ensure that your library has the best titles.
3. Because not all children's families can afford to purchase e-reading devices, provide access to them, either through loan or through in-library use.
4. Incorporate picture book apps and eBooks into library programs for children.
5. Include picture book apps and eBooks on pleasure reading lists.

What Parents Can Do

1. Remember that children enjoy reading both print and eBooks.
2. Ensure that your children have access to digital books either by purchasing them for their collections or by borrowing them from the library.

To Read More

Association for Library Services to Children. American Library Association. 2017. *Digital Media Resources*. Available at: http://www.ala.org/alsc/digital-media-resources. Regularly updated, this web page includes current articles, blog posts, and websites about children and digital media—surveys and other research reports, information about tablets, apps and eBooks, developing library collections, and services.

Koester, Amy, ed. 2014–2015. *Young Children, New Media, and Libraries: A Guide for Incorporating New Media into Library Collections, Services, and Programs for Families and Children Ages 0–5.* Little eLit. Available at: https://littleelit.com/. Starting with a discussion of the role of new media in children's librarianship and an overview of the research on new media, this book continues with chapters on developmentally appropriate practice, evaluation of new media, incorporating new media in story times, and the management of new media. It is an excellent source for public librarians. Published by Little eLit, a collaborative web-based think-tank that began in 2011 as a blog and continues today, gathering resources for librarians and providing a forum for discussion.

References

Cope, Bill, and Mary Kalantzis. 2009. " 'Multiliteracies': New Literacies, New Learning." *Pedagogies: An International Journal* 4: 164–195.

Howard, Vivian, and Maureen Wallace. 2016. "Today's Tech Literacy Tools: Parental Perceptions of Apps for Preschoolers." *Children and Libraries* 14, no. 1: 3–9.

Kress, Gunther. 2000. "Mutimodality." In *Multiliteracies: Literacy Learning and the Design of Social Futures*, 182–202. Edited by Bill Cope and Mary Kalanztis. London, New York: Routledge.

Maynard, Sally. 2010. "The Impact of e-Books on Young Children's Reading Habits." *Public Research Quarterly* 26, no. 4: 236–248.

McKechnie, Lynne (E. F.). 2017. *"Both My Favourites" (Stella, 3 years): A Case Study of One Child's Multimodal Reading Practices.* Paper presented at the annual conference of the Society for the History of Reading, Publishing and Authorship (SHARP). University of Victoria.

McKechnie, Lynne (E. F.), and Kathleen Schreurs. 2017. *"Every Single One Is My Favourite" (Theo, 4 years): Children's Experiences and Perceptions of E-book Reading).* Final Report. 2014 OCLC/ALISE Library and Information Science Research Grant Project. Available at: http://www.oclc.org/content/dam/research/grants/reports/2014/mckechnie2014.pdf.

New London Group. 1996. "A Pedagogy of Multiple Literacies: Designing Social Futures." *Harvard Educational Review* 66: 60–92.

Scholastic. 2017. *Kids and Family Reading Report*, 6th ed. Available at: http://www.scholastic.com/readingreport/files/Scholastic-KFRR-6ed-2017.pdf.

Schreurs, Kathleen. 2013. "Children's E-books are born: How E-books for Children Are Leading E-book development and Redefining the Reading Experience. *Partnership* 8, no. 2: 1–14. Available at: https://journal.lib.uoguelph.ca/index.php/perj/article/view/2744#.Wg19wjdrzIU.

2.5 Children, Libraries, and Reading

The public library is the only local government-funded, educational, and social service freely available to children from birth through adolescence. For that reason, according to Armstrong et al. (1997), it plays a very important role in supporting children in their development as readers. One of the most important services of the public library is provision of large and rich collections for children of all ages. Many studies (see, e.g., Allington 2002; Gottfried, Fleming, and Gottfried 1998; Krashen 2002; McQuillan 1997; Pack 2000) indicate that access to books and magazines is correlated with higher reading achievement.

The opportunity to try out a book with no risks, the importance of no-cost use, the assistance of knowledgeable staff, wide choice of materials in multiple formats, and the ability to browse and freely choose reading material independently—all these factors support readers of all ages. Public libraries are the best place for children to find materials for the FVR that Krashen (2004) has identified as crucial to reading success.

Case 10: "I Need a Book Like That One and That One."

In McKechnie's (1996) study of the use of public libraries by four-year-old girls and their mothers, she encountered many examples of children's insatiable appetites for books. In one such episode, Genevieve had been left by her mother in the children's area with the instruction to select five books for borrowing. When mother returned, Genevieve was sitting cross-legged on the floor, looking through one book from a large pile of picture books that she had collected in front of her.

Mother: Genevieve! How many books do you have?

Genevieve: One more.

Mother: Just one more! Remember how many books I said?

Genevieve: Yup.

Mother: How many?

Genevieve: Four.

Mother: I said five. And I think you've got more than five.

Genevieve: I do. I do have more.

Mother: Ya. We're going to have to put some back.

Genevieve: [Picking up and looking at the books one at a time] I want this one. Where's that one? That one. That one.

. . .

Mother: OK. I leave you for three minutes and look, you've cleaned out the library.

Genevieve: That one. I need a book like that one and that one.

Comments

Genevieve eventually talked her mother into six books. The two of them examined the pile together to figure out which six would be the best to take home. This extract from a library visit transcript is interesting because it shows how important the library's collections—especially the picture books—were to the children who participated in this study ("I need a book."). The public library was uniquely able to satisfy Genevieve's addiction to books.

References

Allington, Richard L. 2002. "What I've Learned about Effective Reading Instruction: From a Decade of Exemplary Elementary Classroom Teachers." *Phi Delta Kappa* 83, no. 10: 740–747.

Armstrong, Chris, Debbie Denham, Judith Elkin, Margaret K. Evans, Roger Fenton, Peggy Heeks, and Ray Lonsdale. 1997. "A Place for Children: The Qualitative Impact of Public Libraries on Children's Reading: Interim Report." *The New Review of Children's Literature and Librarianship* 3: 93–103.

Gottfried, Adele E., Jane Fleming, and Allan W. Gottfried. 1998. "Role of Cognitively Stimulating Home Environments in Children's Academic Intrinsic Motivation: A Longitudinal Study." *Child Development* 69, no. 5: 1448–1460.

Krashen, Stephen D. 2004. *The Power of Reading: Insights from the Research.* Westport, CT: Libraries Unlimited.

Krashen, Stephen D. 2002. "What Do We Know about Libraries and Reading Achievement?" *Book Report* 20, no. 4: 38.

McKechnie, Lynne (E. F.). 1996. *Opening the "Preschoolers' Door to Learning": An Ethnographic Study of the Use of Public Libraries by Preschool Girls.* PhD diss. University of Western Ontario, London, Ontario, Canada.

McQuillan, Jeff L. 1997. *Access to Print and Formal Instruction in Reading Acquisition.* PhD diss. University of Southern California.

Pack, S. 2000. "Public Library Use, School Performance and the Parental X-factor: A Biodocumentary Approach to Children's Snapshots." *Reading Improvement* 37: 161–172.

Chapter 3

Young Adults and Reading

Paulette M. Rothbauer

There has been a sea change in young adult (YA) publishing and reading over the past decade. Not only is YA literature one of the best-selling book markets around the world, but teenagers and young adults themselves exhibit a new knowledge of YA titles as well. In the late 1990s and early 2000s when I first interviewed teenagers about their reading preferences and asked them if they read YA fiction, many of them were hard-pressed to name a single title or author beyond *Harry Potter* or Judy Blume. Today teens can respond at length about their favorite authors, series, and even about their preferred publishers and recommended online sites for reader reviews. In other words, they are experts on a new golden era of literature produced and written for them.

In this chapter, I write about teenagers and young adults as two distinct but coextensive cohorts of people. Libraries tend to define young adults with the concrete age range of 12 to 18 years, while booksellers and publishers have opened the upper bracket to include people into their early- to mid-1920s. In Western culture in particular, younger adults often have more in common with older teens, deferring adult autonomy and independence from their parents until after postsecondary schooling and the attainment of full-time employment.

3.1 Are Young Adults Reading or Not?

There is still a lot of anxiety and confusion in various published reports of the reading habits of young adults. It seems that one headline will proclaim that their reading habits are healthy and on the rise, whereas the next headline will decry the decline of reading among teens. Here's a sample of recent headlines that illustrate this divide:

On the rise-of-reading side:

- "Think Young People Are Looking at Snapchat Instead of Reading? Wrong! Waterstones' Boss Says . . ." (Ashton 2017)
- "Films Fuel Huge Rise in Teenagers Reading" (Harris 2013)
- "Millennials Are Out-Reading Older Generations" (LaFrance 2014)
- "Surge in Young People Enjoying Reading, Figures Show" (*East Anglian Daily Times* 2014)

On the decline-of-reading side:

- "Why Aren't Teens Reading Like They Used To?" (Ludden 2014)
- "Teens Reading Fail" (Hawkes 2017)
- " 'Books Smell Like Old People': Do Teens Read Seriously Anymore?" (Denby 2016)
- "Reading Decline for 15 Year Olds" (Preiss 2013)

Much of the rhetoric on either side of this phenomenon of teen reading is concerned with digitally mediated reading. Interestingly, digital technology can be either the hero or the villain in these stories where it can as easily prompt a fervour of reading among teens as determine their states of attention deficit and distraction (see section 1.4). Concerns about the dangers of screen reading and e-media overload (e.g., *PBS Newshour* 2016) compete with enthusiastic calls for app-based reading (Gupta 2016). However, there is increasing acknowledgement that the "war between printed books and ebooks is over" (e.g., Alam 2017). If news headlines create confusion about whether or not there is a crisis of teen reading, large-scale surveys with representative samples of young people don't do much to quell the debate about whether teens are reading or reading less.

Surveys Say . . .

The Pew Research Center surveys on young Americans' reading habits consistently report that teens read more and read more frequently than older age cohorts. A 2013 survey found that 46 percent of 16- to 17-year-olds read every day. School reading probably inflates these numbers, but 46 percent of teen respondents also said they read books for entertainment (Pew Research Center 2014). Interestingly, a 2016 Pew survey on book reading reports that 18- to 29-year-olds "are more likely than their elders to read books in various digital formats, but are also more likely to read print books as well: 72% have read a print book in the last year, compared with 61% of seniors" (Pew Research Center 2016).

In a synthesis of multiple sources of American large-scale survey data, Common Sense Media's report features somewhat different findings, declaring that as young people reach their teens, their reading drops precipitously (Rideout 2014). Drawing from national education statistics, this research brief also reports persistent gaps among readers of different genders and ethnicities.

The National Endowment for the Arts (NEA) in the United States has been raising alarm bells about the decline in reading among Americans at least since 2004 with the publication of *Reading at Risk* and again in 2007 with *To Read or Not to Read* (see section 4.1). After explaining that the report uses data from multiple national agencies supplemented with survey data from a variety of academic, foundation, and business sources, Dana Gioia, then chairman of the NEA, wrote: "The story the data tell is simple, consistent, and alarming. Although there has been measurable progress in recent years in reading ability at the elementary school level, all progress appears to halt as children enter their teenage years" (NEA 2007, 5). Gioia continued, ending with a call to arms for "parents, teachers, librarians, writers, and publishers, but also for politicians, business leaders, economists, and social activists" asking them to recognize that reading "seems to awaken a person's social and civic sense" and that "books change lives for the better" (NEA 2007, 5). Perhaps this call to arms worked, as two years later, the NEA reported a 21 percent increase in adolescent reading, the first increase in decades. And even more interesting, this increase was not credited to school initiatives but to what Gioia cited as a "broader, community-wide phenomenon" (NEA 2009, 2).

The National Literacy Trust in the United Kingdom has been capturing data on children's reading for the past 20 years, and the latest survey of over 42,000 young people aged 8 to 18 years provides some contrasts to the findings reported in the Common Sense Media brief and NEA studies. The most compelling is that reading enjoyment is on the rise among young people in the United Kingdom with 6 out of 10 young people reporting that they enjoy reading either "very much" or "quite a lot" (Clark and Teravainen 2017, 3). Generally, the Literacy Trust data show positive relationships between reading enjoyment, reading comprehension, and reading scores; children's and teen's self-perceptions of reading skills; time spent reading; and numbers of books read (10–13).

In Canada, statistics on reading for pleasure as reported by children between the ages of 6 and 17 years and by their parents show similar findings (Scholastic Canada 2017). Seventy-nine percent of teens between 15 and 17 years reported that they were currently reading or had just finished reading a book for fun (12). Sixty-five percent of them said that they "like [reading books for fun] a lot" or that they "love it" (17). What's more, 69 percent of teens claimed that "they really enjoy reading books over the summertime" (78). This finding is not surprising, perhaps, when a whopping 94 percent of children said that their favourite books are ones that they picked out themselves (33, 35), and nearly as many said that they were more likely to finish self-selected titles. Even with such high figures for reading enjoyment among the respondents, nearly half of the children had trouble finding books they liked, and, importantly, their parents underestimated their children's ability to find materials that they liked (29). Parents, teachers, and friends play a big role in reading choices, whereas only 11 percent of children surveyed said that librarians encouraged them in reading for fun (39).

The Organisation for Economic Co-operation and Development's Programme for International Student Achievement (PISA) continues to assess the mathematics, science, and reading abilities of 15-year-olds around the world (see Adkins and Brendler 2015). Although PISA measures functional literacy, that is, "an individual's capacity to understand, use, reflect on, and engage with written texts" (O'Grady et al. 2016, 31), findings do warrant our close attention to the promotion of reading proficiency among youth. One of the most relevant findings is the strong association between reading proficiency and educational attainment (see, e.g., Knighton and Bussière 2006). Even if these studies of standardized assessments don't tell us much about what reading means to youth, they do help us understand that supporting reading among young people can have only positive outcomes.

Given the value of reading to young people's present lives and future chances, it can be worrying to many adults to see evidence of trends among youth of less reading, less frequent reading, and less reading proficiency. Trying to respond to the often negative and always conflicting evidence of the large surveys can also feel overwhelming. Quantitative data do a great job of illustrating the shape of trends in reading and library use over time, but smaller-scale studies with qualitative approaches that delve deeply into the reading practices of teenagers sometimes tell us a different story. Despite all of this research on young adults and reading or, perhaps because of it, it can be difficult to know how to support YA readers and how to develop programming and curricula to respond to their interests and habits.

If studies tell us anything, it is that teens *are* reading, and what's more, many of them are *choosing* to read. There is a persistent stereotype of the young adult as a reluctant and unwilling reader forced to read for school who will at the first opportunity choose to engage in other leisure activities—anything but reading. Undoubtedly, you've heard other variations of the problem of reading and young adults. They all amount to the same thing: young adults have a problem, and it is that they cannot or do not like to read. However, 15-year-old Emily explains this as a loss, "I feel like the older generations, like my teachers or something say, " 'Oh kids don't read enough . . .' But there's just no time. I hate that we're teenagers and we have no time to read. But you have school, you have work, you have sports, you have different things to do." The reports of teen reading on the rise, such as the ones featured in this section, support what prominent reading researcher and advocate Stephen Krashen (2004, 2011) has been saying for decades—that contrary to popular belief, if they are supported, teenagers and young adults will voluntarily read and actively choose to read for pleasure.

Research Tells Us: Teenagers' Reading and Writing in Multilingual Contexts

In his six-year ethnographic study with Arabic-speaking families in Sydney, Australia, Ken Cruickshank (2004) reminds us that, when school literacy is the benchmark, the value of "out-of-school" literacies is invisible. Cruickshank outlines three main assumptions that stereotype literacies of ethnic minority parents, youth, and families:

1. the belief that there is a lack of reading materials in the home as a problematic outcome of the "school definition of 'books' . . . as the reading of novels in English for enjoyment,"
2. defining immigrant youth and their families by their ethnic background, in terms of unchanging "traditional" culture, and
3. the "picture of teenagers as passive victims of a cultural gap between their parents and the wider society." (460)

Using data from interviews and observations with 60 Arabic-speaking teachers, students, and community workers, and followed by interviews with 20 families, and then engagement with 5 of these families for an additional four years, Cruickshank offers a richly detailed picture of teenagers' literacy practices within an Arabic-speaking immigrant community. Interestingly, while "all the boys and most of the girls in the wider study" reported that they "hated" reading, and the adults in the study saw the teenagers as "non-readers" and "underachievers," the two-week literacy diaries kept by the young people themselves showed a wide range of home reading and writing practices that played a "pervasive and integral role in their daily lives" (463–465). Cruickshank explains that these teenagers, like their parents and teachers, defined reading as the reading of "school-sanctioned novels." Not only did these teenagers read and enjoy other kinds of YA fiction, but they also read magazines, newspapers, TV guides, computer and gaming manuals, and religious texts and engaged in constant everyday reading and writing associated with shopping, school, and communicating with family and friends. Cruickshank found that over a four-year period, with the rise of digital media technologies and global developments in media markets, teenagers exhibited both improved English usage and formal knowledge of Arabic language.

Cruickshank, Ken. 2004. "Literacy in Multilingual Contexts: Change in Teenagers' Reading and Writing." *Language and Education* 18, no. 6: 459–473.

What Librarians and Teachers Can Do

1. Continue to keep abreast of new studies of teens, literacy, reading, and libraries, while taking with a big grain of salt the media panics about the crisis of teen reading. Follow the media reports back to the original studies and look for definitions of how researchers are defining literacy

and reading. Does "reading" include leisure reading, reading for pleasure, and nonbook materials?

To Read More on Approaches to Teens, Young Adults, and Reading

Journal of Adolescent & Adult Literacy, Wiley-Blackwell.

> Currently edited by Kathleen Hinchman and Kelly Chandler-Olcott, this peer-reviewed journal, published six times a year, is the go-to publication for cutting-edge research on multiple literacies of teenagers and young adults. Its mandate is to provide innovative research-based insights that "improve engagement and achievement among literacy learners ages 12 and older." It is a must-read for anyone concerned with young adults and reading in contemporary society.

Rutherford, Leonie, Lisa Waller, Margaret Merga, Michelle McRae, Elizabeth Bullen, and Katya Johanson. 2017. "Contours of Teenagers' Reading in the Digital Era: Scoping the Research." *New Review of Children's Literature and Librarianship* 23, no. 1: 27–46.

> In this accessible yet systematic literature review, the authors provide a synthesis of recent research on teenagers' reading, an account of academic disciplines invested in the topic, and an orientation to research designs used to approach it. Although the article is concerned with the Australian context, it relies on an international sample of studies that provide insights at global, national, and local scales.

References

Adkins, Denise, and Beth M. Brendler. 2015. "Libraries and Reading Motivation: A Review of the Programme for International Student Assessment Reading Results." *IFLA Journal* 41, no. 2: 129–139.

Alam, Hina. 2017. "Torontonians Are Reading More, Library Says." *TheStar.com*, June 29. Available at: https://www.thestar.com/news/gta/2017/06/29/torontonians-are-reading-more-library-says.html.

Ashton, James. 2017. "Think Young People Are Looking at Snapchat instead of Reading? Wrong! Waterstones' Boss Says . . ." *The Mail on Sunday*, June 11, 83.

Clark, Christina, and Anne Teravainen. 2017. *Celebrating Reading for Enjoyment: Findings from Our Annual Literacy Survey 2016*. London: National Literacy Trust.

Cruickshank, Ken. 2004. "Literacy in Multilingual Contexts: Change in Teenagers' Reading and Writing." *Language and Education* 18, no. 6: 459–473.

Denby, David. 2016. " 'Books Smell Like Old People': Do Teens Read Seriously Anymore?" *The New Yorker*, February 23. Available at: http://www.newyorker.com/culture/cultural-comment/books-smell-like-old-people-the-decline-of-teen-reading.

East Anglian Daily Times. 2014. "Surge in Young People Enjoying Reading, Figures Show." *East Anglian Daily Times*, July 22.

Gupta, Prerna. 2016. "Hooked: How We Got 10 Million Teens to Read." *Medium.com*, April 18. Available at: https://medium.com/@prernagupta/how-we-got-10-million-teens-to-read-fiction-on-their-phones-19a2a475084c.

Harris, Sarah. 2013. "Films Fuel Huge Rise in Teenagers Reading: Movies Including *The Hunger Games* Help Increase Book Sales by 11%." *Mail Online*, June 28.

Hawkes, Steve. 2017. "Teens Reading Fail." *The Sun*, April 19, 1: 18.

Knighton, Tamara, and Patrick Bussière. 2006. *Educational Outcomes at Age 19 Associated with Reading Ability at Age 15*. Culture, Tourism and the Centre for Education Statistics Research papers. Ottawa, ON: Statistics Canada.

Krashen, Stephen. 2004. *The Power of Reading: Insights from the Research*, 2nd ed. Westport, CT: Libraries Unlimited.

Krashen, Stephen. 2011. *Free Voluntary Reading*. Santa Barbara, CA: Libraries Unlimited.

LaFrance, Adrienne. 2014. "Millennials Are Out-Reading Older Generations." *Atlantic.com*, September 10.

Ludden, Jennifer. 2014. "Why Aren't Teens Reading Like They Used To?" *NPR: Morning Edition*, May 12.

National Endowment for the Arts. 2004. *Reading at Risk: A Survey of Literary Reading in America*. Report #46. Washington, DC: National Endowment for the Arts.

National Endowment for the Arts. 2007. *To Read or Not to Read: A Question of National Consequence*. Report #47. Washington, DC: National Endowment for the Arts.

National Endowment for the Arts. 2009. *Reading on the Rise: A New Chapter in American Literacy*. Washington, DC: National Endowment for the Arts.

O'Grady, Kathryn, Marie-Anne Duessing, Tanya Scerbina, Karen Fung, and Madia Muhe. 2016. *Measuring Up: Canadian Results of the OECD PISA Study: The Performance of Canada's Youth in Science, Reading and Mathematics, 2015 First Results for Canadians aged 15*. Council of Ministers of Education, Canada. Available at: https://www.cmec.ca/Publications/Lists/Publications/.../PISA2015-CdnReport-EN.pdf.

PBS Newshour. 2016. "The Drug-Like Effect of Screen Time on the Teenage Brain." May 4. Available at: http://www.pbs.org/newshour/bb/the-drug-like-effect-of-screen-time-on-the-teenage-brain/.

Pew Research Center. 2014. "Younger Americans and Public Libraries." September 10. Available at: http://www.pewinternet.org/2014/09/10/younger-americans-and-public-libraries/.

Pew Research Center. 2016. "Book Reading 2016." September. Available at: http://www.pewinternet.org/2016/09/01/book-reading-2016-methodology/.

Preiss, Benjamin. 2013. "Reading Decline for 15 Year Olds." *The Sydney Morning Herald*, August 16.

Rideout, Victoria. 2014. *Children, Teens, and Reading: A Common Sense Media Research Brief*. San Francisco, CA: Common Sense Media. Available at: https://www.commonsensemedia.org/research/children-teens-and-reading.

Scholastic. 2017. *Kids & Family Reading Report, Canadian Edition*. Available at: http://www.scholastic.ca/readingreport/.

3.2 Young Adults and Fiction Reading

As we move to a close of the second decade of the twenty-first century, the boom in YA publishing and reading does not appear to be slowing down. YA fiction is a worldwide publishing phenomenon that many claim arose from the massive popularity of three franchises: Harry Potter, Twilight, and The Hunger Games. A new reading audience emerged that was turned on to the pleasures of reading by their fanatic interest in Harry, Bella, or Katniss, and they were looking for their next all-consuming reading experience (Withers and Ross 2011).

Others see the buzz around YA literature as the result of the high-quality crossover YA novels that appeal to adult readers as much as to teens, such as those by John Green, Sabaa Tahir, Rainbow Rowell, Angie Thomas, and Sarah J. Maas, among others. A new marketing category has been established in publishing and bookselling—that of the "new adult" to signify readers in the age range of 18 to 25 years (Naughton 2014, 20; also Pattee 2017). This age category is often seen to correspond to trends in society that see young people deferring the spoils of adulthood (e.g., Mortgages! Car payments! Careers! Marriage!) until later and later as high student debt, longer periods of schooling, and low youth employment levels lead to longer dependency on parents, often into young people's mid- to late 20s (Rothbauer 2013).

As we have seen in the past, anything that young people like to or *love* to read in massive numbers is called into question for its mind-rotting and addictive properties. Compare the following two quotes, the first by the authors of a survey of Canadian young people in 1931 and the second published in 2014 that call into question the pervasive practice of adults reading materials intended for younger readers:

> The next step in the encouragement of good reading habits is to keep away from the child objectionable or worthless books . . . if enough good reading is constantly put before him, he will usually find so much of interest in it that undesirable books will make little appeal. There are, of course, exceptions to this rule. An occasional child may be continually exposed to good literature in the home and yet turn to cheap and sensational books. Such a child, however, is likely to need special attention not only to his reading but to his activities, his companions, and his environment in general. (Terman and Lima 1931, 5–6)

> There's a special reward in that feeling of stretching yourself beyond the YA mark, akin to the excitement of graduating out of the kiddie pool and the rest of the padded trappings of childhood: It's the thrill of growing up. But the YA and "new adult" boom may mean fewer teens aspire to grown-up reading, because the grown-ups they know are reading their books. When I think about what I learned about love, relationships, sex, trauma, happiness, and all the rest—you know, *life*—from the extracurricular reading I did in high school, I think of John Updike and Alice Munro and other authors whose work has only become richer to me as I have grown older, and which never makes me roll my eyes. (Graham 2014)

Although the authors' motives are different here, they rely on similar arguments: reading is good, but what some readers like to read is bad, and all readers should put aside those materials that give them pleasure to "read up" the reading ladder, moving on to "good literature" or "grown-up reading." Of course, this rhetoric is counter to the position that the reading that young people (and all people) freely choose to do is by definition "good reading," but it also suggests that readers only ever read one kind of literature, a perception that the research also tells us just isn't true (Davila and Patrick 2010, 207; Manuel 2012, 12–37).

Happily, one of the outcomes of a large and active reading audience for an internationally popular genre of fiction is that we have a related surge of research into the reading preferences of teens and young adults in terms of genre *and* format, along with new knowledge of gendered reading practices too. Decades of research into the reading preferences of young adults tells us that fiction is the most preferred reading genre for both male and female teen readers. Manuel and Robinson (2003) explore some of the assumptions about gendered reading among teens, finding that, contrary to popular belief, girls were as likely as boys to prefer three classic genres: fantasy, action/adventure, and mystery (69–70). Classic genres such as romance and humor also remain popular choices. However, beyond these traditional categories, new themes and styles continue to grow in popularity. Speculative and fantasy fiction (Fichtelberg 2015), dystopia (Day, Green-Barteet and Montz 2014), and contemporary social realism remain trending topics in YA literature (Cart 2016). In addition, some literary agents see a shift in perspectives and voice that reflect increased diversity in terms of authors, characters, settings, and themes (Roback 2016), credited in large part to the #WeNeedDiverseBooks social media movement (Kirch 2014). Taking a closer look at the popularity of new reading preferences can help us understand more about the role of contemporary YA literature in the lives of today's young people. The Young Adult Library Services Association recognized the value of YA literature when it formally adopted a white paper written by Michael Cart (2008) that acknowledged "that whether one defines young adult literature narrowly or broadly, much of its value cannot be quantified but is to be found in how it addresses the needs of its readers."

Teenagers and Young Adults Using Public Libraries

There continues to be a lot of research-based evidence indicating that traditional barriers still exist for teenage library use, even in light of changing service mandates in public libraries that see a stronger focus on non-collections-based services (Agosto 2016). As Denise Agosto and her colleagues write, negative perceptions of libraries and librarians, a preference for self-directed online research, lack of awareness of "non-printed book" services, and a tendency to see libraries as being all about books continue to characterize teens' use of public libraries (for more, see Agosto, Purcell, Magee, and Forte 2015, 319). A study that asked teens to narrate a short personal video about their newly renovated YA public library space found that many of the teen participants were keen readers and that the new library spaces were seen as supporting their leisure reading practices (Agosto, Bell, Bernier, and Kuhlmann 2015). Some research shows that arts-involved youth from low socioeconomic status backgrounds were more likely to have read a book and to have visited a library in the previous year than their less arts-involved peers (Catterall, Dumais, and Hampden-Thompson 2012). Another study using a nationally representative sample of American 12th graders found that regardless of socioeconomic differences, teens who live near well-serviced public libraries use them (Sin 2012, 228). A recent Pew study reports that millennials (i.e., the youngest adult cohort, 18 to 35 years of age) were most likely to have visited a public library in person and public library websites in the previous year (Geiger 2017). Many smaller studies also declare that teens and young adults do not find librarians or libraries particularly useful sources of information about books and reading whether these are small-town teens in Ontario (Rothbauer 2011), Norwegian teens in Oslo (Tveit 2012), or young teens from the East Coast of Canada (Howard 2011).

Case 11: What Teen/YA Readers Say about Libraries and Librarians

Although large-scale surveys have little positive to say about the role of librarians in teens' reading choices, when we look more closely at how they discover more good books to read, librarians and libraries find their way into their stories. From interviews conducted by MLIS students enrolled in my Young Adult Materials class in 2016 ($n = 30$), there is evidence that shows that for many teens a little bit of knowledge of library systems and a positive relationship with library workers can go a long way to supporting their use of the library as a place to find reading materials:

> I went on the library website. I've read everything, so I've got to the point now where I go to the library website and I either go into recommended reads and I go into the different genres and stuff. . . . And then I go through authors and then what they say recommended or I just go through the new books because lately I've run out of old books to read. (Marten, female, age 16)

> So sometimes when I'm looking for a new book and I want something that's related to another book I've already read, then I'll look to see what's on the same "shelf" on the [library] website. (Nick, age 17)

Sasha (age 17), an avid reader of manga and YA fantasy, described the pleasure she experienced as part of YA book club run by "one of the librarians." She had this to say on whether she would join more book clubs:

> I guess, yeah. That's like usually where I find all the really cool books. Because I look online and I see, "oh, that book looks cool," and then my expectations go down low, but usually when it comes to book club books . . . when I read those books, they're actually pretty good.

Some of the age-old barriers to library use exist too: age stereo-types, perceptions of being judged, and lack of privacy. Sally (age 16), from a small town, said that she would be less likely to accept rec-ommendations from older librarians:

> It depends on the age of the librarian. . . . Because if based on like what my grandparents read like a lot of the time, I see like older librarians especially in like [my small town] library . . . I don't know, just way different novels than what I'm interested in and they wouldn't be typically interested in like YA books . . . maybe don't know about YA.

Another reader from a small town, Sara (age 20) described her discomfort with the lack of anonymity in her small public library:

> I find the library . . . to me should be a private place where you go in, you're just who you are. You don't have to hide what you're taking out of the library, you can't be judged for what you're taking out of the library. It's like going into a lingerie store or something—you don't want to be judged for what you're buying. . . . You don't want to be judged for what you're taking out of the library. It's . . . it's per-sonal. What you read is personal. I find that in a small library you don't have that . . . .

Comments

Even this small sample of excerpts from recent interviews with teen-agers and young adults shows us that there continue to be opportunities and challenges for supporting their active library use. For better or worse, libraries figure prominently in their reading accounts. In this set of interviews, readers also praised large retail bookstore strategies of display and read-alike suggestions and they described comparison-searching methods, where participants reported checking library cata-logues against bookstore records and social media reader reviews.

To Read More on Young Adults' Reading of Young Adult Literature

Gaffney, Loretta M. 2017. *Young Adult Literature, Libraries, and Conservative Activism.* Lanham, MA: Rowman & Littlefield.

Gaffney addresses the politics of reading YA literature in the context of American librarianship. The author covers the rise of YA literature and the related responses in library services to young people over time and explores competing conceptions of teen readers, the value of reading for teens, and intellectual freedom and censorship. The book ends with a renewed call for using the lenses of social change and social justice as ways to understand and analyze YA literature and reading.

Heath, Shirley Brice, and Jennifer Lynn Wolf. 2012. "Brain and Behaviour: The Coherence of Teenage Responses to Young Adult Literature." In *The Emergent Adult: Adolescent Literature and* Culture, 139–154. Edited by Mary Hilton and Maria Nikolajeva. London: Ashgate.

This unusual exploration of the neuroscience of the teenage brain in the context of anthropological studies of young adults' reading practices and behavior is by noted literacy scholar Shirley Brice Heath and her colleague Jennifer Lynn Wolf, an education researcher. Brice and Wolf provide an overview of recent developments in brain research and then discuss how adolescents "voluntarily practice repeatedly the imaginative constructions and deciphering of maps, codes, mathematical riddles, foreign languages, and scientific information" (143) when they read YA literature. They then show how such reading corresponds to brain maturation and how together "these give the cognitive insights and social foundations critical to adolescents' development of judgement and foresight. These in turn benefit from the rehearsals and mental practice that result from the "power of imagination" that Young Adult reading expects" (154).

WNDB. WeNeedDiverseBooks.org. Available at: http://weneeddiversebooks.org/ (accessed July 9, 2017).

This nonprofit collective emerged from the advocacy of three authors, Ellen Oh, Malindo Lo, and Cindy Pon, in response to an all-white, all-male membership on a panel at a national book conference in 2014. On their website, their mission statement reads, "We Need Diverse Books™ is a grassroots organization of children's book lovers that advocates essential changes in the publishing industry to produce and promote literature that reflects and honors the lives of all young people." The social media hashtag #WeNeedDiverseBooks continues to be used to tag relevant issues and titles. WNDB has also created a book discovery app called "Our Story" to help connect young readers with diverse stories by authors from marginalized communities. WNDB is an important resource that functions as a clearinghouse for information and advocacy on multicultural literature, publishing, and reading for young people.

References

Agosto, Denise E. 2016. "Hey! The Library Is Kind of Awesome! Current Trends in US Public Library Services for Teens." *Public Libraries* 55, no. 5: 30–39.

Agosto, Denise E., Jonathan Pacheco Bell, Anthony Bernier, and Meghan Kuhlmann. 2015. " 'This Is Our Library, and It's a Pretty Cool Place': A User-Centered Study of Public Library YA Spaces." *Public Library Quarterly* 34: 23–43.

Agosto, Denise E., Michelle Purcell, Rachel M. Magee, and Andrea Forte. 2015. "Teens, Libraries, and Social Media: Myths and Reality." *Public Library Quarterly* 34, no. 4: 318–327.

Cart, Michael. 2008. "The Value of Young Adult Literature." Young Adult Library Services Association (YALSA), American Library Association. Available at: http://www.ala.org/yalsa/guidelines/whitepapers/yalit.

Cart, Michael. 2016. *Young Adult Literature: From Romance to Realism*, 3rd ed. Chicago: Neal-Schuman/ALA.

Catterall, James S., Susan A. Dumais, and Gillian Hampden-Thompson. 2012. *Arts and Achievement in At-Risk Youth: Findings from Four Longitudinal Studies*. Research Report #55. Washington, DC: National Endowment for the Arts.

Davila, Denise, and Lisa Patrick. 2010. "Asking the Experts: What Children Have to Say about Their Reading Preferences." *Language Arts* 87, no. 3: 199–210.

Day, Sara K., Miranda A. Green-Barteet, and Amy L. Montz, eds. 2014. *Female Rebellion in Young Adult Dystopian Fiction*. Farnham, Surrey, UK: Ashgate.

Fichtelberg, Susan. 2015. *Encountering Enchantment: A Guide to Speculative Fiction for Teens*, 2nd ed. Santa Barbara, CA: Libraries Unlimited.

Geiger, Abigail. 2017. "Millennials Are the Most Likely Generation of Americans to Use Public Libraries." *Fact Tank: News in the Numbers*, Pew Research Centre, June 21. Available at: http://www.pewresearch.org/fact-tank/2017/06/21/millennials-are-the-most-likely-generation-of-americans-to-use-public-libraries/.

Graham, Ruth. 2014. "Against YA." *The Slate Book Review, Slate.com*, June 5. Available at: http://www.slate.com/articles/arts/books/2014/06/against_ya_adults_should_be_embarrassed_to_read_children_s_books.html.

Howard, Vivian. 2011. "What Do Young Teens Think about the Public Library?" *The Library Quarterly* 81, no. 3: 321–344.

Kirch, Claire. 2014. "BookCon Controversy Begets Diversity Social Media Campaign." *Publishers Weekly*, May 1. Available at: https://www.publishersweekly.com/pw/by-topic/childrens/childrens-industry-news/article/62094-diversity-social-media-campaign-goes-viral.html.

Manuel, Jacqueline. 2012. "Reading Lives: Teenagers' Reading Practices and Preferences." In *Teenagers and Reading: Literary Heritages, Cultural Contexts and Contemporary Reading Practices*, 12–37. Edited by Jacqueline Manuel and Sue Brindley. Kent Town, South Australia: Wakefield Press.

Manuel, Jackie, and Dennis Robinson. 2003. "Teenage Boys, Teenage Girls and Books: Re-viewing Some Assumptions about Gender and Adolescents' Reading Practices." *English Teaching: Practice and Critique* 2, no. 2: 66–77. Available at: http://education.waikato.ac.nz/research/files/etpc/2003v2n2art6.pdf.

Naughton, Julie. 2014. "New Adult Matures." *Publishers Weekly* 261, no. 28 (July 14): 20.

Pattee, Amy. 2017. "Between Youth and Adulthood: Young Adult and New Adult Literature." *Children's Literature Association Quarterly* 42, no. 2: 218–230.

Roback, Diane. 2016. "Bologna 2016: Agents Talk Children's and YA Trends." *Publishers Weekly*, March 11. Available at: https://www.publishersweekly.com/pw/by-topic/international/trade-shows/article/69644-bologna-2016-agents-talk-children-s-and-ya-trends.html.

Rothbauer, Paulette. 2011. "Rural Teens on the Role of Reading in Their Lives." *Journal of Research on Libraries and Young Adults* 1, no. 2. Available at: http://www.yalsa.ala.org/jrlya/2011/02/rural-teens-on-the-role-of-reading-in-their-lives/.

Rothbauer, Paulette. 2013. "Imagining Today's Young Adults in LIS: Moving Forward with Critical Youth Studies." In *Transforming Young Adult Services: A Reader for Our Age*, 171–188. Edited by Anthony Bernier. Chicago: Neal-Schuman Publishers.

Sin, Sei-Chang Joanna. 2012. "Modeling the Impact of Individuals' Characteristics and Library Service Levels on High School Students' Public Library Usage: A National Analysis." *Library and Information Science Research* 34, no. 3: 228–237.

Terman, Lewis M., and Margaret Lima. 1931. *Children's Reading: A Guide for Parents and Teachers*, 2nd ed. Toronto: Ryerson.

Tveit, Åse Kristine. 2012. "Reading Habits and Library Use among Young Adults." *New Review of Children's Literature and Librarianship* 18, no. 2: 85–104.

Withers, Hannah, and Lauren Ross. 2011. "Young People Are Reading More than You." *McSweeney's*, February 8. Available at: https://www.mcsweeneys.net/articles/young -people-are-reading-more-than-you.

3.3 Reading and Identity

The ways in which young people discover and enact various aspects of their emerging identities have become a major strand of literacy research in recent years (Hinchman and Appleman 2010, xvii). There is widespread agreement that reading is an ally in the construction of identity at a crucial time in a young person's life. The concept of developing a personal identity is widely understood to be a process of defining the self in relation to others based on self-categorization and group identification and is held to be one of the major tasks of adolescence (Cotterell 1996, 5). The relationships readers create with fictional characters and worlds allow readers to test and explore various identities. Louise Rosenblatt (1994, 145) suggests that reading can play a critical role in this identity work:

> Literary texts provide us with a widely broadened "other" through which to define our world and ourselves. Reflection on our meshing with the text can foster the process of self-definition in a variety of ways.

Reading connects with identity along such variables as ethnicity, class, sexual orientation, gender, disability, language, geography, religion, and age. Especially useful are qualitative studies that begin with real readers in order to examine the role of reading among young people who are negotiating intersecting aspects of their identity. Such studies show again and again the importance for readers of encountering authentic cultural representation and the reflection of lived experiences in the texts with which they engage. They also show that identities are contextual—some aspects of identity are sanctioned and rewarded whereas others emerge through cultural conflict (Francois 2011). In his studies of the literacies of young black men, David Kirkland (2011) shows how important it is to find a "fit" between young people's ideologies and reading materials. The role of adult mentors and mediators can often be critical in connecting marginalized youth with meaningful texts.

Underlying many of these claims for reading is the assumption that a certain kind of reading is central to identity growth (Alsup 2010, 2). Most of the young people in these studies are speaking of the power of narrative to change their lives, the kind of narrative accounts of experience found in *stories*. Novels, biographies, autobiographies, and short stories "read" in a variety of formats (traditional hardcovers and paperbacks, fanfiction, film and video, music, poetry, comics, and magazines) enable young people to imagine new possibilities, while at the same time establishing boundaries for identity. Dennis Sumara describes this process as a "re-weaving of the reader's self that alters the reader's interactions with the world" (1996, 80). This kind of reading affords a certain pleasure in finding oneself in the text while also functioning as a way to gather and organize information about the larger world and one's place in it. Using a qualitative case-study approach with 16- and 17-year-old readers, Erin Spring explicitly theorizes the relationship between geographical place and youth identities both inside and outside of texts (2016).

In short, reading supports young adults as they negotiate various elements of their personal and social identities. Research also shows us that voluntary reading of YA literature leads to shifts in young people's self-perceptions *as* readers (Ivey and Johnston 2013). Voluntary reading engagement helps teens to establish identities as readers—to see themselves as people who read and who like to read. It is clear from qualitative reading research with young adults and teens that, for some, claiming an identity *as a reader* is a significant act of self-definition central to their understanding of self. What's more, claiming a reading identity as a teenager can be a resistant act in an adult world that has rendered such an identity as nonexistent or invisible (Learned 2016; Rothbauer 2009; Smith and Wilhelm 2009).

Case 12: LGBTQ YA Readers

In the past decade, there has been a surge in research that looks at the role of YA literature with LGBTQ characterizations and themes for its potential to disrupt or support heteronormativity (e.g., Blackburn, Clark and Nemeth 2015; see also Chapman 2015 for research on the provision of such literature in English public libraries). There is also a boom in publishing of YA titles with LGBTQ content (see Cart and Jenkins 2006 for a comprehensive bibliography of such titles published over time). Mollie Blackburn and Ryan Schey (2017, 46) note that in school contexts one is still more likely to find representations of LGBTQ people and experiences that function "as windows" for teen readers to help them understand experiences that are different from their own than to find studies in which LGBTQ YA readers use "literacy events and practices as mirrors." In previous research (Rothbauer 2004a, 2004b), I explored how voluntary reading mediates the pressures of negotiating lesbian, bisexual, and queer identities among YA women. The starting point of this research is that reading provides a safe, self-regulating, private way to explore identity. Most of my participants actively sought to find themselves reflected in their reading choices. The following two excerpts are particularly salient articulations of this theme:

> I think [reading] helps to validate my own life. That's what I look for in a book, and that's what I gain from reading certain kinds of books . . . acceptance and validation even though I have it all around

me, I still look for it. I like to read other people's experiences and say, yeah I'm having a similar experience, or, yeah I can associate with this character, therefore what I'm feeling is normal. And so I think that is my number one goal when I'm looking for books and when I'm reading, I'm trying to associate with the book, and kind of make myself feel better, you know, make myself feel normal, I think. (Keri, age 20)

[Reading] is a way that I better understand myself . . . When I go out to get a book at the library because I want to read, that's generally what I'm looking for. Sometimes I just read because I'm bored or I read because there's nothing else to do, or sometimes I read because I want to know this information . . . but mostly the big purpose . . . is to be able to look at something from another perspective and kind of twist that around in my brain and see to better understand myself and better be able to interact. (Nicky, age 18)

What Librarians, Teachers, and Parents Can Do

1. Educate yourselves about aspects of intersectional youth identity. Pay respectful attention to how young people adopt and resist categories to describe themselves and others. Avoid exclusionary language and practices and always check your assumptions. And, remember, identity practices are dynamic and always changing.

2. Be careful about reading identity "off" of books and other kinds of reading materials, and be aware of the tensions of under-representation. For example, just because a young person identifies as "queer" doesn't mean that person wants to read books only with queer characters in them. Such books will be of interest to a wide range of readers too. On the other hand, when it is difficult to find yourself represented in the kinds of stories that you want to read, any help in identifying materials will likely be appreciated!

To Read More on Reading and Identity

Hinchman, Kathleen A., and Deborah A. Appleman, eds. 2017. *Adolescent Literacies: A Handbook of Practice-Based Research.* New York: Guilford Press.
The purpose of this handbook is to "provide examples of research that share what practice-based research has shown about how literacies are situated in adolescents' evolving identities, about the contexts within which adolescents locate the literacies in their lives, about the multiple texts of literacies, and about what we have come to identify as effective classroom literacy instructional practices" (16). The first section on "Adolescent Literacies and Identities" includes essays by leading literacy researchers that address the ways that literacies and identities are co-constructed by young people from a variety of diverse contexts and backgrounds.

Moje, Elizabeth Birr, and Allan Luke. 2009. "Literacy and Identity: Examining the Metaphor in History and in Contemporary Research." *Reading Research Quarterly* 44, no. 4: 415–437.

A challenging read, but worth the effort, this article reviews the use of "literacy-and-identity" metaphors in a wide selection of literacy studies. Drawing from identity theory and literature, the authors begin with five conceptions of identity: (1) difference, (2) sense of self/subjectivity, (3) mind or consciousness, (4) narrative, and (5) position. They then explore how each of these metaphors for identity has entailments and consequences for our understanding of literacy and identity.

References

Alsup, Janet E., ed. 2010. *Young Adult Literature and Adolescent Identity across Cultures and Classrooms*: *Contexts for the Literary Lives of Teens*. New York: Routledge.

Blackburn, Mollie A., Caroline T. Clark, and Emily A. Nemeth. 2016. "Examing Queer Elements and Ideologies in LGBT-Themed Literature: What Queer Literature Can Offer Young Adult Readers." *Journal of Literacy Research* 47, no. 1: 11–48.

Blackburn, Mollie V., and Ryan Schey. "Adolescent Literacies Beyond Heterosexual Hegemony." In *Adolescent Literacies: A Handbook of Practice-Based Research*, 38–60. Edited by Kathleen A. Hinchman, and Deborah A. Appleman. New York: Guilford Press.

Cart, Michael, and Christine A. Jenkins. 2006. *The Heart Has Its Reasons: Young Adult Literature with Gay/Lesbian/Queer Content, 1969–2004*. Lanham, MD: Scarecrow Press.

Chapman, Elizabeth L. 2015. Provision of LGBT-Related Fiction to Children and Young People in English Public Libraries: A Mixed-Methods Study. PhD diss., Information School, University of Sheffield. Available at: http://etheses.whiterose. ac.uk/11802/.

Cotterell, John. 1996. *Social Networks and Social Influences in Adolescence*. London: Routledge.

Francois, Chantal. 2011. Review of "Handbook of Adolescent Literacy Research." *Harvard Educational Review* 81, no. 2: 371–380.

Hinchman, Kathleen A., and Deborah A. Appleman, eds. 2017. *Adolescent Literacies: A Handbook of Practice-Based Research*. New York: Guilford Press.

Ivey, Gay, and Peter H. Johnston. 2013. "Engagement with Young Adult Literature: Outcomes and Processes." *Reading Research Quarterly* 48, no. 3: 255–275.

Kirkland, David E. 2011. "Books Like Clothes: Engaging Young Black Men with Reading." *Journal of Adolescent & Adult Literacy* 55, no. 3: 199–208.

Learned, Julie E. 2016. " 'Feeling Like I'm Slow Because I'm in This Class': Secondary School Contexts and the Identification and Construction of Struggling Readers." *Reading Research Quarterly* 51, no. 4: 367–371.

Rosenblatt, Louise M. 1994. *The Reader, the Text, the Poem: The Transactional Theory of Literary Work*. 1978. Reprint, Carbondale: Southern Illinois University Press.

Rothbauer, Paulette M. 2004a. *Finding and Creating Possibility: Reading in the Lives of Lesbian, Bisexual and Queer Young Women*. PhD diss., Faculty of Information and Media Studies, The University of Western Ontario, London, Ontario.

Rothbauer, Paulette M. 2004b. " 'People Aren't Afraid Anymore but It's Hard to Find Books': Reading Practices That Inform the Personal and Social Identities of

Self-Identified Lesbian and Queer Young Women." *Canadian Journal of Information and Library Science* 28, no. 3: 53–74.

Rothbauer, Paulette M. 2009. "Exploring the Placelessness of Reading among Older Teens in a Rural Municipality." *The Library Quarterly* 79, no. 4: 465–483.

Smith, Michael W., and Jeffrey D. Wilhelm. 2009. "Boys and Literacy: Complexity and Multiplicity." In *Handbook of Adolescent Literacy Research,* 360–371. Edited by Leila Christenbury, Randy Bomer and Peter Smagorinsky. New York: Guilford Press.

Spring, Erin. 2016. "Place and Identity in YA Fiction." In *Identities and Subjectivities,* Volume 4, Geographies of Children and Young People, 1–23. Edited by Nancy Worth, Claire Dwyer, and Tracy Skelton. Singapore: Springer.

Sumara, Dennis J. 1996. *Private Readings in Public: Schooling the Literary Imagination.* New York: Peter Lang.

3.4 Digital Reading

Once we accept that reading means more than just the reading of books, we must take some account of other modes of narrative engagement that are popular with young adults. What matters is that young people are engaging with text in sustained ways that are meaningful, pleasurable, and voluntary. For example, young people tell us they are drawn to anime fictions because they care about the characters, they want to know what happens to them, and when they can't know what happens (as happens due to sporadic access), they will fill in the blanks themselves, creating and distributing their own fanfictions. In the process they "have fun, exercise one's imagination, and avoid boredom . . . [they] develop and solidify relationships with various friends, online and otherwise" (Chandler-Olcott and Mahar 2003). Young people interacting with multiple narrative forms across different media still rely on traditional literacy skills, in some cases with considerable refinement, in order to make sense of new formats and media. Playing a favorite computer game continues to involve "integrating information across multiple texts, relating textual meanings to personal experience, and composing complete messages in the form of stories and reports for actual audiences" (Guthrie and Metsala 1999, cited in Moje 2002). Ellen Forsyth (2010) makes these links explicit in her analysis of what gamers say about gaming and reading, and she shows how what gamers report as being of high interest corresponds to readers' advisory elements of appeal.

The "how" of reading matters less when the interests of young people motivate their reading choices. In a study of young teen readers published in 2002, Margaret Mackey found that issues of personal salience were extremely important in their selection of texts and that the content of the text often outweighed considerations of format (15). Recent research into the format preferences of teen readers shows that while they are living tech-saturated lives and regardless of the perceived benefits of eBooks (e.g., convenience and ease of access, privacy, customizable interfaces, access to embedded dictionaries and other resources) many still prefer print (Gray and Howard 2017; Merga 2015; Tveit and Mangen 2014).

Some researchers argue that popular and alternative forms of texts introduce students to stories they might never otherwise encounter (see, e.g., Schwartz 2002 on graphic novels). A danger lies in a tendency to privilege traditional print literacy. According to David Buckingham (as cited in Williams 2003), young people quickly learn that conversations about media use take place in the "margins of school life" and that there is a certain amount of "institutional hostility" toward popular culture in general. Other unsanctioned reading and writing is often denigrated by adults, including technology-mediated literacy practices associated with social media, gaming, music-sharing sites, and fanfiction, but research tells us that young people consume and create meaning from a variety of popular media texts.

Engaging in online conversations with authors and other readers on fanfiction sites can be empowering to teen readers "in a way that tips the balance of power and the ownership of text toward the reader" (Parkin 2010, 62). The values of peer-based reciprocity and encouragement through critical "beta-reading" (i.e., volunteering to give feedback) of writing submitted to online fanfiction sites rely on literacy skills and knowledge but more importantly create a culture of engagement and excitement for reading and writing (Black 2008, 41–42; also, Martens 2016). However, even general online reading has positive outcomes for teens, as reported by the advocacy group People for Education (2011, 4):

> PISA results show that fifteen year-olds who are extensively engaged in online reading activities, such as reading e-mails, chatting on line, reading news online, using an online dictionary or encyclopaedia, participating in online group discussions and searching for information online, are generally more proficient readers than students who do little online reading.

Case 13: Voices of Real Readers Reading (and Writing) Online

Many of the readers in a set of interviews from my Young Adult Materials class ($n = 30$) articulated the ways in which they would extend the story worlds in which they were invested. Sometimes readers sought out fanfiction, as in the case of Sasha (a female fantasy reader, age 17), who said:

> Sometimes, when I'm reading a book and then I finish it, and I feel like I want to read more from it. Even though it's not from that author, it's still like re-experiencing those characters again. Like, I've read so much fanfiction on Harry Potter.

Rebecca (age 19) responded at length to a question about being a fan, highlighting the connections that can be made with other readers:

> When someone recommends a book to me, I like to read it, because then that's a connection to them. If you say, "I love this book, you should read it", I go, "Well, why did they like it?" And then you read

it, and maybe you didn't like it. . . . Where is the break down? Or if you really love it, then you can share collectively, which is why you have fandoms and stuff like that. Like huge, because people just want to feel connected to other people, and that's maybe the only thing they have in common, that they love this book, movie, or whatever.

Others are like Nancy (an active book blogger, age 17), who moved her thoughts about books online. Nancy's comments about blogging show how much pleasure she gets from reading and from sharing what she reads through writing:

> My blog is mostly where I talk about books because if you're not interested in books you're not following my blog. It's nice, like I love answering comments or talking about books or talking about something I said in my review . . . because these people care about books where my friends don't really. . . . Like the thing that brings me so much pleasure, I'd love someone else to read what I wrote. I [blog] to practice writing and then it's just so much fun to share my opinions on books.

The last word goes to Sophie (an avid online reader, age 22), who paradoxically did not see herself as "one of those people who tends to read consistently and often." She describes the intense experience of getting consumed by a book "all in one go" and then her wariness of finding new fanfiction "because it's like another thing that I'm going to get really into." Later in the interview, she says that, because she is not finding the book she wants to read ("South-Western pulpy supernatural detective story with a female lead"), she'll write her own: "I'll read books or fanfiction that's like, 'oh that's a brilliant line, or oh, I should write a book that's this,' so by reading it gives me more ideas of what to do both in terms of writing and artistic pursuits."

Comments

When prompted, almost all the young adults in this sample, whether they identified as readers or not, described active engagement with story through reading books, playing games, or writing. Even more importantly, they valued these literacies for the feelings of pleasure they generated and for the sense of community that they encouraged.

To Read More on Young People Reading Online

Martens, Marianne. 2016. *Publishers, Readers, and Digital Engagement*. London: Palgrave Macmillan.

Featuring YA literature trends, brands, and online platforms, Martens explores the roles of author, reviewer, reader, and marketer in the context of online environments designed to invite YA participation in the world of books they love to read. Martens looks at the fraught voluntary labor of teens as they engage in "participatory reading experiences via publishers' and authors' interactive websites and use of social media" and what this means for publishing, readership, and the traditional gatekeepers of YA literature, namely librarians, teachers, and parents.

Tosenberger, Catherine. 2014. "Mature Poets Steal: Children's Literature and the Unpublishability of Fanfiction." *Children's Literature Association Quarterly* 39, no. 1: 4–27.

Tosenberger makes an impassioned case for considering the value of fanfiction as a genre of literature and as a means for young people to exercise knowledge, agency, and autonomy. She writes, "Young readers today enter a world in which, with the click of a button, they can find an enormous number of free stories that extend, explore, and challenge the narratives adult institutions have deemed fit for their consumption. And even better, these young readers can—and do—speak up themselves: fanfiction readers easily become fanfiction writers and find not just generalized encouragement, but an entire community eager to read their efforts and to help them develop their own voices."

References

Black, Rebecca W. 2008. *Adolescents and Online Fan Fiction.* New York: Peter Lang.

Chandler-Olcott, Kelly, and Donna Mahar. 2003. "Adolescents' Anime-Inspired 'Fanfictions': An Exploration of Multiliteracies." *Journal of Adolescent and Adult Literacy* 46, no. 7: 556–566.

Forsyth, Ellen. 2010. "From Assassins Creed 2 to the Five Greatest Warriors: Games and Reading." *APLIS* 23, no. 3: 117–128.

Gray, Robyn, and Vivian Howard. 2017. "Young Adult Use of Ebooks: An Analysis of Public Library Services and Resources." *Public Library Quarterly* 36, no. 1: 1–14.

Guthrie, John T., and Jamie L. Metsala. 1999. "Literacy in North America." In *Literacy: An International Handbook*, 381–384. Edited by Daniel A. Wagner, Richard L. Venezky, and Brian V. Street. Boulder, CO: Westview Press.

Mackey, Margaret. 2002. *Literacies across Media: Playing the Text.* London: Routledge Falmer.

Martens, Marianne. 2016. "Reading the Readers: Tracking Visible Online Reading Audiences." In *Plotting the Reading Experience: Theory, Practice, Politics*, 263–277. Edited by Paulette Rothbauer, Kjell-Ivar Skjerdingstad, Lynne (E. F.) McKechnie, and Knut Oterholm. Waterloo, ON: Wilfrid Laurier University.

Merga, Margaret K. 2015. "Do Adolescents Prefer Electronic Books to Paper Books?" *Publications* 3, no. 4: 237–247.

Moje, Elizabeth Birr. 2002. "Re-framing Adolescent Literacy Research in a Digital World." *Reading Research and Instruction* 41, no. 3: 211–228.

Parkin, Rachel Hendershot. 2010. "Breaking Faith: Disrupted Expectations and Ownership in Stephenie Meyer's Twilight Saga." *Jeunesse: Young People, Texts, Cultures* 2, no. 2: 61–85.

People for Education. 2011. *Reading for Joy.* Toronto. Available at: http://www.people foreducation.ca/document/reading-for-joy/.

Schwartz, Gretchen E. 2002. "Graphic Novels for Multiple Literacies." *Journal of Adolescent and Adult Literacy* 46, no. 3: 262–265.

Tveit, Åse Kristine, and Anne Mangen. 2014. "A Joker in the Class: Teenage Readers' Attitudes and Preferences to Reading on Different Devices." *Library & Information Science Research* 36: 179–184.

Williams, Bronwyn T. 2003. "What They See Is What We Get: Television and Middle School Writers." *Journal of Adolescent and Adult Literacy* 46, no. 7: 546–554.

3.5 Reading Comics *by Lucía Cedeira Serantes*

In this section, comics are understood to be an umbrella term referring to different expressions and formats taken by the comics medium, such as webcomics, comic strips, manga, graphic novels, trade paperbacks, or French albums. Historically, comics have been a popular reading material for youth, their content and communities an important part of youth culture (Wright 2003). Educational and cultural institutions and the mainstream media, on the other hand, have looked askance at comics, often attacking their value as reading materials for young people. Researchers, educators, and librarians, who noted the great popularity of comics with teens, generally had one of two responses: either they openly condemned comics as harmful or they found ways to use the popularity of comics as an enticement in schools and libraries (e.g., Jacobs 2013). Much research on comics either explains the form itself (e.g., Cohn 2013) or discusses the stories being told (e.g., Abate and Tarbox 2017). However, with the exception of fan studies, little research has been published on how readers consume and engage with comics. Comics have grown in complexity and diversity, offering a multimodal, multilayered reading experience. Nevertheless, it is commonplace to find articles that focus on teen readers of comics as readers who lack reading skills—reluctant readers or readers at risk. Other articles look for potential applications of the medium, or examples suggesting that comics are suited for English language learners or visual readers.

Three Disciplines Look at Comics

It is not easy to find research at the intersection of reading, comics, and teens. Library and Information Science (LIS), Education, and Media Studies each offers different and complementary perspectives on teens reading comics, but the experience of the real reader is usually missing in action. Interest in comics reading can be tracked back to the first wave of popularity of comics during the 1930s and 1940s (e.g., Frank 1944; Witty 1941; Wolf and Fiske 1949). Many of these studies were negative about the use of comics for either pleasure reading or educational purposes (see Tilley 2012, 2013). These historical articles offer interesting points of comparison against which to measure contemporary attitudes, showing how much (or relatively little) things have changed in the understanding, use, and care for comics and for their readers.

Media Studies has singled out as its core subject of research the comics fan, often young and male. However, studies such as those from Brown (2001) and Pustz (1999) paved the way to more diverse and inclusive approaches to comics audiences, such as the work of Canadian scholar Benjamin Woo (2011, 2012). A 2002 American Library Association pre-conference dedicated to graphic novels marked an explosion in LIS literature about comics. The goal of this LIS work has largely been to offer professionals the necessary information and tools to be able to select and integrate comics into library collections and programs. This professional objective has left little room to explore the reasons for readers' attraction to comics (Cedeira Serantes 2013). The few researchers and professionals who study real comics readers (e.g., Kan 2013; Snowball 2005, 2008; Zabriskie 2010) often challenge stereotypes, delving deeply the comics-reading phenomenon. Snowball deepens the connection between comics and reluctant readers; Zabriskie looks at how graphic novels provide teens a sense of belonging in libraries; and Kan expands on who should be considered a comics reader.

In Education, the recognized importance of research on everyday literacy practices of teens highlighted the possibilities of popular culture materials, comics among them, as educational tools. The series of articles by researcher Shari Sabeti (2011, 2012, 2013) still represent one of the most stimulating examples of research about readers. Her work with a group of high school students who were members of an extra-curricular graphic novels reading club raises questions about agency, identity, and power when reading and working with graphic novels. A more expansive understanding is slowly developing due to a combination of several factors: the slow but steady inclusion of comics in teachers' and librarians' education (Downey and Davidson 2012; Williams and Peterson 2009); the recognition of comics in awards or the development of comics-focused lists; comics' presence in new curricular requirements, such as Common Core (Monnin 2013); and the diversification of the comics publishing field, for example, with the increasing availability of comics for children (Burnett 2016) and informational comics (Clark 2014).

What Do Real YA Readers Say about Their Experience Reading Comics?

To address the gap in research on real YA readers who read comics, I designed a research project for my doctoral dissertation that aimed to make readers' voices central to a study of comics and reading (Cedeira Serantes 2014). I interviewed nine females and eight males, between the ages of 17 and 25. I recruited participants from three different sites in London, Ontario: the public library, a comics store, and a university with a large, undergraduate population. Some participants were beginner comics readers and others had been readers since childhood. These readers did not "grow out of comics" or "move on" to other kinds of reading materials. They enriched their comics reading, evolving in their taste and practices (Cedeira Serantes, forthcoming 2018).

Two particularly relevant themes that emerged from the study were (1) the interaction between the experience of time and comics reading and (2) the materiality of reading. Comics are often characterized as a "quick read" and are therefore often recommended for reluctant readers. However, my research participants pointed to a duality in reading comics: there is the possibility both of reading fast and of taking time when reading. One participant, Kalo, explains "how you can control the flow of time and also leave it up to the reader to go through at their pace." Baa praised how much comics can communicate and "you can finish them in a day." Devi, on the other hand, liked to "spend a lot of time on a page." Comics adapt to these readers' fast and busy lives, but they can also help to create moments for contemplation (Cedeira Serantes 2016). Another participant, Shade, was adamant about how a print comic is "the closest thing you're going to get to holding an idea."

I found Shade's comment so intriguing that I asked successive participants what they thought about print and digital reading. These readers were not luddites or collectors, but many discussed how certain comics needed to be read in print format. They talked about holding a comic or touching the paper as central to their reading experience (see section 1.4 for more on print versus screens). Many explained that, when they preferred print versions, the preference was not a choice *against* digital. They chose the format in the context of how print comics or digital comics adapt (or not) to their everyday life and to their desired reading experience. Their choice of format was also related to how they see themselves as readers. Shade again says it very simply and directly: "[t]he paper, the book, the whole package of it in one physical thing, I guess I prefer that." These readers' insights enhance our understanding not just of comics reading, but of reading in general as a multifaceted, everyday practice in the midst of a media-saturated and accelerated life experience.

To Read More on Young Adults and Comics Reading

Botzakis, Stergios, Rachelle Savitz, and David E. Low. 2016. "Adolescents Reading Graphic Novels and Comics." In *Adolescent Literacies: A Handbook of Practice-Based Research*, 310–322. Edited by Kathleen A. Hinchman and Deborah A. Appleman. New York: The Guilford Press.

In a collection that follows up on Donna Alvermann's pioneering work on adolescent literacies, this selected chapter is full of examples of how comics can enrich and transform teaching. Classic functions of comics are described as motivational or visual literacy tools, but the chapter also examines how students' interest in comics beyond the classroom creates opportunities to take up questions about the exploration and formation of identity and how comics can provide opportunities for teachers to foster interdisciplinary collaboration in schools.

Goldsmith, Francisca. 2017. *The Readers' Advisory Guide to Graphic Novels*. Chicago: ALA.

An updated edition, this guide is concerned with comics reading and readers of all ages. It responds to stereotypes, effortlessly expanding the range of readers who should be considered comics readers and providing suggestions on how to support and expand their reading interests. Goldsmith's annotated selections always go beyond popular and classic titles. As a pioneer of comics advocacy in LIS, Goldsmith shares her rich understanding of and potential for the medium and its readers.

Tilley, Carol L. 2014. "Comics: A Once-Missed Opportunity." *Journal of Research on Libraries and Young Adults* (May): 1–18. Available at: http://www.yalsa.ala.org/jrlya/2014/05/comics-a-once-missed-opportunity/.

An example of Tilley's exemplary historical research into the relationship between comics and librarianship, this paper draws on 1950s vignettes with real teens as the main protagonists and examines them as examples of how comics reading created spaces and communities for participatory culture, creative expression, and civic engagement outside the purview of librarians and libraries. Tilley encourages contemporary librarians to use these examples as an inspiration to reflect upon practices that they might be presently neglecting.

References

Abate, Michelle Ann, and Gwen Athene Tarbox, eds. 2017. *Graphic Novels for Children and Young Adults: A Collection of Critical Essays*. Jackson: University Press of Mississippi.

Brown, Jeffrey A. 2001. *Black Superheroes, Milestone Comics, and Their Fans*. Jackson: University Press of Mississippi.

Burnett, Matia. 2016. "What the Kids Are Reading: The Booming Business of Children's Graphic Novels and Comics." *Publishers Weekly*, November 8. Available at: https://www.publishersweekly.com/pw/by-topic/childrens/childrens-industry-news/article/71982-what-the-kids-are-reading-the-booming-business-of-children-s-graphic-novels-and-comics.html.

Cedeira Serantes, Lucía. 2013. "Misfits, Loners, Immature Students, Reluctant Readers: Librarianship Participates in the Construction of Teen Comics Readers." In *Transforming Young Adult Services: A Reader for Our Age*, 115–135. Edited by Anthony Bernier. New York: Neal-Schuman.

Cedeira Serantes, Lucía. 2014. *Young Adults Reflect on the Experience of Reading Comics in Contemporary Society: Overcoming the Commonplace and Recognizing Complexity*. PhD diss., Faculty of Information and Media Studies, The University of Western Ontario, London, Canada. Available at http://ir.lib.uwo.ca/etd/2075/.

Cedeira Serantes, Lucía. 2016. "When Comics Set the Pace: The Experience of Time and the Reading of Comics." In *Plotting the Reading Experience: Theory, Practice, Politics*, 217–232. Edited by Paulette Rothbauer, Kjell-Ivar Skjerdingstad, Lynne (E. F.) McKechnie, and Knut Oterholm. Waterloo, ON: Wilfrid Laurier University.

Cedeira Serantes, Lucía. Forthcoming 2018. "The Possibilities of Comics Reading: Uncovering a Complex and Situated Reading Experience in Canada." In *Young People Reading: Empirical Research Across International Contexts*. Edited by Evelyn Arizpe and Gabrielle Cliff-Hodges. London: Routledge.

Clark, J. Spencer. 2014. "Teaching Historical Agency: Explicitly Connecting Past and Present with Graphic Novels." *Social Studies Research & Practice* 9, no. 3: 66–80.

Cohn, Neil. 2013. *The Visual Language of Comics: Introduction to the Structure and Cognition of Sequential Images*. New York: Bloomsbury Academic.

Downey, Elizabeth M., and Karen Davidson. 2012. "Graphic Novels in Graduate-Level Library and Information Studies Literature and Materials Courses." *New Review of Children's Literature and Librarianship* 18, no. 1: 67–83.

Frank, Josette. 1944. "What's in the Comics?" *Journal of Educational Sociology* 18, no. 4: 214–222.

Jacobs, Dale. 2013. *Graphic Encounters Comics and the Sponsorship of Multimodal Literacy.* New York: Bloomsbury Academic.

Kan, Kat. 2013. "What Kinds of Kids Read Comics?" *Knowledge Quest* 41, no. 3: 30–33.

Monnin, Katie. 2013. "Aligning Graphic Novels to the Common Core Standards." *Knowledge Quest* 41, no. 3: 50–56.

Pustz, Matthew. 1999. *Comic Book Culture: Fanboys and True Believers.* Jackson: University Press of Mississippi.

Sabeti, Shari. 2011. "The Irony of 'Cool Club': The Place of Comic Book Reading in Schools." *Journal of Graphic Novels and Comics* 2, no. 2: 137–149.

Sabeti, Shari. 2012. "Reading Graphic Novels in School: Texts, Contexts, and the 'Work' of Critical Reading." *Pedagogy, Culture & Society* 20, no. 2: 191–210.

Sabeti, Shari. 2013. "'A Different Kind of Reading': The Emergent Literacy Practices of a School-Based Graphic Novel Club." *British Educational Research Journal* 39, no. 5: 835–852.

Snowball, Clare. 2005. "Teenage Reluctant Readers and Graphic Novels." *Young Adult Library Services* 3, no. 4: 43–46.

Snowball, Clare. 2008. "Teenagers Talking about Reading and Libraries." *Australian Academic & Research Libraries* 39, no. 2: 106–118.

Tilley, Carol L. 2012. "Seducing the Innocent: Fredric Wertham and the Falsifications That Helped Condemn Comics." *Information & Culture* 47, no. 4: 383–413.

Tilley, Carol L. 2013. "'Superman Says, "Read!"' National Comics and Reading Promotion." *Children's Literature in Education* 44, no. 3: 251–263.

Williams, Virginia Kay, and Damen V. Peterson. 2009. "Graphic Novels in Libraries Supporting Teacher Education and Librarianship Programs." *Library Resources & Technical Services* 53, no. 3: 166–174.

Witty, Paul. 1941. "Children's Interest in Reading the Comics." *Journal of Experimental Education* 10, no. 2: 100–104.

Wolf, Katherine, and Marjorie Fiske. 1949. "The Children Talk about Comics." In *Communications Research, 1948–1949*, 3–50. Edited by Paul Lazarsfeld and Frank Stanton. New York: Harper and Bros.

Woo, Benjamin. 2011. "The Android's Dungeon: Comic-Bookstores, Cultural Spaces, and the Social Practices of Audiences." *Journal of Graphic Novels and Comics* 2, no. 2: 125–136.

Woo, Benjamin. 2012. "Understanding Understandings of Comics: Reading and Collecting as Media-Oriented Practices." *Participations* 9, no. 2: 180–199.

Wright, Bradford W. 2003. *Comic Book Nation: The Transformation of Youth Culture in America.* Baltimore, MD: Johns Hopkins University Press.

Zabriskie, Christian. 2010. "Graphics Let Teens OWN the Library." In *Graphic Novels and Comics in Libraries and Archives: Essays on Readers, Research, History and Cataloging*, 167–176. Edited by Robert G. Weiner. Jefferson, NC: McFarland & Co.

3.6 Young Adults Reading and Reaching Out

Reading is commonly seen to be a private, individual activity conducted in solitude. However, research shows that even when young people read alone, the act of reading remains profoundly social. Books and other reading materials function as what sociologist James Paul Gee has called " 'artifacts' of thinking, feeling, believing, valuing, and acting that can be used to identify oneself as a member of a socially meaningful group or social network or to signal (that one is playing) a socially meaningful role" (Gee 1996, 131).

Reading materials will attract specific communities of readers who share similar reading tastes, often related to genre: science fiction, romance, horror, comics, gaming, fanfiction, poetry, and so on. Sometimes it works the other way around too—specific communities draw together certain kinds of readers who in turn share common reading interests: youth claiming certain kinds of cultural identities, youth committed to various social and political causes, or youth who share leisure interests. Diverse communities of readers exist, and social connections are frequently mediated through reading that provides opportunities to establish or foster a membership in specific communities. Perhaps one of the most obvious examples concerns the myriad Harry Potter fandoms (now 20 years old and counting) that emerged almost immediately (facilitated by the Internet) when the series was launched in 1997. The fan base deepens with every successive generation of readers. A reader need not participate in any fan activities online or face-to-face to be able to share in this reading phenomenon: the only requirement for making connections with others is familiarity with the stories.

Social Media and YA Communities of Reading

Social media that are associated with contemporary YA literature allow for unprecedented access to authors, publishers, and other readers. American YA literature sensation John Green rivals J. K. Rowling for the sheer size of community associated with his literary and digital media creations. Green is the best-selling author of a number of YA titles, including *The Fault in Our* Stars and *Paper Towns*, which are also feature films. Green produces content for several media platforms with an active follower presence on YouTube, Instagram, Facebook, Tumblr, and over five million followers on Twitter (see http://www.johngreen books.com for more on Green's media presence). Fans of all ages claim identities as Nerdfighters (Green) or Potterheads (Rowling) and find each other in what Simone Murray has called the "digital literary sphere" (2015, 313). But fans also meet in a variety of face-to-face communities from national conventions to small-town book clubs, fan appreciation events, or literature classrooms.

The *uber* success of authors such as Rowling and Green is difficult to replicate, but teens who want to connect with others over reading will find that most YA authors now have a presence online. Beyond author and publisher sites, however, young people also find community on popular review sites and YA lit promotional feeds on social media that are organized by reading interest. To give just two examples: on Twitter, people who want to connect with authors, publishers, and readers through LGBTQIA and YA Lit, there is @YA_Pride feed; for middle grade and YA lit on disabilities, there is @DisabilityInLit. Marcella Purnama looked at Goodreads for reviews of John Green's books and found that "the more emotion readers show online, the more they interact with others about the books"

(Purnama and Davis 2016). Online communities enable sharing of feelings for books, authors, characters, plots, and more, but they also provide a forum for practicing digital content creation, which in turn supports information literacy development more generally (Harlan, Bruce, and Lupton 2012). Interestingly, one large-scale study of Australian youth (Merga 2015) found that avid readers were less likely to be heavy users of social media, perhaps because they are too busy reading books!

Young Adult Readers on Reading with Friends and Family

Reading is social for young people too in the ways that they interact around reading with friends (Merga 2014) and family (Knoester and Plikuhn 2016). In her focus group research with young teens, Vivian Howard (2008) found that for many "reading takes place almost exclusively in a social context and is seen as an effective way to cement peer friendships. These teens actively seek to read the same materials as their closest friends and use reading (talking about reading, exchanging reading material, following the same series) as a form of social bonding" (108–109). In my Young Adult Materials class interviews with YA readers, age 15 to 23 years, we asked several questions about how reading and recommendations were shared. All readers gave examples of sharing reading whether with close friends, or, more distantly, with classmates and teachers, or with random followers (i.e., "Facebook friends") on social media like Tumblr or Reddit. These readers also highly valued peer-based recommendations, often claiming that they only really trust people who are the same age. Additionally, many preferred to give and receive information about books and reading with mutual knowledge of reading interests.

Case 14: Reflecting on a Reading Conversation

When asked if he shared his reading with anyone, Nick (an avid fantasy reader, age 17) described the exchanges he had with his girlfriend. The excerpt begins with Nick's response to a question about how he finds science fiction and fantasy books to read:

Nick: I guess I'd probably just ask someone. I definitely know a few people who know a lot about books so I'd ask one of them. Like my girlfriend, she knows a lot about books so I'd probably just ask her.

Interviewer: Do you and your girlfriend share reading interests?

Nick: Yeah, a lot of them. She definitely reads more than me though! [laughs]

Interviewer: But you two talk about books?

Nick: Yeah, all the time. ... We usually talk about books that we've both read, which is cool because sometimes we have really different opinions. ... One of the books we talked about recently was *A Court of Thorns and Roses* [by Sarah J. Maas], which is a fantasy, kind of fairy tale book. And we both really liked some parts and didn't enjoy other parts, so it made for a good discussion. ... I really liked the colorful prose and plot moments where the protagonist is thrown into life or death situations. And what I didn't like, this sounds like a huge nitpick but whatever, what I didn't like was a riddle that was supposed to be really hard for the protagonist to solve but seemed to me was really obvious. And then my girlfriend read that same book, and she didn't like the portrayal of um, romantic relationships and sexuality because it was done in a not great way. Like the protagonist, who's a woman, there are some moments where it's glossed over that she's not being treated very well by male characters in the book. And that's something that didn't really register for me when I was reading it. I mean, I read the same words I guess, but it didn't register. But then when I talked to my girlfriend about it, I was able to see the book in a different light.

Comments

Not all readers want this kind of exchange. But for those who do, this excerpt nicely illustrates the pleasures of conversations about reading—sharing likes and dislikes, learning and reflecting on different responses to the same texts, and sharing a reading experience or event that makes the book that much more memorable and enjoyable.

What Librarians Can Do

1. Create time and space for conversations about reading—face-to-face when possible but also online when appropriate. In libraries this can be done through formal book clubs, through scheduled light socializing about books and reading, or via "passive programming" by creating ways for teens to encounter venues for sharing their thoughts about what they read (e.g., comments boxes or boards, online review sites, library publications).

References

Gee, James Paul. 1996. *Social Linguistics and Literacies: Ideology in Discourses*, 2nd ed. PA: London: Falmer Press.

Harlan, Mary Ann, Christine Bruce, and Mandy Lupton. 2012. "Teen Content Creators: Experiences of Using Information to Learn." *Library Trends* 60, no. 3: 569–587.

Howard, Vivian. 2008. "Peer Group Influences on Avid Teen Readers." *New Review of Children's Literature and Librarianship* 14, no. 2: 103–119.

Knoester, Matthew, and Mari Plikuhn. 2016. "Influence of Siblings on Out-of-School Reading Practices." *Journal of Research in Reading* 39, no. 4: 469–485.

Merga, Margaret K. 2014. "Peer Group and Friend Influences on the Social Acceptability of Adolescent Book Reading." *Journal of Adolescent & Adult Literacy* 57, no. 6: 472–482.

Merga, Margaret K. 2015. "Are Avid Adolescent Readers Social Networking about Books?" *New Review of Children's Literature and Librarianship* 21, no. 1: 1–16.

Murray, Simone. 2015. "Charting the Digital Literary Sphere." *Contemporary Literature* 56, no. 2: 311–339.

Purnama, Marcell, and Mark Davis. 2016. "Authors, Get Thee to Social Media: Exploring the Rise and Rise of YA Books." *The Conversation*, April 12. Available at: https://theconversation.com/authors-get-thee-to-social-media-explaining-the-rise-and-rise-of-ya-books-57281.

3.7 To Read More on Special Communities of YA Readers

In the years since we published *Reading Matters*, we have seen the enormous success of YA literature publishing, and there has been a related rise in research interest in what YA readers do with this literature. Nonetheless, today it can still be difficult to locate reading studies with teen and young adults who are marginalized by class, ethnicity, and geography (and other variables). To conclude this chapter, I've highlighted a small selection of notable work to draw our attention to issues of access, representation, and politics of reading among communities of youth that tend to be invisible and understudied.

Rural Youth

Like much research with humans, qualitative research with teen and YA readers often relies on convenience samples with people to whom researchers have easier access (i.e., people living in university cities and towns). It can be harder to find out about the perspectives of youth living in rural and remote communities. I interviewed teens about reading who lived in a small farming community to explore to what extent they might have been marginalized from an active culture of reading due to their distance from urban centres and, at the time, due to slow and sporadic Internet access. This research revealed that, even though most of the teens were prolific readers, there was little evidence of a culture of shared or supported reading (Rothbauer 2009, 2011). Kim Becnel and Robin Moeller (2015) found a similar lack of reading culture in their study of reading with 10th-grade students from rural North Carolina, this despite the high degree engagement with YA literature and reading. Studies like these raise questions about the role public and school libraries can play to encourage reading in communities with little evidence of support for youth reading especially in out-of-school contexts.

Indigenous Youth

Canadian researcher Erin Spring (2016a) has recently launched a collaborative project working with young Blackfoot teens living on a reserve in Alberta to investigate "the ways in which [these] young readers reflect on their social, cultural, and place-based identities while reading culturally relevant, local fiction." Taking an ethnographic and multiliteracies approach, Inge Kral and Jerry Schwab (2012) report on the out-of-school literacies of indigenous youth in remote Australia, finding rich opportunities for scaffolding reading and writing practices through digital media play and production. Debbie Reese (2017) brings attention to high-quality American Indian children's and YA literature and reveals both that there is growing field of excellent literature to read and to promote and that there is a lot of work still to be done to understand how such texts are received and used by young people.

Immigrant/Migrant Youth

In 2013, youth between 15 and 24 years, represented about one-eighth (28.2 million) of the 232 million migrants worldwide (Cortina, Taran, and Raphael 2014, 2), and these numbers are growing. Young people, their families, and communities are negotiating the challenges of migration, and research tells us that digital media and literacies play a significant role in building and maintaining connections with others in home and adopted nations (e.g., Lam 2009; Leurs 2015). It is, however, still difficult to identify studies of migrant youth as readers, even with the emergence of a strong field of literature for youth that features immigrant and settlement narratives (e.g., Brown 2011; Naidoo and Dahlen 2013). Erin Spring (2016b) explores "the temporal dimensions of place, identity, and the reading experience" with two young women who migrated to Toronto with their families from Seoul, Korea, and Moscow, Russia, respectively. In this close-grained analysis we learn how the migration experiences of these two readers interact with their negotiation of place, collective identity and belonging.

Incarcerated Youth

There is a small body of empirical research literature on the positive outcomes for incarcerated youth who participate in reading interventions to improve literacy and learning skills (see Harris et al. 2006; O'Cummings et al. 2010; Styslinger, Gavigan, and Albright 2017). There are even fewer studies on how youth involved with correctional facilities make meaning from texts. Stephanie Guerra (2012) provides a starting point for learning more about reading engagement among at-risk and incarcerated youth in her work on the potential of using urban fiction in literacy instruction with such youth.

References

Becnel, Kim, and Robin A. Moeller. 2015. "What, Why, and How They Read: Reading Preferences and Patterns of Rural Young Adults." *Journal of Adolescent & Adult Literacy* 59, no. 3: 299–307.

Brown, Joanne. 2011. *Immigration Narratives in Young Adult Literature: Crossing Borders.* Lanham, MD: Scarecrow Press.

Cortina, Jeronimo, Patrick Taran, and Alison Raphael, eds. 2014. *Migration and Youth: Challenges and Opportunities.* Global Migration Group. Available at: http://www.unhcr.org/globaltrends2016/.

Guerra, Stephanie F. 2012. "Using Urban Fiction to Engage At-Risk and Incarcerated Youths in Literacy Instruction." *Journal of Adolescent & Adult Literacy* 52, no. 5: 385–394.

Harris, Pamela J., Heather M. Baltodano, Alf Redo J. Artiles, and Robert B. Rutherford. 2006. "Integration of Culture in Reading Studies for Youth in Corrections: A Literature Review." *Education & Treatment of Children* 29, no. 4: 749–778.

Kral, Inge, and Robert G. (Jerry) Schwab. 2012. *Learning Spaces: Youth, Literacy and New Media in Remote, Indigenous Australia.* Canberra, Australia: ANU E Press. Available at: http://www.oapen.org/search?identifier=459851.

Lam, E. 2009. "Multiliteracies on Instant Messaging in Negotiating Local, Translocal, and Transnational Affiliation: A Case of an Adolescent Immigrant." *Reading Research Quarterly* 44, no. 4: 377–397.

Leurs, Koen. 2015. *Digital Passages: Migrant Youth 20.0: Diaspora, Gender and Youth Cultural Intersections.* Amsterdam: University of Amsterdam Press. Available at: http://www.doabooks.org/doab?func=search&query=rid:17216.

Naidoo, Jamie Campbell, and Sarah Park Dahlen, eds. 2013. *Diversity in Youth Literature: Opening Doors through Reading.* Chicago: ALA Editions.

O'Cummings, Mindee, Sarah Bardack, and Simon Gonsoulin. 2010. *Issue Brief: The Importance of Literacy for Youth Involved in the Juvenile Justice System.* Washington, DC: National Evaluation and Technical Assistance Center for the Education of Children and Youth Who Are Neglected, Delinquent, or At Risk (NDTAC). Available at http://www.neglected-delinquent.org/nd/docs/literacy_brief_20100120.pdf.

Reese, Debbie. 2017. *American Indians in Children's Literature.* Available at: https://americanindiansinchildrensliterature.blogspot.ca/p/about.html.

Rothbauer, Paulette M. 2009. "Exploring the Placelessness of Reading among Older Teens in a Canadian Rural Municipality." *The Library Quarterly* 79, no. 4: 465–483.

Rothbauer, Paulette M. 2011. "Rural Teens on the Role of Reading in Their Lives." *Journal of Research on Libraries and Young Adults*, February 14. Available at: http://www.yalsa.ala.org/jrlya/2011/02/rural-teens-on-the-role-of-reading-in-their-lives/.

Spring, Erin. 2016a. "Everyone Knows a Junior: Blackfoot Children and Their Books." *Bookbird* 54, no. 1: 55–60.

Spring, Erin. 2016b. "The Experiences of Two Migrant Readers: Freedom, Restriction, and the Navigation of Adolescent Space." *Jeunesse: Young People, Texts, Cultures* 8, no. 1: 227–247.

Styslinger, Mary E., Karen Gavigan, and Kendra Albright, eds. 2017. *Literacy Behind Bars: Successful Reading and Writing Strategies for Use with Incarcerated Youth and Adults*. Lanham, MD: Rowman & Littlefield.

Chapter 4

Adult Readers

Catherine Sheldrick Ross

At the heart of this chapter on adult readers lie some crucial questions: How do enthusiastic readers differ from people who say they don't enjoy reading? What is the nature of the reading experience for avid readers? What role does reading play in their lives? How can librarians and other allies of pleasure reading support readers in finding enjoyable books and in sharing their reading with others?

4.1 The Who, What, Where, and When of Reading

For more than three-quarters of a century, large-scale studies of reading have asked, "Who reads what and how much in what part of the country?" and have reached certain fairly stable conclusions. Women read more than men. Men are more likely than women to be nonbook readers, but that still leaves a lot of book-reading men. Younger people used to read more than those over age 50, but now some studies report an expansion of reading among people age 60 and over as baby boomers continue their book-reading habit in retirement. A finding that has remained unchanged over decades of survey research is that college-educated people and people with higher annual incomes read the most. Engagement in reading climbs in lockstep as one goes up the socioeconomic ladder. The most robust single predictor of an individual's participation in reading is level of education, which is of course related to income level and occupation group. Occupation group is more important than age when it comes to predicting whether or not a person is a book reader. Whites read more than nonwhites, but recently some studies in the United States show black readers closing the gap.

Studies that examine literacy skills have found that younger adult readers have better literacy skills than older ones (despite the widespread belief that literacy rates are falling and that readers who are now of retirement age experienced a superior quality of elementary education in comparison with those readers of the present day—see section 3.1). People who are avid readers as adults often got their start in childhood, come from reading families, and continue to enjoy reading as they grow older. Nevertheless, over the course of a lifetime, the amount of time people spend reading can wax and wane, depending on what else is happening in their lives, such as the birth of children or retirement from employment. The BookTrust study (2013, 9) in the United Kingdom found, for example, that among both men and women, people over 60 were the most likely to report reading books for pleasure "daily" or "at least weekly."

As Table 4.1 indicates, studies have consistently found that the vast majority of the population reads *something*, at least half the population reads books, and about 10 to 20 percent are avid readers for whom being a reader is a crucial part of their identity. Some people read only newspapers, some read newspapers and magazines but not books, but book readers usually also read newspapers and magazines. In Europe, northerners read more books than do those in the south. In Scandinavia, for example, 90 percent of Swedes and 82 percent of Danes responding to a Eurobarometer survey (2013) reported having read at least one book in the last year in comparison with 51 percent of Romanians, 50 per cent of Greeks, and 68 percent in the European Union (EU) as a whole. This means that aggregated summaries can obscure significant regional differences within continents, within countries, and within provinces and states.

Because in modern economies, some 95 percent of people report having read "something" in the past year, surveys typically give weight to book reading as a key indicator of reading, sometimes further qualifying book reading by *purpose* (e.g., "for other reasons than work or study"—Eurobarometer 2013); *type of material* (e.g., "literary reading" but not nonfiction—NEA 2004, 2007, 2009); or *format* (e.g., print, eBook, audiobook—Zickuhr and Rainie 2014). Some surveys now ask about online reading such as reading fanfiction or reading stories or poems on Facebook or Wattpad (e.g., Australian Council for the Arts 2017). The Australian study (2017, 9) reports that, in comparison with five years earlier, "there has been a strong shift toward spending more time reading overall (including Internet, social media, blogs, magazines, books and newspapers), and a slight shift toward spending less time reading books."

Table 4.1

Percentage of the Population That Reads

Study	All readers %	Book readers %	Frequent readers %
Link & Hopf (1946)	—	50	20
Leigh (1950)	85 to 90	50	25
Ennis (1965)	—	49	15
BISG (1978)	94	55	25
Gallup (1978)	—	75	24
Guldberg (1990)	—	54	—
Book Marketing Ltd. (2000)	96	70	12
Createc (2005)	—	87	13
NEA (2004)	—	57	24
NEA (2009)	—	54	—
BookTrust (2013)	—	86	21
Environics (2013)	—		—
Eurobarometer 399 (2013)	—	68	—
Pew (2014)	—	76	—
Australia Council for the Arts (2017)	—	92	41

The readership studies cited in Table 4.1 have been sponsored by organizations with different specific interests. Studies initiated by library associations or by book sellers/book publishers want to know *where* people get books (libraries, bricks-and-mortar bookstores, online bookstores, used-book outlets, borrowing from friends and relatives), *what genres* they prefer, and *how they find out* about books (reviews, social media, word-of-mouth from friends, recommendations of a librarian or bookseller, information on the book itself such as the cover and blurb). Sponsors of the study determine its scope and how "reading" is defined. Hence the series of studies sponsored by the National Endowment for the Arts (NEA)—*Reading at Risk* (2004), *To Read or Not to Read* (2007), and *Reading on the Rise* (2009)—limited its interest to "literary reading," which was defined as reading novels, short stories, plays, or poetry, but not nonfiction. This privileging of fiction is notable because it is in marked contrast to the practice of earlier studies, where the most highly prized reading was nonfiction. In some studies, the nationality of the author or publisher also matters. Countries with smaller domestic markets such as Canada, Australia, Norway, and Sweden are concerned to protect local authors and publishers from a flood of foreign materials. Accordingly, national studies are designed to find out how many people are reading/buying home-grown books and authors. The Australian study *Reading the Reader* (2013, 5) reported that 65 percent of the Australians surveyed said that they enjoy fiction by Australian writers, 59 percent said they enjoy Australian-authored nonfiction, and 42 percent report being interested in books and writing about Indigenous Australia.

Earlier Studies of Adult Leisure Reading

If we look just at North America, we find that adult leisure reading has been studied for decades in a variety of contexts. Two early studies of reading deserve special mention. In 1942 Ruth Strang published *Exploration in Reading Patterns*, based on case studies of 112 persons ranging in age from 13 to over 50 and ranging in economic status from very poor to very wealthy. Her data included demographic data, scores on the vocabulary test of the Terman-Merrill intelligence test, reading test scores on three assigned articles, and interview data on the use of leisure time, magazines in the home, current reading, sources for books, and reading preferences and aversions. From the analysis of these data based on case studies, Strang (1942, 2–5) derived seven generalizations including the following, which subsequent research has amply supported:

- Each person's reading pattern is complex and unique because of the hundreds of single factors that influence a person's reading. These factors include age, occupation, vocational demands, geographic location, availability of reading matter, community customs, the influence of close friends and family members, childhood experiences that support or discourage reading, the reader's sense of himself or herself as a reader—in short a whole series of environmental factors that interact with the individual's biological nature.

- A relationship exists between a reader's interest in and enjoyment of a text, the reader's estimate of the text's difficulty, and the reader's proficiency in reading it.

- People read with their experience and their emotions. "What a reader gets out of a passage depends, in large measure, on what he brings to the passage."

- "An individual's reading pattern has a central core or radix which, more or less, determines its nature."

Of equal significance as a groundbreaking, pioneering study of reading is Philip Ennis's *Adult Book Reading in the United States* (1965). Ennis combined qualitative and quantitative methods. One section analyses 18 lengthy, tape-recorded interviews with readers, while another section presents responses to the NORC Amalgam Survey of June 1965 administered to a national sample of some 1,500 respondents. Ennis was particularly interested in explaining "the processes of making and keeping the book reading audience" (33). The first problem he confronts is how to define what is meant by a reader. He says, "We might say that there are two major components in defining a reader: an objective measure of his book reading, whereby we can establish the threshold of being 'in' or 'out' of the category, and the person's own definition of himself as someone who reads books" (40). Ennis concluded, as have many subsequent studies, that the most accurate test of a reader was to ask about the number of books read in a given period (e.g., the last six months), the amount of time spent reading, and the number of books in the home.

Ennis wanted to understand the processes involved in making and keeping the book-reading audience. Hence he considered magazine and newspaper reading only insofar as they functioned as stepping stones to book reading. In particular, Ennis was interested in finding "the various combinations of experiences in childhood and in school with those in adult life that hold people within the reading habit, lead them into it in later life, and prevent them from slipping out of it" (33). By correlating survey respondents' answers regarding whether or not they were book readers as children and whether or not they were currently book readers, Ennis produced a four-cell matrix of regular readers (those who read books both in childhood and currently), deserters (those who used to read books but stopped), late starters, and nonreaders of books. Of the 1,466 respondents, 58 percent read books in childhood and 42 percent did not. At the time of the survey, about half of the respondents (49 percent) read books and the other half did not. The cross-tabulation is where it gets interesting: 35 percent read books both in childhood and currently; 15 percent were late starters who didn't read books in childhood but currently read books; about one-quarter were deserters (24 percent); and another quarter (27 percent) were consistent nonreaders of books at both time periods. So book-reading children were more than twice as likely as the non-book-reading children to be readers as adults, but late starters still made up almost a third of current book readers.

Philip Ennis (11–12) found that reading was, if anything, even more complex than Ruth Strang had reported. He came to the following conclusions, which have also held up remarkably well in subsequent studies:

- While there was enormous diversity in the books read by readers, "the diversity of reading interests should not be construed as a cacophony of books ... In most cases, in fact, the person's reading had immediate and obvious relevance to his life."
- "People read about what they want to believe and tend to select books that are in some way familiar."
- "People reject or block out vast areas of books" on grounds that resisted probing or analysis, such as, "I'm not interested in fiction at all. I don't know why. It just can't sustain my interest at all."

At the end of the 1970s, the Book Industry Study Group (BISG) commissioned what became a landmark study of adult reading in the United States: *The 1978 Consumer Research Study on Reading and Book Purchasing* (1978), conducted by the market research company Yankelovich, Skelly, and White. The study's objectives were to distinguish readers from nonreaders, to identify the types of materials people read, and to find out *why* people read. For the quantitative phase of the study, 1,450 in-depth, one-hour interviews were conducted in 165 U.S. cities, with randomly chosen Americans, aged 16 and over. The sorting "in" or "out" question used in this study was whether a respondent had read any book, any magazine, and any newspaper in the past six months. Only 6 percent of the BISG sample said they had *not* read any format in the past six months, while 94 percent had read at least a newspaper. Thirty-nine percent read only newspapers and/or magazines and were labeled nonbook readers. Fifty-five percent were book readers, defined as such because they reported having read at least one book in the past six months.

The reading of formats was cumulative. Some readers read only newspapers and/or magazines and not books. But there is almost no one (2 percent of the population) who reads books exclusively and does not also read newspapers and magazines. A big difference between book readers and people who read only newspapers and/or magazines is that the *book readers were far more likely to report that they read for pleasure*. Summarizing the 1978 BISG study, the principal investigators said, "In general, we find that reading for pleasure, a pattern of consistently heavy reading, and a view of books as best able to satisfy a number of reading 'motivations' were those factors linked with heavy reading and with a commitment to books in particular" (McEvoy and Vincent 1980, 137).

Not to be outdone by the book industry, in the same year as the BISG study the American Library Association commissioned the Gallup Organization to undertake a large-scale national study reported in *Book Reading and Library Usage* (1978). Gallup conducted 1,515 telephone interviews with a representative national sample of adult Americans in order to find out who reads books, what book they read last, where they obtained the last book, what was their frequency of visiting a public library, what they used the library for, and what was their satisfaction with library services. Not unexpectedly, "heavy" readers were more likely to be women, from 18 to 34 years of age and with some college education (Gallup 1978, 14). About half of all respondents (51 percent) had visited a public library in the last year, including 9 percent who visit the library every two weeks (22).

Glass Half Empty or Glass Half Full?

Studies are governed by the preoccupations, fears, and anxieties of the era that produced them. By the year 2000, new worries came to the fore, particularly the impact of the Internet culture. If 50 percent of a national population in a high-income country reads books for pleasure—that is, for reasons other than for work or study—is this good or bad? Authors of reading studies come to diametrically opposite conclusions, depending on whether or not they have a vested interest in using the study as a call to arms for educational restructuring (more testing, more phonics), for more investment in cultural institutions, or for other reforms. An interesting case is the series of reports published by the NEA starting with *Reading at Risk* (2004) and followed by further reports in 2007 and 2009. The 2004 study was drawn from the literature portion of a large-scale survey, Survey of Public Participation in the Arts (SPPA), that was conducted in 2002 by the Census Bureau with a survey sample of 17,000 adult Americans. It turned out that in 2002, 56.6 percent of respondents claimed to have read a book for leisure (not for work or study) and 46.7 percent claimed to have read literature (novels, short stories, plays, or poetry)—down by 4 percent and 7 percent, respectively, from a similar SPPA study conducted in 1992.

A press release for *Reading at Risk* warned, "Literary Reading in Dramatic Decline ... Fewer Than Half of Americans Now Read Literature." In this press release, then NEA chair Dana Gioia was quoted as saying, "This report documents a national crisis. ... The decline in reading among every segment of the adult population reflects a general collapse in advanced literacy. To lose this human capacity—and all the diverse benefits it fosters—impoverishes both cultural and civic life." The NEA report (2004, vii) blamed "our society's massive shift toward electronic media for entertainment and information," claiming, "The decline in reading correlates with increased participation in a variety of electronic media, including the Internet, video games, and portable digital devices." This increased participation is presented as a bad thing because book reading requires "active engagement" in contrast to the "passive participation" engendered by electronic media: "Even interactive electronic media, such as video games and the Internet, foster shorter attention spans and accelerated gratification" (vii). (See sections 1.1 and 1.4 for more on the talk about active book reading versus passive screen watching.) A follow-up study *To Read or Not to Read* (NEA 2007) supported the conclusions of *Reading at Risk* by summarizing additional data from studies of all kinds of voluntary reading with a particular focus on youth (see section 3.1). Chairman Dana Gioia called the 2007 study "a call to action" (6).

Meanwhile, the Department of Canadian Heritage commissioned a national survey of Canadians, which was reported in *Reading and Buying Books for Pleasure* (Createc 2005, 4). The Createc report announced somewhat smugly that "Canadians appear to be distinctly different from their American counterparts," whose reading the NEA had just described as falling off a cliff. In Canada, "Contrary to certain alarmist claims that there is a trend towards a lower reading rate in our society or that the Internet has had harmful effects on reading habits, this national survey has shown that reading for pleasure remains a solidly established and widespread habit with little or no change over the last 15 years" (4). But wait! The lost literary readers of America were found a few years later— 16.6 million of them. Dana Gioia explained in his Preface to a new NEA report, *Reading on the Rise* (2009), that friends of reading everywhere—"millions of parents, teachers, librarians, and civic leaders"—were roused to action by *Reading at Risk* and together turned things around through the introduction of thousands of programs, such as NEA's own Big Read program (see section 4.7).

Less interested in promoting literary reading than in examining social inequity, the BookTrust survey (2013) found that England is divided into two nations: the advantaged, who read books, and the marginalized, who watch screens and play video games. BookTrust, which calls itself "the UK's largest reading charity," sponsored an England-wide telephone survey in 2013 of the reading habits of 1,500 adults, using a quota sample to make sure that the survey respondents were representative of the population at large in terms of gender, age, and socioeconomic status. As an organization, BookTrust believes that reading can transform lives. Through its Bookstart program, which celebrated 25 years of operation in 2017, BookTrust provides free books and resources that reach 2.5 million children a year. The BookTrust survey was designed to tease out the attributes and attitudes that distinguish reluctant readers and nonreaders from avid, committed readers. Researchers used postal codes to link survey results with preexisting national data that measured various dimensions of deprivation (income, employment, health, education, crime, living environment) of the area in which respondents lived. The *BookTrust Reading Habits Survey 2013* found that the higher their socioeconomic group, the more satisfied people are with their lives and the more often they read.

The researchers used cluster analysis to sort participants into segments, based on reading habits and reading frequency. They defined a segment as "a group of respondents who share common characteristics" while differing in their characteristics from respondents in other segments. Nine segments were identified, ranging from segment 1 (Bookworms) to segment 9 (Don't read) in decreasing steps of engagement with reading (7). Here is how the upper and lower anchor points are described in the BookTrust report (2013):

Segment 1: Bookworms (6 percent)

- Bookworms devour paperback, hardback and e-books, getting through 12 books a month.
- They have an average of nearly a thousand (994) books in their house.
- They are more likely than average to be aged over 60 (and retired), female, and highly educated.
- They are the happiest of all the segments.

Segment 9: Don't read (10 percent)

- This segment has very low levels of reading. Three-quarters do not read any books in a typical year.
- Many in childhood did not have stories read to them by their parents and did not enjoy reading at school.
- They are more likely to be younger (particularly 18–29 age group) and over two-thirds are male. They are also more likely than average to be from DE Socio-Economic group, and to have no qualifications.
- They are significantly more likely than any other segment to have had a poor experience of reading when a child. Over half (56 percent) did not enjoy reading at school, 43 percent were not read to by their parents, and 31 percent were not encouraged to read by their parents when growing up.

The "Don't read" segment is far more likely than any of the other segments to agree with such statements as: "I often start reading a book, but get bored after a few chapters"; "I cannot find the time to read"; "Reading is hard work"; and "I find reading boring."

But What Do These Studies Really Tell Us?

First some caveats. The majority of the large national surveys are based on telephone interviews with random, stratified samples of at least 1,000 people. Usually now these are random-digit-dial surveys by landline and cell phone. Most use quotas to ensure that the sample's age, gender, and region match census information and have a margin of error of ±3. Even when the questions asked are the same from one survey to the next, changes in responses of two or three percentage points either way can happen by chance and are nothing either to crow about or be despondent over. Surveys that report questionnaire data on percentages of readers are only roughly comparable because studies ask different questions and define differently what counts as being a reader. As noted earlier, typically reading studies use an "in or out" sorting question to determine whether or not the survey respondent is a reader (or a book reader or a literary reader) or not. Then they correlate reading with demographic variables such as sex, age, education, occupation, family income, and place of residence.

Because studies vary in their operational definitions of a "reader," variations in the size of the reading population is an artifact of the question asked. So much depends on the kind of material counted and the time period specified. Some studies are interested only in voluntary reading done by choice ("excluding reading done for work or study"), while others count all kinds of reading, including work-related reading and blogs, and all formats including audiobooks. Findings also vary depending on whether the sorting question used is "Are you currently reading a book?" or "Have you read a book in the past six months?" or "Have you read a book in the past year?" or "Have you read a book recently?" The latter question is problematic on two counts: what individual survey takers understand by "recently" and what they understand by "reading a book." As Ennis (1965, 6) noted early on about the challenge of surveying readers, "It became clear during the course of the interviews . . . that there was a wide range of calendar time contained in the notion of 'recently.'" Similarly, without guidance, questionnaire respondents vary dramatically in what they count as "reading a book," with some people counting it only if they read the whole book from cover to cover and other people counting it when they consult a section of a reference book or cook book.

The "all the way through or part of the way through" qualification is an attempt to address this methodological problem, but it has the effect of expanding what gets counted as being a book reader. So compare two findings, both from 1978: Gallup found that 75 percent of Americans are readers, whereas the BISG found that 55 percent of Americans are readers. To get the 75 percent figure, the Gallup study had asked if the respondent had read "any kind of a book all the way through or part of the way through" in the past year. In contrast, the BISG study asked whether they had read at least one book in the past six months.

Despite justified skepticism about the accuracy of any particular number for the percentage of the population who read books, the accumulation of demographic research conducted over some 80 years demonstrates one thing beyond question. While there is nothing magical about the book format in itself, choosing to read books for leisure means having the literacy skills effortlessly to make sense of extended text. "Reading books" turns out to be a useful proxy for a lot of other things that are considered socially desirable: engagement with the world, being in the know, the ability to use texts to satisfy one's active curiosity about the world and one's place in it, access to the specialized literacies that are associated with professional careers that pay the highest salaries, and the possession of social capital and status associated with education.

Research Tells Us

A survey of 1,520 American adults by the Pew Research Center found that about a quarter of them (26 percent) report that they have *not* read a book "in whole or in part" in the past year, whether in print, electronic, or audio form. Summarizing the study, Andrew Perrin (2016) asks, "So who, exactly, are these non-book readers?" Nonbook readers are more likely to be men than women (31 percent versus 21 percent), more likely to have high school or less education than to have graduated from college (40 percent versus 13 percent), more likely to have an annual income below $30,000 than above $75,000 (33 percent versus 17 percent), and more likely to be Hispanic than black or white (40 percent versus 29 percent and 23 percent, respectively). Perrin reports that the demographic groups that are least likely to read are also least likely to have visited a library in the past year. Nevertheless, this still leaves a lot of people who are in the "least likely to read" categories who in fact *do* read books and *do* visit libraries.

What Libraries Can Do

1. Keep in mind the importance of accessibility and make it easy and convenient for people to find reading materials of all kinds, not just books, and at all levels of difficulty and demandingness. If the library's brand is story, make it easy for people to find engaging stories across a variety of formats, including audiobooks.

References

Australia Council for the Arts. 2017. *Reading the Reader: A Survey of Australian Reading Habits.* Macquarie University. Available at: http://www.australiacouncil.gov.au/ workspace/uploads/files/readers_survey_summary_final_v-592cf39be2c34.pdf.

Book Industry Study Group. 1978. *The 1978 Consumer Research Study on Reading and Book Purchasing.* New York: Yankelovich, Skelly and White, Inc.

Book Marketing Limited. 2000. *Reading the Situation: Book Reading, Buying and Borrowing Habits in Britain.* London: Library and Information Commission.

BookTrust. 2013. *BookTrust Reading Habits Survey 2013.* Available at: https://www .booktrust.org.uk/usr/library/documents/main/1576-booktrust-reading-habits-report -final.pdf.

Createc. 2005. *Reading and Buying Books for Pleasure: 2005 National Survey, Final Report.* Department of Canadian Heritage. Available at: http://data.library .utoronto.ca/datapub/codebooks/utm/srbb05/srbb05_report.pdf.

Ennis, Philip H. 1965. *Adult Book Reading in the United States: A Preliminary Report.* (National Opinion Research Center Report, no. 105). Chicago: National Opinion Research Center.

Eurobarometer 399. 2013. *Cultural Access and Participation.* European Commission. Available at: http://ec.europa.eu/commfrontoffice/publicopinion/archives/ebs/ebs_399_en.pdf.

Gallup Organization. 1978. *Book Reading and Library Usage: A Study of Habits and Perceptions.* Conducted for the American Library Association. Princeton, NJ: Gallup Organization.

McEvoy, George F., and Cynthia S. Vincent. 1980. "Who Reads and Why?" *Journal of Communication* 30, no. 1: 134–152.

National Endowment for the Arts. 2004. *Reading at Risk: A Survey of Literary Reading in America.* Research Division Report #46. Washington, DC. Available at: http://arts.gov/publications/reading-risk-survey-literary-reading-america-0.

National Endowment for the Arts. 2007. *To Read or Not to Read: A Question of National Consequence.* Research Report #47.Washington, DC. Available at: http://arts.gov/sites/default/files/ToRead.pdf.

National Endowment for the Arts. 2009. *Reading on the Rise.* Available at: http://arts.gov/file/2574.

Perrin, Andrew. 2016. "Who Doesn't Read Books in America?" *Pew Research Center,* November 23. Available at: http://www.pewresearch.org/fact-tank/2016/11/23/who-doesnt-read-books-in-america/.

Strang, Ruth. 1942. *Explorations in Reading Patterns.* Chicago: University of Chicago Press.

Zickuhr, Kathryn, and Lee Rainie. 2014. "A Snapshot of Reading in America in 2013." *Pew Research Center.* Available at: http://www.pewinternet.org/2014/01/16/a-snapshot-of-reading-in-america-in-2013/.

4.2 Why (Not) Read?

Large-scale studies summarized in section 4.1 such as the *BookTrust Reading Habits Survey* (2013, 43–51) tell us how many people there are at different levels of reading engagement from least to most. The BookTrust study also highlights some significant differences in readers' lifelong relationship with reading, starting in childhood. The 21 percent in the "Don't Read" and "Don't Like Reading" categories in the BookTrust study typically were not read to as children. As adults, they avoid reading whenever possible, do not find reading to be either fun or relaxing, and say that whenever they try reading a book they get bored after a few chapters. The 21 percent in the "Love to Read" and "Bookworms" categories typically were read to regularly as children. As adults, they read every day for enjoyment, buy books for themselves and others, and enjoy talking about books and getting them as presents.

Nevertheless, answers to the crucial question of *why* some people choose to read and others don't remain elusive. National reading surveys ask respondents to pick answers from a menu of already formulated options including "Always have read" for why they read and "Lack of time" or "I find reading boring" for why they don't. But when unenthusiastic readers say that reading is "boring" or they find it "hard to concentrate" or they have a "short attention span" or they "have no time" or "prefer other activities," it usually means that there is a misalignment between the reader's skills and the demands of the text. Boring texts are usually either too easy or, more likely, too difficult for the reader. For many unengaged readers, the thought of reading conjures up feelings of inadequacy, frustration, failure, and memories of childhood humiliation at school.

This section is an attempt to piece together from multiple sources the evidence to answer the "Why (not) read" question by looking in particular at the most engaged readers. What are avid readers like? *What satisfactions, benefits, and rewards do avid readers get from reading that are closed off to people who don't choose to read? The Future of Reading*, sponsored by Arts Council England, uses the terms "highly engaged readers" and "unenthusiastic readers" to differentiate the two poles of reading engagement. Unenthusiastic readers understand the benefits that reading is supposed to bring—especially utilitarian benefits such as gaining knowledge—even if they themselves personally experience few such benefits (Creative Research 2009, 8). In contrast, highly engaged readers acknowledge the utilitarian benefits but put more weight on pleasure, relaxation, the excitement of discovery, and the delight in a good story. In short, we know that there are stark statistical differences between unengaged readers and avid readers. But to tease apart these differences, we need to turn to more fine-grained evidence such as interviews with readers, reading diaries, and readers' own accounts and self-statements.

Frustrated Readers

The key difference between highly engaged readers and low-engagement readers is that for the latter group reading is *hard*, akin to the laborious decoding of a document written in a barely understood language. Whereas accomplished readers breeze through stretches of text with apparent effortlessness, nonreaders say that they have trouble "getting into" a book. In *Speaking of Reading*, which is a distillation of interviews with readers, Nadine Rosenthal (1995, 25) provides a similar picture of what it is like for adults who "are able to read, but can't seem to concentrate long enough for their minds to engage with the words to create meaning." Her chapter, "Frustrated Readers," includes the following accounts:

Janice: I read one word at a time. I don't skip anything because I'm afraid I'll miss something (29).

Rich: Sometimes I still have difficulty comprehending what I'm reading . . . so I'll have to read it over and over. . . . I've gone through it two and three times, and I'm not going to try to decipher it anymore, it's just too frustrating." The adolescent is rekindled in me, and I just bail out (33).

Kevin: Reading is a waste of time for me unless I understand the book, which is rare. I guess people who read all the time must get something out of it that I just haven't experienced (36).

Nancy: I feel that my eyes stutter—I'm not able to see the words fast enough, smooth enough. . . . As a reader, I can't get the information in, in a fluid, effortless way. I start books, yet very seldom do I finish them (45).

Titus: I want to read, but I start and then I get lost and have to go back. I get stuck or lost or forget what I just read. I have to read things over and over. Sometimes I read and get stuck on all the words I don't know. Or I read the paragraph real slow to try to remember what I just read, but I can't . . . I get frustrated; it just drags on and on (49).

These frustrated readers live at the opposite pole from frequent readers who say that reading is like breathing. For avid readers, the act of reading itself becomes transparent. The mediating role of words on the page drops from consciousness and the reader is drawn effortlessly into the textual world. In contrast, frustrated readers engage in a painful word-by-word struggle, as their descriptions of their reading experience reveals: "so slowly that I lost the flow," "one word at a time," "just bail out," "decipher," "my eyes stutter," "get lost," "stuck on all the words I don't know," and "drags on and on." Whereas confident readers may choose to read certain passages slowly to savor the language and prolong the pleasurable experience, frustrated readers approach reading as a painful task of decoding, letter by letter and word by word. With attention focused on sounds and letters, these slow readers have trouble making sense of or remembering what they read. So they may start all over again from the very beginning and sometimes they just give up.

What Avid Readers Say about Why They Read

Wendy Lesser begins her book *Why I Read* (2014, 3) with an acknowledgment that reasons for reading are complex and ultimately mysterious: "It's not a question I can completely answer. There are abundant reasons . . . many of them mutually contradictory." She says that her reading is to a certain extent "a compulsion. As with all compulsions, its sources prefer to stay hidden." Lesser's characterization of reading reminds us that for avid readers reading is such a big part of who they are that the "Why read?" question is hard to answer, as it was for Ivor, one of the most committed readers in my study:

> That is very difficult. I wish I could say, "I read because of this" or "Reading is important because of this." But I can't, because there are so many reasons that it's important. It's like that terror of losing my arms or losing my eyesight. I can't say that I read as an escape, because I don't. It may sound as though I read as an escape—all this talk about going to another world—but it's not really escaping because I'm always fully prepared to come back. Why do I read? I read to learn. Probably if I had to say why I read that would be it. I read to learn. Which is not to say that I only read books of a strictly educational nature. But, whenever I read, I feel as though I'm assimilating what I read into this—almost like a one-man folk memory. Oh, this is so hard! Reading is, you see, just so huge to me—so huge that it's so hard to quantify it and say, "This is true" and "This is not true." (Ivor, graduate student, age 26)

For Ivor and many other committed readers, reasons for reading can be hard to disentangle because they are all bound up, one in another. Readers pick up book to be entertained by a good story, but then learn something about the world or about themselves. Readers read to be transported to another world, but learn something that they take back and use in their everyday life. Avid readers in my study all agreed on one thing: reading gives them something that can't be experienced any other way.

This value goes beyond the instrumental and utilitarian. Certainly they agree that by reading a lot they improve their level of literacy, increase their vocabulary, become better writers, and, consequently, do better at school and in their careers. But that's not *why* they read. Committed readers are apt to say that reading is part of their identity. In answer to a question about why they read and the importance of pleasure-reading in their lives, participants in my study of avid readers called reading "almost a necessity," "absolutely sacred," "a passion," and "like eating and sleeping." They said:

- For me to read is to live.
- If I were stuck on a desert island without books, I would go crazy.
- My panic is to be in the house without anything to read. That makes me just absolutely, totally panic stricken. I can't live without reading. Blindness probably scares me more than anything.

Talk of blindness was a common response to the interview question, "What would it be like if for one reason or another you *couldn't* read?" The typical reaction was initially a horrified statement that the situation was unthinkable. One person said emphatically, "What sort of question is that! That's not an option! If I'm going on an overnight somewhere, I will bring *two* books because I read a number of books at a time." Another person said, "I wouldn't be me. I wouldn't be the person I am if I didn't read or wasn't able to read. It frightens me to think that something like reading can create you or at least influence who you are so much, because if I wasn't able to read I wouldn't be me. It frightens me, so I don't even want to consider it as an option." When Toyne and Usherwood (2001) adopted the same question, "What would it be like if . . . you *couldn't* read?" they got the same alarmed responses from readers in the United Kingdom—talk of blindness and suggestions of methods of coping such as memorizing texts or writing one's own texts. Then came panicky statements that the loss would be "devastating," "a huge gap," "like dementia, I would be dying," "it would be suicide, it would be like murder" (Toyne and Usherwood 2001, 47–48). In short, for avid readers, reading is so much a part of their identity that they say, "I wouldn't be me" if I couldn't read.

Finding without Seeking

For some people who grow up in small communities and feel like ugly ducklings, reading provides a lifeline to a larger world. In Elizabeth Strout's novel *My Name Is Lucy Barton* (2016), the narrator explains how she grew up poor and ostracized, living until the age of 11 with her family in a cold and draughty garage with access to only a trickle of running water in a makeshift sink, her father so damaged by his war experience that he is unpredictable and frightening. Lucy's favorite book in childhood was about two happy girls with a nice mother who move to a new town for the summer. "In this new town there was a girl named Tilly—Tilly!—who was strange and unattractive because she was dirty and poor and the girls were not nice to Tilly, but the nice mother made them be good to her. This is what I remember from the book: Tilly" (Strout 2016, 24). Lucy gives a copy of this special book to her own daughter, Chrissie, for her eighth birthday. And Chrissie's response to the book with Tilly in it: "Mom, it's kind of a dumb book" (74). Well-loved and economically secure, Chrissie may not even have noticed Tilly, who appears to be a secondary character in a book about the two happy girls.

Strout's fictional representation of the unpredictable way in which a book comforts, reassures, or inspires has many counterparts in my interviews with avid readers. I have called this phenomenon "finding without seeking" (Ross 1999). A book initially chosen for pleasure ends up helping readers cope with life outside the book. Readers read the book within the context of their own lives, their own preoccupations acting as a filter to highlight certain parts of the book—sometimes a minor character such as Tilly whom other readers may skip over—that address their particular concerns. In my study, Rebecca (social worker, age 34) said, "I feel that what I got out of books was definitely mediated by my own needs. There's a process that goes on where you are thinking about certain things in your life, and you do pick out relevant bits and pieces from your reading that mean something to you." Anna (homemaker, age 35) explicitly referred to a benevolent process in which wide and frequent reading, especially of fiction, produces answers to current concerns, without the need for active seeking:

> I find that what I'm reading and what I'm thinking about as I'm read-
> ing help my whole adjustment to the world when I'm not actually sit-
> ting down reading. I feel that the circular nature of life and art is very
> important. I don't separate them. What I'm getting out of the art is
> very important to the life. It's often difficult to say to oneself,
> "There's a problem that I'm working through now. I'm going to go
> out and look for books which deal with it." But if you read widely
> and frequently, you can't help but coming against the problems in lit-
> erature which you find useful in life and vice versa. I don't actively
> go seeking.

In short, one of the great mysteries of reading is the unpredictability of the strong connection a book will make with a particular reader at a particular time. Commenting on this phenomenon, Toyne and Usherwood (2001, 42) quote Alan Bennett's reflection that "something in the book speaks to part of you that is just waiting to be spoken to." A case in point: in Diane Osen's *The Book That Changed My Life* (2002), author Cynthia Ozick recalled being 17 and reading Henry James's "The Beast in the Jungle" in a story anthology that her brother had brought home from the library. She says, "Reading it, I felt it to be the story of my own life—which was strange, since it's about an elderly gentleman who suddenly discovers that he has wasted his years" (123).

The Role of Reading in Readers' Lives

So what role does reading play in the lives of committed readers? What makes avid readers so different from unengaged readers, such that reading provides rewards to committed readers that are unimaginable to nonreaders. Research studies that are the most helpful in exploring the "Why read?" question typically gather data through open-ended interviews and focus group discussions. They arrive at their analytic categories from the bottom up by examining what readers say rather than from the top down using preestablished categories.

Jackie Toyne and Bob Usherwood's *Checking the Books* (2001, 25–52) offers one helpful typology of reasons why people say they read "imaginative literature," by which is meant novels, plays, and poetry. This typology is based on discussions held with 29 focus groups of both users and nonusers of libraries, located in nine different public libraries. Analyzing answers to the prompt, "What contribution, if any, does the reading of imaginative literature bring to your life?" Toyne and Usherwood developed the following categories, illustrated in each case with statements from readers:

- Escapism (relaxation, opportunity to abandon the here and now)
- Means of escape (escape into other worlds, escape through association, escape through aesthetic pleasure)
- Reading for instruction (practical knowledge, literary skills, lessons about the world, reliability of instruction)
- Self-development (personal insight, insight into the "other")
- Location of reading in people's lives (reading as a bodily function, exercise the imagination, reading as identity).

Jessica E. Moyer (2007) explored the multiple purposes that reading fiction serves in the lives of readers. In a study based on questionnaires and interviews with library users, Moyer (2007, 74–75) concluded that readers read fiction for pleasure, but then derive significant educational benefits that she categorized as follows: (1) learning about yourself and gaining insight into other people and relationships, (2) learning about other cultures and other time periods, (3) life enrichment and intellectual growth, and (4) gaining different perspectives and being challenged to think in a different way. In Copenhagen, Gitte Balling (2016) conducted group and individual interviews focusing on the reading experience with members of a reading group and with LIS students. She concluded that reading has a "dual role": "Reading ... on the one hand is relaxing and entertaining and on the other hand creates knowledge and experience" (Balling 2016, 44).

Using in-depth qualitative interviews with 11 immigrant Russian readers, Keren Dali (2014, 28) asked, "What are your reasons for leisure reading?" All the readers gave multiple reasons, both personal and interpersonal. Personal reasons given for reading included "entertainment; escapism; pleasure; relaxation; consolation, comfort, and reassurance; stimulating dreams and imagination;

learning to forgive and to understand other people . . . ; recovering from negative life experiences; developing and defining self-identity; emotional maturation; reliving the past; self-help; acquiring a new lifestyle and/or getting new perspectives on life; information; education; and—No reason, really . . . I just like it." Dali's article makes a helpful conceptual distinction between two kinds of reasons why people say they read that are often lumped together: *expectations* that motivate a reader to pick up the book in the first place and *outcomes* after the book is read. Hence a reader could be motivated to choose a book by an expectation of pleasure and escapism, but the outcome might be getting a new perspective that offers a way of coping with a problem.

Interviewees in reading studies are usually anonymous. When famous people are interviewed about reading, as in Michiko Kakutani's interview (2017) with Barack Obama, we have extra information about context because we already know a lot about the life of the reader. Here is what President Obama said a week before he left the Oval Office about how reading has helped him:

> I think that I found myself better able to imagine what's going on in the lives of people throughout my presidency because of not just a specific novel but the act of reading fiction. It exercises those muscles, and I think that has been helpful.
>
> And then there's been the occasion where I just want to get out of my own head. [Laughter] Sometimes you read fiction just because you want to be someplace else.
>
> And perspective is exactly what is wanted. At a time when events move so quickly and so much information is transmitted, the ability to slow down and get perspective, along with the ability to get in somebody else's shoes—those two things have been invaluable to me. Whether they've made me a better president, I can't say. But what I can say is that they have allowed me to sort of maintain my balance during the course of eight years, because this is a place that comes at you hard and fast and doesn't let up.

Here Obama identifies the same elements that other less famous readers mention: connection with others and the "ability to get in somebody else's shoes," escape "to get out of my own head" and be taken "someplace else," and "the ability to slow down and get perspective" and "maintain my balance."

And here is one further piece for the mosaic, a piece that points us toward one of the themes discussed next. In his book-length account of his lifelong relationship with books and reading, *One for the Books* (2012), Joe Queenan says emphatically that his reason for reading—and that of most book lovers—is the desire for escape or "to be somewhere else."

> I know why I read so obsessively. I want to be somewhere else. . . . I am convinced that this desire to escape from reality—on a daily, even an hourly basis—is the main reason people read books. Intelligent people, that is. . . . I think this compulsion is fairly common. . . . [M]ost book lovers . . . read to escape to a more exciting, more rewarding world. (4)

Reading for Escape

In my project of interviewing avid readers, I tried to get at the "Why read?" question by adding a new question in 2010 and 2011 on the role of reading: "What would you say is the role that reading plays in your life?" There were 57 interviewees who answered this question: 19 males and 38 females between the ages of 22 and 82, with the majority in their 20s and 30s. The first thing that stands out from an analysis of the responses is that the bedrock for discretionary reading is pleasure. Through reading, these readers say, they get many benefits—they learn things about the world and about themselves, they get new perspectives that give them a broader outlook and help them solve problems, they get a more empathetic understanding of other people, they regulate their own mood, and so on. *But if the experience were not pleasurable, they wouldn't do it.*

The most frequently mentioned role is reading for escape. Unprompted, 44 percent (25 interviewees) explicitly used the term "escape" to describe a role that reading plays in their lives. An additional 16 percent (9 interviewees), while not using the actual term "escape," nevertheless described their reading in ways that implied reading for escape. Perhaps less surprising than the high percentage of self-identified escapist readers is the very positive way interviewees characterized reading for escape. In earlier studies, the terms "escape" and "escapism" have often been used pejoratively, sometimes to describe a way of reading and sometimes to categorize whole genres as "escapist literature." For example, in a UNESCO report, Richard Bamberger (1975, 21) summarized a typology of motives for reading consisting of four primary types: informative reading, escapist reading, literary reading, and cognitive reading. The reader of escapist reading "wants to escape reality, to live in a world without responsibilities and limits. . . . Considered purely from its content, escapist reading is predominantly negative. . . . Picture magazines and cheap novels owe their existence to the addiction to escapist reading." In contrast, the 60 percent (34 interviewees) who talked about their own reading in terms of escape saw escapist reading in positive terms. They might agree that for them reading is a compulsion verging on "addiction," but characterized reading for escape as healthy—in fact something that recharged their batteries and helped them cope in their everyday life.

"Reading for escape," as described by these 34 avid readers, turns out to be a many-faceted concept. To start with, there is the distinction that readers made, either implicitly or explicitly, between "escaping from" and "escaping to." The "escaping from" readers said that reading an engrossing book was a good way to "block out" or keep at bay the stresses, worries, or what one reader called "the humdrum" of everyday life. They consider such reading to be therapeutic, two readers going so far as to say it kept them "sane." Toyne and Usherwood (2001, 26–35) found very similar results when they asked focus group members, "What contribution, if any, does the reading of imaginative literature bring to your life?" Noting that the first response provided was usually "escapism," they cautioned that we can understand the role of reading for escape only by examining it "within its social context," which is to say within the life of the reader (27). They found that, depending on the particular daily pressures facing readers, the "intensity of the need to escape" varied a lot from those who read for escape as a form of pleasant relaxation after a hectic day to those whose reading was literally a "lifesaver" (30).

Here are some examples from my study that illustrate the range of ways that "escape-from" reading is said to help readers: "It's an escape from real life. You can forget about your issues while you are reading"; "It's an escape from stuff that's happening, at work or in my social life—from that daily grind, and into a story line"; "Reading gives you a private little space where you take that time for yourself. You block out everything else that's going on in the world"; "It's a source of clarity—just clearing my mind of anything that's bothering me and putting me into a position where I don't have to worry about real life and whatnot around me ... It's a good way to reset"; "I'm very high-strung and I worry about things a lot. I feel that reading helps me refocus my brain and think that I don't have to worry about all this stuff. Reading is very much a necessity in order to have a balanced life"; Reading is a way "to kind of get out of my head"; "I was a really shy kid and [am still somewhat shy], but there is something about books that releases you from whatever inhibitions that you have around other people so that you just live the moment with the characters and it's sort of an escape"; "Whatever is happening in your life at the time, reading is a way of turning away from that and getting lost in the book." In summary, reading is a way of coping with the stresses of life by providing a barrier that blocks out negative things, a private sanctuary, a reset button, a way to refocus, a source of balance, and a release. It takes a lot of different metaphors to capture the nuanced ways in which "escaping from" reading can be therapeutic.

The other side of "escape from" is "escape to"—the magic act that Emily Dickenson celebrates in: "There is no Frigate like a Book / To take us Lands away." When I mentioned in an email to a friend that I was writing something on "what people mean when they say they read for escape," she wrote back: "Escape: into other possibilities for living a life; vicarious drama and/or experience; armchair travelling. Opening each new book is a chance for adventure and for hope." Such reading is a form of transport, taking readers into worlds more exciting and more intense than the everyday. These escapist readers wanted the experience of immersion and transport, of "living there" or "imagining that you're right there." They said, "It doesn't matter what else is going on—I'm in the book; I'm part of the book." They talked about "being completely absorbed in what I'm reading," "oblivious" to their immediate environment, and "caught up" in an imaginative journey to another world where they "experience something new and fresh." This is the positive, hopeful, and zestful aspect of escape. Now the emphasis is placed not on what is being left behind but on the world that the reader is entering. Annabel (student, age 25) said, "Ever since I was little, it's always been about escapism, and not necessarily because I had a life that I wanted to escape *from*, but just something sort of fun and adventurous to escape *into* for a little while, and then come back out." The key is the nature of the experience that the reader chooses. As Craig (retired skilled tradesman, age 67) put it in an interview conducted before the 2010–2011 set of interviews: "If I'm going to escape, well then let's escape to where I want to go. I want to acquire some knowledge about different times and different things—to know what happens in Iceland, in early England, between the stars. If you are going on a trip, that is escapism. But you will pick the place where you want to go, whether that place is Banff Springs or Las Vegas." A common metaphor for "escape to" is the journey. As one of Gitte Balling's interviewees put it, "I wouldn't call it an escape, perhaps rather a journey. A reality journey—a journey into another reality" (Balling 2016, 44).

The reader, not the book, determines whether or not the reading experience will provide a satisfactory escape. Some readers require high-adrenaline books, while others need safety and a reassuring ending. Scarlet (commercial credit analyst, age 26) explains that romance novels with their happy endings are enjoyable precisely *because* the plots of fiction differ from the plots of real life: "People ask me all the time: 'You know that stuff is not real, right?' I'm like, 'Yes, I really know that.' It's not real. It doesn't happen in the real world, which is why I like it so much." To be a successful vehicle for escape, a book needs to be challenging enough to keep the reader interested but not so challenging that it requires a special effort of concentration. It needs to offer safe entry into a world that the reader enjoys living in for a while—engaging, but not threatening. Annabel said that although she was glad that she had read *Blindness* by José Saramago, "depressing and terrifying" as it was, she "would never want to escape into that book."

Depending on what else is going on in the reader's life, the escape book may need to be intense and suspenseful, or it may need to be familiar and comforting, as in the case of Susan Chira (2016). In a *New York Times* article, Chira describes how, in a vigil at the hospital fearing for the life of a loved one, she "turned to reading for solace" specifically to Jane Austen's *Pride and Prejudice*. She said, "Not just any book would do. I couldn't get through a new book; it was too hard to summon the energy to concentrate. I needed the comfort and relative ease of familiarity." On the other hand, Dale (accountant, age 52) needed the pull of suspense to keep her reading while coping with the pain of cancer. She described herself, before cancer, as a voracious reader, a "bookaholic," who, for most of her life, had read "history, biographies, science, science fiction, romance, mysteries, thrillers—you name it—there wasn't a book I didn't read." Now she reads mostly thrillers, being "harder to please now, but it has to do with pain levels":

> I have discovered that with my current pain level, getting deeply involved in a mystery will keep me reading, whereas, with anything without the suspense, the pain gets in the way. I start not being able to focus. But a mystery or thriller where there is suspense will pull me—pull at me to keep reading and keep my focus, despite the pain.

Back-and-Forth Traffic: Reading for Connection

In what seems like a contradiction, many who said they read for escape also said that they read for connection. Some 20 interviewees (35 percent) mentioned that they valued reading as a way of getting connected to the world. Reading, they said, puts you in another person's shoes and helps you see the world through someone else's eyes. Reading is a lifeline. Sometimes the very qualities that make reading an escape also make it a source of connection. By providing a means of armchair travel to places, situations, and worlds not available in your everyday life, reading opens you to new perspectives and ideas, which you can carry back into your everyday life. And as Joseph Gold (2002, 61) points out in *The Story Species*: "Reading Literature constitutes a very efficient behaviour for acquiring experience" that is "relatively risk-free and energy saving."

A recurring theme is the back-and-forth traffic between the book and the world or the book and the self. Reading involves retirement from the world and then a return, possibly bearing unexpected treasure. Readers talk of "balance," "dialogue," and "coming back." In Ivor's account quoted at the beginning of this section, he says, "It may sound as though I read as an escape—all this talk about going to another world—but it's not really escaping because I'm always fully prepared to come back." Adrian (student, age 25) explains how reading is part of a back-and-forth movement between the self and the world that provides intellectual growth and balance:

> Reading really balances my life. Reading helps me grow. I can be out in the world and talk to people and hang out and discuss things. Then when I go back and read something, or something deep that moves me, then it changes my perception that much. Then I go back out in the real world. It's a sort of a back-and-forth thing and it really balances things out.

For Kirsti (translator, age 38), reading is a three-way transaction among book, world, and self. Reading is a way of connecting with other people but it is also "a dialogue with yourself":

> I value the connection to other human beings. . . . Reading can appear to be a one-way street, where you simply take in what the author writes, but I find it's also a dialogue with yourself. You receive something from the story. You question yourself. You question what you knew before you read this. You ask, Does this reading experience change anything in your life or in the way you think? So there's that part of it—the part that makes me ponder human thought and my own thought process.

When interviewees elaborated on how reading connects them with the world, they typically mentioned the awakening of new interests, the way reading opens the mind, the way reading about other people and other cultures offers new perspectives, and the way what is learned during reading feeds back into everyday life. Here are some examples. For Liam (student, age 35), the reading he enjoys sparks his interest in the world around him because "reading has this infectious quality to it . . . leading to other places and other bits of knowledge": "It can take you from place to place to place to place. So if I read a story about characters who dream, suddenly it makes me want to learn more about dreaming, the biological aspects of dreaming, the cultural significance of dreaming, the mythological aspects of dreaming." Abigail (student, age 23) says, "Reading opens my mind to the way other people think. I think of it sort of as a sociological experiment." Eleanor (conservation biologist, age 28) says, "I get different perspectives on how I look at the world, it helps me grow as a person, and to consider more viewpoints when I am thinking about or looking at a situation." A comment by Brandon (student, age 27) takes us back to the theme of the two-way traffic between the world of the book and the reader's own life: "I like that I get new insight into different situations. It's interesting to see how a woman may view being marginalized, or how a survivor from the Holocaust felt. I can learn about people's different life experiences and then I can reevaluate my own."

Research on reading and empathy by the research group lead by Toronto cognitive psychologists Keith Oatley (2011) and Raymond Mar supports claims by readers who said that they *become* the characters they read about. For example, Melanie (student, age 25) said, "You can see yourself in the characters you are reading about." Monica (retired teacher, age 59) said, "I am one of those people who can put myself in someone else's shoes and *be* that character. I find myself able to relate to the character—I'm usually the heroine of the story but I can be the villain too." Dale (accountant, age 52) said, "A book allows you to experience the people's thoughts so you really do become them while you're reading it. You get to empathize and understand their logic and their way of thinking." So how does this work? Mar, Oatley, and colleagues (2006b, 2009) have used the research tools of psychology to study the connection between reading and empathy and between reading and "theory-of-mind," which is the ability to attribute mental states—beliefs, intentions, desires, knowledge—to others and to understand that other people's mental states may differ from one's own. Mar and Oatley say that fiction provides a safe "simulator" environment in which readers have a chance to experience the thoughts and emotions of others. Their research found that the more fiction that people read, the better they did in a test of empathy and theory-of-mind (Mar, Oatley et al., 2006a, 2009).

Previous studies (Ross 1999; Sabine and Sabine 1983) had claimed that reading changes readers. But, because these studies were based on readers' accounts, they could be challenged as anecdotal. So Maja Djikic, Keith Oatley, and colleagues (2009) tested under laboratory conditions the hypothesis that reading fiction can transform the self, as measured by changes in traits and emotions on before-and-after measures. After they had completed a set of questionnaires including the Big-Five Inventory (BFI) and an emotion checklist, 83 undergraduates in the experimental group read Chekhov's short story "The Lady with the Toy Dog." The matched control group read a text with the same content that was "controlled for length, readability, complexity, and interest level." Then traits and emotions were measured again. The conclusion: "The results show the experimental group experienced significantly greater change in self-reported experience of personality traits than the control group, and that emotion change mediated the effect of art on traits."

The Reading Paradox

The reading paradox is that reading can fill contradictory needs often simultaneously: to escape from the world and to connect with other people, to be relaxed and to be stimulated, to be solitary and to be social, to confirm ideas you already have and to be opened up to new ideas. Over and over, in self-reports, readers say: Books give me comfort, make me feel better about myself, reassure me that I am normal because characters in books have feelings like mine. Books provide confirmation that others have gone through similar experiences and survived. Books are a way of recharging my batteries and they help me keep my life in balance when day-to-day pressures are intense. Books help me clarify my feelings, change my way of thinking about things, help me think through problems in my own life, help me make a decision, and give me the strength and courage to make some major changes in my own life. They give me a sense of mastery and control, give me courage to fight on, make me think that if the hero(ine) can overcome obstacles then so can I, give me the hope to rebuild my life, and help me accept things I can't change. They broaden my horizons; provide a window into other lives and other societies; and put me in touch with a larger, more spacious world. In short, reading is like the patent medicines advertised in nineteenth-century religious magazines: it will do anything you want it to do. It will calm you down or stimulate you. It will provide an escape from life's problems, or it can allow you to confront these problems at one remove within the safety of the world of the book.

Case 15: Plugged in, in a very grand way

One of the most committed readers in the avid readers study, Sarah (library assistant, age 40) talks about why reading has been important throughout her life.

Sarah: Books became increasingly more important through my childhood and my adolescence. I had a really desperately unhappy childhood and adolescence and, when I got to be in my teens, books became a place for me to go. They became a way of escape. They also became a way of establishing a certain self-esteem that I wouldn't have had otherwise. I could read, so I couldn't be all that stupid. I read big thick books, so I must be really, essentially, a smart person. And even at that age I recognized the value of having that control over language. I realized that books contributed to that and I loved language. I loved the way that words were used. So even though I had no other accomplishments, books were sort of like a lifeline for me. They provided me a place to go to be away from my situation. And they also provided me with a sense of self respect. I really feel that they sustained me. . . .

I know reading is a solitary activity and you think of someone who reads as an introvert because they're not socializing, but I never felt that way. I always felt that books were a connection with humanity and not just with my little world. My world was very narrow because it was a small town, which was at the end of the earth. But I was connected, I felt, to the whole universe when I was sitting there reading. I was connected to all of history. I was connected to great minds and wonderful thoughts all of humanity. I was . . . plugged in, in a very grand way.

Comments

This passage illustrates the complexity of the "Why read?" question. Here Sarah starts off with escape—books as a getaway from unhappy surroundings—but soon interweaves contrasting themes of engagement, empowerment, control over language, and a connection with all humanity. Reading experts sometimes set up polarities and value only one element of the dyad: facing up to life/escape, encountering the new/repeating the familiar, shattering expectations and values/confirming them, opening doors to the new/returning home to the familiar. Readers are more apt to say they value *both* elements in the dyad to different degrees at different times, depending on what else is going on in their lives.

To Read More

Raymond Mar and colleagues have a well-established research program related to the psychology of fiction, especially the role of literary fiction in enhancing empathy. You can find ongoing reports of work on such topics as "Literariness and Empathy," "Moods and Stories," and "Fiction and Imaginative Resistance" in the blog *OnFiction* (http://www.onfiction.ca/).

References

Balling, Gitte. 2016. "What Is Reading Experience?" In *Plotting the Reading Experience: Theory/Practice/Politics*, 37–53. Edited by Paulette Rothbauer, Kjell Ivar Skjerdingstad, et al. Waterloo, ON: Wilfred Laurier University Press.

Bamburger, Richard. 1975. *Promoting the Reading Habit. Reports and Papers on Mass Communication*, no. 72. New York: UNESCO.

BookTrust. 2013. "BookTrust Reading Habits Survey 2013." Available at: https://www.booktrust.org.uk/usr/library/documents/main/1576-booktrust-reading-habits-report-final.pdf.

Chira, Susan. 2016. "In Trying Times, the Balm of Jane Austen." *New York Times*, December 23, 2016. Available at: https://www.nytimes.com/2016/12/23/books/review/in-trying-times-the-balm-of-jane-austen.html.

Creative Research. 2009. *The Future of Reading: A Public Value Project*. Arts Council of England. Available at: http://www.creativeresearch.co.uk/uploads/files/Future-Reading-Report.pdf.

Dali, Keren. 2014. "From Book Appeal to Reading Appeal: Redefining the Concept of Appeal in Readers' Advisory." *The Library Quarterly* 84, no. 1: 22–48.

Djikic, Maja, Keith Oatley, Sara Zoeterman, and Jordan B. Peterson. 2009. "On Being Moved by Art: How Reading Fiction Transforms the Self." *Creativity Research Journal* 21, no. 1: 24–29.

Gold, Joseph. 2002. *The Story Species: Our Life-Literature Connection*. Markham, ON: Fitzhenry and Whiteside.

Kakutani, Michiko. 2017. "Transcript: President Obama on What Books Mean to Him." *New York Times*, January 16. Interview Available at: https://www.nytimes.com/2017/01/16/books/transcript-president-obama-on-what-books-mean-to-him.html.

Lesser, Wendy. 2014. *Why I Read: The Serious Pleasure of Books*. New York: Farrar, Straus, and Giroux.

Mar, Raymond A., Keith Oatley, et al. 2006a. "Bookworms versus Nerds: Exposure to Fiction versus Non-fiction, Divergent Associations with Social Ability, and the Simulation of Fictional Social Worlds." *Journal of Research in Personality* 40: 694–712.

Mar, Raymond A., Keith Oatley, and Jordan B. Peterson. 2006b. "Exploring the Link between Reading Fiction and Empathy." *Journal of Personality* 74: 1047–1078.

Mar, Raymond A., Keith Oatley, and Jordan B. Peterson. 2009. "Exploring the Link between Reading Fiction and Empathy: Ruling Out Individual Differences and Examining Outcomes." *Communications* 34: 407–428. Available at: http://www.yorku.ca/mar/Mar%20et%20al%202009_reading%20fiction%20and%20empathy.pdf.

Moyer, Jessica E. 2007. "Learning from Leisure Reading: A Study of Adult Public Library Patrons." *Reference & User Services Quarterly* 46, no. 4: 66–79.

Oatley, Keith. 2011. *Such Stuff as Dreams: The Psychology of Fiction*. Oxford: Wiley-Blackwell.

Osen, Diane, ed. 2002. *The Book That Changed My Life: Interviews with National Book Award Winners and Finalists*. New York: The Modern Library.

Queenan, Joe. 2012. *One for the Books*. New York: Viking Books.

Rosenthal, Nadine. 1995. *Speaking of Reading*. Portsmouth, NH: Heinemann.

Ross, Catherine Sheldrick. 1999. "Finding without Seeking: The Information Encounter in the Context of Reading for Pleasure." *Information Processing and Management* 35: 783–799.

Sabine, Gordon, and Patricia Sabine. 1983. *Books That Made the Difference*. Hamden, CN: Library Professional Journal.

Strout, Elizabeth. 2016. *My Name Is Lucy Barton*. New York: Random House.

Toyne, Jackie, and Bob Usherwood. 2001. *Checking the Books: The Value and Impact of Public Library Book Reading*. Sheffield, UK: Department of Information Studies, The University of Sheffield.

4.3 The Reading Experience

In her book about rereading the classics of science fiction, *What Makes This Book So Great*, novelist Jo Walton (2014) notes that most literary critics don't consider the reading experience itself—they stick to interpreting texts. Declaring herself *not* a proper literary critic, Walton talks about her own experiences with reading throughout her collection of essays as well as in three pieces entirely about reading practices: "Why I Reread," "Gulp or Sip," and "Do You Skim?" The details that she provides about her own reading practices raise questions about reading experience in general. Do other avid readers share these approaches to reading and to what extent? What are the various dimensions along which the reading experience can vary from one reader to another? Walton's discussion of her own reading practices suggests some larger themes: rereading books, books as friends, safe reads, the risk of disappointment in starting a new book, one's ideal relationship with a book, preferred places for reading, remembering a book by remembering the circumstances of its reading, fitting reading into the interstices of the day, laying in supplies so that one won't run out of things to read when away from home, reading one book at a time versus having several on the go simultaneously. Here is Walton describing her own experience reading—and rereading—books:

> When I re-read, I know what I'm getting. It's like revisiting an old friend. An unread book holds wonderful unknown promise, but also threatens disappointment. A re-read is a known quantity. (Walton 2014, 18)
>
> My ideal relationship with a book is that I will read it for the first time entirely unspoiled. I won't know anything whatsoever about it, it will be wonderful, it will be exciting and layered and complex and I will be excited by it, and I will re-read it every year or so for the rest of my life, discovering more about it every time and every time remembering the circumstances in which I first read it. (19)
>
> I don't think of reading as something I have to stop to do. I read in the interstices of my day. . . . I carry my book around with me and read on the bus, on the metro, or if I'm waiting for someone. If I'm going out, I check that I have enough to read to last me. I generally read one book at a time, but occasionally I'll read a big heavy hardback at home and take a little light paperback out with me. (402)
>
> I read in cafes and tea houses. I don't think of this as going there especially to read, any more than I think of going there to breathe. I will be reading and breathing while I am there drinking tea, that goes without saying. (403)

In general, our best sources about the reading experience come from readers' accounts that tease out the embodied experience of reading in time and space such as: (1) reading memoirs, (2) posted answers on online discussion groups to questions such as "What Is It Like to Be a Voracious Reader?" and "Do You Finish a Book You Don't Like?" (Quora); and (3) research studies based on intensive interviews with readers.

Sources: Reading Memoirs

Reading memoirs come in two categories: short accounts by individual readers, often celebrity readers, that are solicited by an editor and collected into a book form; and self-initiated, book-length explorations by a single author. In the former category, the following are good examples: G. Robert Carlsen and Anne Sherrill's *Voices of Readers* (1988), Arlene Perly Rae's *Everybody's Favorites* (1997), Diane Osen's *The Book That Changed My Life* (2002), and Antonia Fraser's *The Pleasure of Reading* (1992/2015). In the latter category, sharply realized, personal accounts of the reading experience can be found in these reading memoirs: Lynne Sharon Schwartz's *Ruined by Reading* (1996), Wendy Lesser's *Nothing Remains the Same* (2002), Sara Nelson's *So Many Books, So Little Time* (2003), Patricia Meyer Spacks's *On Rereading* (2011), Joe Queenan's *One for the Books* (2012), Will Schwalbe's *The End of Your Life Book Club* (2012) and Books for Living (2017), and Rebecca Mead's *My Life in Middlemarch* (2014).

Carlsen and Sherrill's *Voices of Readers* (1988) remains a valuable source of self-reports by readers because it includes so many verbatim accounts. To engage teachers-in-training in thinking about the experience of books and reading, Robert Carlsen asked students to write a "reading autobiography" or protocol in which they reflected on their experience of learning to read. This book is a selection of statements from the thousands of reading protocols collected from the 1950s to the 1980s, organized by chronological age of the reader at the time of the reported experience and by themes such as learning to read, reading aloud, places for reading, what books do for readers, sources for books, and libraries and librarians. On the topic of connection to fictional characters, one reader recalled a vivid childhood experience of identification: "But in that First Reader, oh so vividly, I remember the story of the little red hen—and I *was* that hen" (1988, 61). Concerning favorite places to read, Carlsen and Sherrill's readers recalled an "overstuffed red velvet chair," a "reading corner" created in an upstairs room of an old farmhouse, reading "behind the fireplace, next to the woodpile," and in "the seclusion of the haymow or the attic" (51–52). Many readers were self-critical, describing themselves variously as "an undiscriminating reader," someone who reads "too slowly," or an overly submissive reader who reads "too passively; I read without a fight" (54–55). Then there are the various ways that readers create their own versions of the books they read by rereading favorite passages or by jumping over whole scenes, as in this case: "My favorite animal book was *Bambi*, but I always skipped the pages that had the pictures of the forest fire, because they terrified me" (77).

In *Everybody's Favorites* (1997), Arlene Perly Rae distills responses from 150 well-known Canadian writers, artists, performers, politicians, and athletes who responded to her invitation to "Think of a special book you read as a child or teenager, a book that woke you up, stirred your soul or changed your life. A book you love." Alice Munro's response is a reflection on the impact of her childhood reading of L. M. Montgomery's *Emily of New Moon:* "In this book, as in all the books I've loved, there's so much going on behind, or beyond, the proper story. There's life spreading out behind the story—the book's life—and we see it out of the corner of the eye" (Rae 1997, 94–95). Poet Dennis Lee reported that when he thinks back to his childhood years "of passionate reading, to their hungry joy, the flash I get is not of a particular book. What I remember is a discovery I made when I was—how old? . . . The discovery was: *There were books that came in series*" (Rae 1997, 125).

In *The Pleasure of Reading*, British author Antonia Fraser (1992/2015) asked 43 writers to provide a short essay on their early reading and influences and what they enjoy currently. Here is a sampling of statements by readers that point to specific, embodied ways of experiencing reading:

> In old age I go back to masterpieces—Stephen Spender (Fraser 1992/2015, 7).
>
> I read to be entertained and to find laughter. I read to escape from boredom. I read, in part at least, to be scared—John Mortimer (65).
>
> Reading for me is tied inextricably to place—Emma Tennant (157).
>
> The same gluttony [for books that I felt in childhood] characterizes my reading today. And I am as indiscriminate now as I was then—Gita Mehta (195).
>
> [T]here are some first readings you can always remember. Open the book again, and the place and time of the first impression come back at you, like a sharp smell or a strong flavour—Hermione Lee (225).
>
> I read for the feel of an invented world, its colour and shadow—Alan Hollinghurst (241).
>
> These days I read in blocks. I choose a writer and read everything over a period of weeks or months—Jeanette Winterson (279).

Turning to single-authored reading memoirs, we can find in Lynne Sharon Schwartz's engaging book *Ruined by Reading: A Life in Books* (1996) a goldmine of details about the reading experience. She ranges over such topics as the voluptuous pleasure of reading late at night when immersion in the experience can be prolonged and uninterrupted ("sometimes at the peak of intoxicating pleasures, I am visited by a panic: the phone or doorbell will ring, someone will need me or demand I do something"—30); the worry over forgetting what has been read; not finishing books or throwing books out; possession ("There were some books I wanted to possess even more intimately than by reading. I would clutch them to my heart and long to break through the chest wall, making them part of me"—67); visualization ("Some readers may run their own private films as each page turns, but I seem to have only spotty fleeting images, a floaty gown, a sofa, a grand ballroom, or a patch of landscape"—77).

Will Schwalbe's *The End of Your Life Book Club* is remarkable for the way it so richly situates the reading experience within the lives of two readers—the author and his mother, Mary Anne Schwalbe. They began their informal book club after Mary Anne was diagnosed with terminal pancreatic cancer. The discussion itself happened during the waiting times of doctors' appointments and cancer treatments. They talked about the books themselves—28 books give their names to chapter titles from Wallace Stegner's *Crossing to Safety* to Alice Munro's *Too Much Happiness*. But they also talked about their own lives, including childhood favorites (Will was obsessed with *Lord of the Rings*; Mary Anne with *Gone with the Wind*). They both loved the opening sentence of novels, a favorite being "The small boys came early to the hanging" from Ken Follett's *The Pillars of the Earth* (18). Mary Anne, who had spent so much of her time in war zones on behalf of refugees, was "drawn to books with dark themes, as they helped her understand the world as it is, not as we wish it would be." Her son was "drawn to books with dark themes mostly because I always feel better about my life in comparison" (29). Books such as Somerset Maugham's *The Painted Veil* gave them a framework for discussing "courage in general and Mom's in particular," which otherwise Mary Anne would decline to talk about. Schwalbe notes, "Books had always been a way for my mother and me to introduce and explore topics that concerned us but made us uneasy" (14).

In *My Life in Middlemarch*, Rebecca Mead reflects on a lifetime of reading George Eliot's masterpiece. As a 17-year-old growing up in a seaside town in the southwest of England, Mead (2014, 2) "identified completely with Miss Dorothea Brooke, an ardent young gentlewoman who yearns for a more significant existence." At that first reading, she says, "I loved *Middlemarch*, and I loved being the kind of person who loved it" (6). *Middlemarch* was "the one book [she] never stopped reading" and the one she came back to when she wanted to reflect on "the strange potency of a great book—the way a book can insert itself into a reader's own history, into a reader's own life story, until it's hard to know what one would be without it" (16). Mead's book is partly a literary biography of George Eliot; partly an account of the characters, incidents, themes, and sources of *Middlemarch*; and partly an account of Mead's lifelong relationship "with a particularly cherished book." Noting that most "serious readers" can point to a book of central importance in their lives, she says, "I choose *Middlemarch*—or *Middlemarch* chose me—and I cannot imagine life without it" (213). In her rereadings over decades, the book changed dramatically, as her sympathies expanded under the "crash course in emotional sympathy" (160) provided by *Middlemarch* as both Dorothea Brooke and Reverend Edward Casaubon come to regret their incompatible marriage. Reading *Middlemarch* at Dorothea's age, Mead could understand Dorothea's misplaced hopes that in marrying the much older Casaubon she would be helpmeet to a great man of learning; reading it in her 30s, she regarded Casaubon as "contemptible and repellent," but having reached the age of Casaubon, she felt "a tender sense of kinship with that sad, proud, desiccated man" (163). Mead quotes Eliot: "Art is . . . a mode of amplifying experience and extending our contact with our fellowmen beyond the bounds of our personal lot" (158). Claiming that George Eliot's fiction is all about "generating the experience of sympathy," Mead quotes from Eliot's letter to John Blackwood, "My artistic bent is directed not at all to the presentation of eminently irreproachable characters, but to the presentation of mixed human beings in such a way as to call forth tolerant judgment, pity, and sympathy" (159). (See section 4.2 for a discussion of Oatley and Mar's work on empathy, the modern equivalent of what Eliot meant by sympathy.)

Sources: Interviews with Readers

To get an understanding of the reading experience of ordinary readers as opposed to elite readers who write about their own reading, we can turn to another source: open-ended, qualitative interviews with readers, or, to use Ian Collinson's term, "everyday readers." In *Everyday Readers*, Collinson (2009) used semi-structured interviews with 4 men and 17 women recruited in New South Wales, Australia, with the goal of discovering the complex nature of everyday book-reading culture. To avoid the common pitfall of trying to deduce reading experience from examining the texts read, Collinson takes the austere position in his analysis of excluding mention of specific texts altogether and focussing instead on reading as it is situated in specific times and places and in specific social contexts. Collinson's readers, who are mostly between the ages of 20 and 35, describe reading as an activity that they do in reclaimed time snatched from daily routines: "While I'm cleaning my teeth ... while I'm walking to the train station"; "in bed before I sleep"; "on my exercise bike" (34). Time was almost always mentioned as a constraint: Natasha would read "a whole stack of good books like *The Shipping News*" while on holiday but far fewer during the work year; Georgina decided not to buy a long, enticing book because "I've got too much on this week, it's too long, I'll leave it till next week"; and Winston explained not rereading by saying, "I want to reread *Crime and Punishment* and I just don't think I will because there is so much other stuff to read" (36–37). Eric described himself as "always looking for checks and balances, I suppose to make certain I'm reading something that is worthwhile, so that I'm not going to waste my time" (37). Interviewees said that their preferred reading mode was private, silent, and uninterrupted, but most have "trained themselves" to "negotiate a place of reading within the shared domestic space of the home," by blocking out the environmental distractions of television and conversations or by retreating to a bedroom (45–47).

Avid readers in my study, in discussing their reading experience, ranged over additional themes:

On choosing books

- At one stage I decided I was going to read the whole library, entirely, all the fiction. I never read nonfiction. I would start at the A's and work down to the Z's. After a few months, I realized I was never going to finish the A's so I started to be more selective and it took me five years to reach the D's. I never got past the D's because then I read Dickens and Dostoevsky and I got held up on them [laughter] another five years. (Sarah, library assistant, age 40)
- I think that's why I'm so careful about [choosing a book]. I don't just pick up any book and read it. Because if I get disappointed, then I get put off, and I get really mad. I get mad at myself for wasting my time. (Marsha, student, age 26)
- It's like finding a gold mine and following the vein when you find a good author like Salmon Rushdie. (Dorothy, public affairs writer, age 30)

On the desired reading experience

- If you're a runner and feeling very fit, you'd go out and tackle 10 miles. And if you're just absolutely pooped, you might just walk around the block. Romantic suspense or a Robert Ludlum I would put in the walking-around-the-block category. You know the style; you know what to expect; and you know what it's going to expect of you. (Lisa, medical doctor, age 38)
- When you immerse yourself in the world of J. R. R. Tolkien or Stephen R. Donaldson, you know you're going to be in that world for a long time. So that makes you invest yourself quite a bit into that world because you know it's something you can be in and enjoy and walk around in for quite some time. (Charles, program coordinator, age 23)

- With books that I really, really know that I'm going to enjoy, I read really slowly—it may take me 10 minutes to read a couple of pages. [I'm] making it last as long as possible. (Zoe, student, age 24)
- I can read anywhere but my ideal reading scenario is: "My cookies here, my cup of coffee here, preferably a couch but a good armchair will suffice with a blanket. Winter is better than summer. The whole 'curling up with a book'—it's a snugly kind of [experience]." (Madeline, student, age 22)

On the emotional dimension of reading

- I can't read a book that pushes me too far away from the central characters. If the author is continuously expecting me to dislike or feel alienated from the characters, then I can't satisfactorily read the book, because the experience of reading that I like is to get soaked in the material. (Elizabeth, PhD student in English, age 35)
- Quite regularly I am very sad when I come to the end [of a novel]. Not because people die, although that saddens me, but because I have to go back again. I have to leave that world behind; but I find another one. (Ivor, graduate student, age 26)

On the aftermath of reading

- I read a book of [Alice Walker's] and it will stay with me; I'll be mulling it in my mind as I do the dishes. (Tina, youth support worker, age 25)
- I like books where I can savor a section; I'll mark them and then I'll go back. I won't re-read the whole book, but I will read passages. (Jean, teacher librarian, age 44)

Dimensions of the Pleasure Reading Experience

As we see, readers vary, but there are patterns to the variation (Ross 2001). Some, like Wendy Lesser (2002), Patricia Meyer Spacks (2011), and Jo Walton (2014), reread books, whereas others say there are so many new books out there that they can't afford the time to reread—and besides rereading a beloved book might be a disappointment that would ruin the book forever. Some require conditions of quiet and privacy to read, some have preferred times and places to read, and still others say they read anywhere, any time, whenever a few minutes present themselves. Some voracious readers read many books on the go at the same time, whereas another reader might spend the entire summer with Roberto Bolaño's *2666* or David Foster Wallace's *Infinite Jest* (see section 1.2). Some like Jo Walton feel duty bound to read every word, whereas others perform guilt-free skimming. Many can recognize their own experience in Sara Nelson's description of falling in love with a book in *So Many Books, So Little Time* (2003, 33): "For me, the feeling comes in a rush: I'm reading along and suddenly a word or phrase or scene enlarges before my eyes and soon everything around me is just so much fuzzy background. The phone can ring, the toast can burn, the child can call out, but to me they're all in a distant dream."

The varieties of ways to experience reading seem to expand the longer we consider the question, as do the dimensions along which readers may vary in their reading practices. The model provided, "What Kind of Reader Are You?," is an attempt to draw from the data of reader statements reported in this section and elsewhere in the book some of the key ways in which pleasure readers differ. These varieties of difference should be considered dimensions along which variation can occur, and not a dichotomous yes or no, this or that. Imagine a seven-point Likert scale in which one anchor point is given a 1 and the other end of the scale gets a 7, and you as a reader may find yourself anywhere along the scale. It goes without saying that there is no preferred answer—all of these ways of reading are good.

This model is intended to capture the experience of avid readers, who will have a more detailed and elaborated mental map of leisure reading than will an unengaged reader. Someone who never cooks has a limited vocabulary and classification scheme for cooking as compared with a passionate cook who can distinguish many kinds of food treatments from fermentation to grilling, different regional and national cuisines, different types of ingredients, and different types of specialized implements for food preparation. Experienced readers, unlike novice readers, will recognize and find themselves somewhere along these dimensions of variation in reading.

What Kind of Reader Are You?

Before reading: Goals, predispositions, and self-set rules

Do you approach reading the way an athlete might approach a workout: that if it's not hard, challenging, and disciplined, it produces no gain? Or do you think of reading as a gift of self-indulgence that you give yourself?

Do you feel that there are types of books that you *should* read—or should *try* to read *more often*? Or do you feel that the right book for you is the one you will enjoy?

Do you have a reading plan of books that you hope to read in the next six months or a list of recommended books that you intend to seek out? Or do you find plans overly constraining and generally read whatever comes to hand?

Do you feel guilty about reading for pleasure and perhaps set limits—no reading until certain tasks are done? Or do you think that reading needs no apologies?

Do you choose a book to suit your mood, either to chime with your current mood or to change it? Or is your choice unaffected by mood?

Do you seek out serendipitous discovery and let chance direct your reading, picking up books at random that look interesting? Or do you usually choose books because they have been pre-selected by trusted advisors, reviews, or lists of best sellers or prizewinners?

What do you read?

When you read for pleasure, do you choose nonfiction because you like to learn about real things? Or do you usually pick fiction?

Do you have a preferred format that accounts for the majority of your pleasure reading? Or do you pick the format—hardcover, paperback, screen, audiobook—depending on the venue in which the reading occurs—such as in bed, on the patio, on a beach, on public transit?

Are you a selective reader of "important books"? Or are you an omnivore who reads everything at all levels from genre books to classics? (See section 1.2.)

Do you have a favorite genre of fiction or nonfiction that you tend to read most often? Or do you read across a wide spectrum of genres?

Do you have a particular core interest that is at the heart of all your reading? Or do you seek variety, being eclectic and interested in everything?

Do you follow an interest from book to book in a daisy chain, such that something in one book triggers an interest that leads to the next book? Or not?

When you really enjoy a book, do you go on an author binge and read everything by that author? Or do you read individual titles, not strings of authors?

Do you enjoy reading books in a series? Or do you prefer self-contained one-off books?

Do you reread? Or do you say that there are so many books out there that you can't afford the time to reread?

What reading experience do you prefer?

Do you savor the first sentences of certain novels and remember particular favorite opening lines? Or is it the book as a whole that counts?

Do you enjoy fast-paced page-turners with lots of plot twists? Or do you prefer slowly unfolding books where the appeal is well-developed characters? (See section 4.6 on elements of appeal and the "four doorways" of plot, character, setting, and language.)

Do you enjoy books that reflect/support your current worldview? Or do you like to have the everyday surface of the given world broken open by a book that challenges and unsettles?

Do you enjoy books that push the boundaries, experiment with formal structures, and play with literary conventions? Or do you prefer more traditional forms where literary technique is unobtrusive and attention is focused on the presentation of realistic characters?

Are your favorite books those that have a strong emotional impact? Or do you prefer books that are very smart and make you think?

Are some books, however well written, just too intense, jarring, or painful to read because of their subject matter or treatment? Or do you think it's a plus when an author takes on tough subjects with dark themes and doesn't pull any punches?

If the narrator or central character is unlikeable and fails to engage your sympathy, does that spoil the book for you? Or do you admire the way the author pulls off a risky play in urging you to expand your sympathies?

Do you enjoy big fat novels with lots of detail and many characters, where you can prolong your engagement with the imagined world? Or do you prefer short, spare books?

When you are into a pleasurable book, do you experience "transport" so that you feel that you are "right there" in the world of the book, oblivious to all around you? Or do you keep your feet firmly in the real world?

Do you surrender to the text and get absorbed uncritically into its world, possibly describing yourself as "enthralled" or "captivated"? Or do you almost always read with your critical faculties alert so as to note just how the text is constructed to produce its effects?

How do you read?

Do you have rituals to enhance the reading experience—a reading nook, a favorite chair, a beverage? Or are the external circumstances of reading unimportant?

Can you read anytime and anywhere, always carrying reading materials with you? Or do you require special conditions for reading, such as uninterrupted time or a private location with no distractions?

As soon as you finish one book, do you start another right away, so that you are always reading? Or do you allow a gap between books?

Do you have several books on the go at once? Or do you finish one book before starting another?

Do you skim books or even jump over entire sections that look unpromising? Or do you feel you owe it to the author or to yourself to read every word?

Do you feel compelled to finish a book? Or are you able to put it down, if you aren't enjoying it?

Are you usually a fast reader, zipping through text in a headlong rush? Or do you read slowly, pausing to reflect and possibly make notes?

Do you start novels at the beginning and read straight through? Or do you read out of order, dipping in here and there, and perhaps even reading the ending first?

Do you read with a pencil in hand to underline key phrases or write marginalia? Or do you prefer to let nothing take you out of your immersion in the reading experience?

After reading

Is there a bleed through between reading and your frame of mind, such that your reading changes your mood—depresses you, cheers you up, or comforts you? Or do you keep your reading life separate from your everyday life?

Do you think that reading makes you a better person with expanded sympathies? Or do you scoff at this idea and point out that Hitler was a great reader?

If you have enjoyed a book, do you also want to experience other versions such as the movie or audiobook? Or do you avoid these other versions?

Do you think it important to remember details about your reading, perhaps keeping a record of your reading in the form of a list, reading diary, or entry in a social media site such as Goodreads. Or do you not find it important to remember details because what you enjoy is the experience of reading itself, not its residue afterwards?

When you remember a well-liked book, do you recall the circumstances of reading it: How you got the book, the place where you were when you read it, who else was with you at the time? Or do these background details disappear because your focus was on the book itself?

Do you keep books once you have read them because their physical presence is important to you? Or do you give them away?

Do you like to discuss your reading with others? Or is reading for you a more personal and solitary enjoyment?

Does your pleasure reading translate into action in the world—such as going on a literary pilgrimage or taking up a social cause or buying a hat like the one worn by a favorite character? Or does what happens in the book stay in the book?

To Read More

Mendelsund, Peter. 2014. *What We See When We Read: A Phenomenology with Illustrations*. New York: Vintage Books.

A work of outstanding originality and playfulness by cover designer Mendelsund (see section 4.5). Mendelsund combines text and plentiful illustrations to investigate how, as readers, we fill in the gaps and construct fully rounded characters from fragments such as slender hands, a stray curl of hair, or dark eyes, constantly making little adjustments in our mental pictures of characters "amending them, backtracking to check on them, updating them when new information arises" (41).

Rothbauer, Paulette, Kjell Ivar Skjerdingstad, Lynne (E. F.) McKechnie, and Knut Oterholm. 2016. *Plotting the Reading Experience: Theory/Practice/Politics*. Waterloo, ON: Wilfrid Laurier University Press.

In June 2013, an international conference held in Oslo, Norway, on "Researching the Reading Experience" drew scholars from North America, Norway, Denmark, Sweden, the United Kingdom, the Netherlands, and Australia. Organized by reading researchers from Oslo and Akershus University College in Norway and from The University of Western Ontario in Canada, the conference produced a permanent record in the form of conference proceedings, *Plotting the Reading Experience*, coedited by Paulette Rothbauer and colleagues (2016). Most papers examine the reading experience of contemporary "everyday readers" and emphasize what's going on with the reader, not the texts.

References

Carlsen, G. Robert, and Anne Sherrill. 1988. *Voices of Readers: How We Came to Love Books*. Urbana, IL: National Council of Teachers of English.

Collinson, Ian. 2009. *Everyday Readers: Reading and Popular Culture.* London and Oakville, CT: Equinox.

Fraser, Antonia, ed. 1992/ 2015. *The Pleasure of Reading,* 2nd ed. London: Bloomsbury.

Lesser, Wendy. 2002. *Nothing Remains the Same: Rereading and Remembering.* Boston, MA: Houghton Mifflin.

Mead, Rebecca. 2014. *My Life in Middlemarch.* New York: Crown Publishers.

Nelson, Sara. 2003. *So Many Books, So Little Time: A Year of Passionate Reading.* New York: Berkley Books.

Osen, Diane, ed. 2002. *The Book That Changed My Life: Interviews with National Book Award Winners and Finalists.* New York: The Modern Library.

Queenan, Joe. 2012. *One for the Books.* New York: Viking.

Quora. "Do You Finish a Book You Don't Like?" Available at: https://www.quora.com/Do-you-finish-a-book-you-dont-like.

Quora. "What Is It Like to Be a Voracious Reader?" Available at: https://www.quora.com/What-is-it-like-to-be-a-voracious-reader.

Rae, Arlene Perly. 1997. *Everybody's Favourites: Canadians Talk about Books That Changed Their Lives.* Toronto, ON: Viking.

Ross, Catherine Sheldrick. 2001. "What We Know from Readers about the Experience of Reading." In *The Readers' Advisor's Companion,* 77–95. Edited by Kenneth D. Shearer and Robert Burgin. Englewood, CO: Libraries Unlimited.

Schwalbe, Will. 2012. *The End of Your Life Book Club.* New York: Alfred A. Knopf.

Schwalbe, Will. 2017. *Books for Living.* New York: Alfred A. Knopf.

Schwartz, Lynne Sharon. 1996. *Ruined by Reading: A Life in Books.* Boston, MA: Beacon Press.

Spacks, Patricia Meyer. 2011. *On Rereading.* Cambridge, MA and London: Harvard University Press.

Walton, Jo. 2014. *What Makes This Book So Great: Re-reading the Classics of Science Fiction and Fantasy.* New York: Tom Doherty Associates Book.

4.4 Respecting Readers

If reading has the power to transform, then this power could be dangerous—dangerous to established structures of church or state or dangerous to the individual. An individual might *get ideas* about sexuality or heretical doctrines or witches or political resistance deemed dangerous by someone else, usually someone else protecting established powers of church or state. Who gets to decide? Should individuals be free to choose reading material for themselves? Or should that reading be channelled, constrained, or suppressed by authorities and guardians who claim to know best? What are the costs to the individual of making so-called poor choices of reading material? The loss of one's immortal soul, which was the justification for the Catholic church's *Index* of banned books? An antisocial career choice induced by reading about glamorous drug dealers, which is the rationale for banning urban fiction in prisons? A distorted picture of the world resulting from reading "fake news" or other misinformation on the Internet? Or merely a waste of reader's time spent reading inferior books when so many brilliant masterpieces remain unread, which was the justification librarians formerly used to suppress series books? This question of who gets to choose leads to themes of censorship, prohibited books, and ritual book burnings. But it also leads to questions about the legitimacy of would-be authorities' attempts to constrain other people's reading, especially the reading of youth and prisoners—both groups deemed to be peculiarly susceptible to harmful influences from books. And ultimately it leads to questions about respecting readers and respecting readers' choices (or not). We know that for avid readers, the freedom to choose is sacrosanct. This section considers ways in which readers' choices can be violated—from Nazi bonfires to the more everyday curtailments in schools and prisons.

Prohibited Reading: From Bonfires to Everyday Constraints

In the twentieth century, the most infamous example of prohibiting reading was practiced in Nazi Germany, accompanied by parades, speeches, and of course bonfires. As Umberto Eco (Carriere and Eco 2011, 254) has pointed out, Nazi bonfires were perpetrated as curative agents to cleanse "degenerate art" from a culture infected by noxious books. In May 1933, the German Student Association burned 25,000 volumes by liberals, pacifists, communists, Jewish writers, and others whose work was considered "un-German." Hitler's Propaganda Minister Joseph Goebbels gave a rousing speech to a cheering crowd of 40,000 people, declaring, "No to decadence and moral corruption! Yes to decency and morality in family and state! I consign to the flames the writings of Heinrich Mann, Ernst Gläser, Erich Kästner." Among other books seized from university libraries and consigned to the flames were works by Sigmund Freud, Karl Marx, Bertolt Brecht, Thomas Mann, and Erich Maria Remarque as well as works by foreign authors such as Marcel Proust, Emile Zola, H. G. Wells, Ernest Hemingway, Jack London, and Helen Keller (Bosmajian 2006, 165). This was the beginning of ritual burnings of books at more than 50 German universities.

The horror inspired by Nazi ritual book-burnings has entered the collective imagination and has been kept alive by dystopian fiction in which bonfires consume first books and eventually people. Ray Bradbury's *Fahrenheit 451* (1953) gets its title from the temperature at which book paper ignites and starts to burn. In the nightmare world imagined by Bradbury, books are outlawed and a "fireman" is a person who burns things—books together with houses in which books have been hidden. Fire has often been the censor's tool of choice because of its symbolic association with purging, cleansing, and purification. Zealots have been the most assiduous book-destroyers, spurred on by an unwavering belief that they are in the right: the knights of the Fourth Crusade who destroyed the Imperial Library of Constantinople on the grounds that the Eastern Orthodox Church was heretical; the Spanish who burned piles of Mayan and Aztec codex books, considering them "superstition and lies of the devil"; the Maoists who destroyed books during the Cultural Revolution in China; the Khmer Rouge who destroyed 80 percent of the books in the National Library of Cambodia; and ISIS forces who burned books in the Mosul University Library in Iraq.

Ritual book-burnings occupy an extreme place in the restriction of reading and the disrespecting of readers. Here is a more everyday example. In March 2013, the Chicago Public Schools issued a directive to restrict access, for all grades below grade 11, to *Persepolis, The Story of a Childhood* (2000). *Persepolis* is Marjane Satrapi's autobiographical graphic novel about growing up in Iran during the Iranian Revolution of 1979, living through the carnage of the Iran-Iraq War, and being sent for her own safety to high school in Vienna. Written in French, *Persepolis* was translated into multiple languages, has sold some 1.5 million copies worldwide, was ranked fifth by *Newsweek* on its list of the decade's 10 best fiction books, was made into an award-winning film, and has been widely praised for its resistance to political and religious repression.

So why try to remove it from schools in Chicago? Book-restrictors typically argue that susceptible readers must be protected from harm by wise guardians. In the case of Satrapi's book, the head of the Chicago Public Schools explained that the offending book contains "graphic language and images" and "powerful images of torture." Contacted in Paris by the *Chicago Tribune* (Ahmed-Ullah and Bowean 2013), Satrapi said, "It's shameful. . . . These are not photos of torture. It's a drawing and it's one frame. . . . Seventh graders have brains and they see all kinds of things on cinema and the internet. It's a black and white drawing and I'm not showing something extremely horrible. . . . They have to give a better explanation." Opposition to this book-restriction was swift. Unfortunately for the book-restrictors, Chicago is also the headquarters of the American Library Association (ALA), which is a powerful ally of the freedom to read. With its Office for Intellectual Freedom and its Freedom to Read Foundation, the ALA advocates for free access to books. It produces the *Journal of Intellectual Freedom & Privacy*, sponsors Freedom to Read week, and compiles data on "challenges, bannings, and burnings" in American schools and libraries. After an intervention on March 15, 2013, by Barbara M. Jones, executive director of the Freedom to Read Foundation, the Chicago Public Schools quickly backpedalled on its restriction of access to *Persepolis* (Peterson 2013).

Censoring, banning, restricting, challenging, and prohibiting books—these are all responses to the dangerous power that prohibitors fear in books. The means of keeping books away from readers may be violent, as in ritual bonfires. Or it may be milder, such as removing *Persepolis* from a school reading list or reshelving a challenged book from the children's library to closed shelving, to the non-circulating reference collection, or to a "parent's shelf" (Jenkins 2011, 447). Or it could be the "spot and seize" maneuver practiced by guards in jails and prisons.

Reading behind Bars

Reading in jails and prisons is a special case where the freedom to read is advocated in theory but constrained in practice. The International Federation of Library Associations and Institutions (IFLA) has articulated guidelines for library services to prisoners, which state:

> An incarcerated person has not relinquished the right to learn and to access information, and the prison library should offer materials

and services comparable to community libraries in the "free" world. Restrictions on the access to library materials and information should be imposed only when such access is known to present a danger to prison security. ... The prison library should provide the offenders with the opportunity to develop literacy skills, pursue personal and cultural interests, as well as life-long learning.

With more than 2.3 million people behind bars, the United States locks people up at a higher rate than any other country in the world, a rate that has quadrupled since "tough-on-crime" policies were introduced in the 1980s. (The incarceration rate in the United States is 666 per 100,000 as compared with the UK rate at 147 per 100,000, Canada at 114, Norway at 74, Sweden at 53, and Japan at 45—World Prison Brief). In the 1980s, the general failure of the rehabilitative goals of prisons lead to a "nothing works" doctrine with contrasting outcomes in different parts of the world. In Scandinavian countries, the recognition that prisons failed to rehabilitate lead to a reduction in incarceration rates. In the United States, it lead to increased incarceration rates and an emphasis on the punitive role of prisons. Worldwide, prisoners' rights to read is an issue that affects the lives of millions.

The prison setting provides a dramatic case study of the tension between guardians-know-best theories and the value of reader choice. In *Running the Books*, Avi Steinberg (2010) describes his initiation into his new job hired to run Boston's prison library. In his first weeks on the job, he asked people about the role of the prison library and almost everyone gave him a different answer. Some thought it "coddled the inmates and gave them a place to plan and commit crimes. Some thought it was an effective way to numb inmates to the reality of captivity, to calm their nerves. ... Some staff believed it was a place to awaken, not numb, inmates" (50–51). The problem is that if books give people ideas, guardians can't predict or control what ideas they will get. Steinberg offers for consideration the contrasting cases of two famous prisoners who read avidly while incarcerated: Malcolm X, who "underwent a major transformation in a prison library," and James 'Whitey' Bulger, the murderous Boston crime boss who "refined his notoriously ruthless tactics, and his method of systematic, brutal repression, by making a careful study of military history" (52).

In her ethnographic study of the reading of women prisoners, *Reading Is My Window* (2010), Meagan Sweeney provides an overview of how, in the U.S. penal system, the balance shifted between freedom to read and prison security. According to Sweeney, in the late nineteenth century and first 80 years of the twentieth century, reading was viewed as a therapeutic tool that helped to correct prisoners' alleged character flaws, made prisoners more docile, and fostered compliance with social norms. By the 1980s, this therapeutic view of reading was replaced by the view that reading was a potentially disruptive practice that fostered empowerment and resistance—undesirable outcomes in an overcrowded prison system that was becoming more punitive than rehabilitative. Sweeney (2010, 41) noted, "Library and penal officials also engaged in heated debate about the proper model for a prison library: should the library be governed by corrections-oriented goals, or should it follow the 'multi-service, user-oriented model of the public library,' which assumes prisoners' right to library service 'regardless of correctional goals.' "

The American Library Association's response to tightening restrictions on what prisoners were allowed to read was to adopt in 1982 the "Resolution on Prisoners' Right to Read," updated in 2010 in the *Prisoners' Right to Read* document, which affirmed: "The right to choose what to read is deeply important, and the suppression of ideas is fatal to a democratic society. The denial of the right to read, to write, and to think—to intellectual freedom—diminishes the human spirit of those segregated from society." Sweeney (2010, 43–44) states that, despite such defenses, "penal objectives increasingly outweigh prisoners' right to read." As an example, she pointed to the banning by Texas penal authorities of Toni Morrison's *Paradise* from all state prisons on the grounds that it threatens security, containing "information of a racial nature" that "a reasonable person" would construe as intending to "achieve a breakdown of prisons through inmate disruption, such as strikes or riots."

Which items are likely to be banned from prisons? For her doctoral thesis on censorship in prison libraries, Tammi Arford (2013) conducted a qualitative study based on a survey of librarians in U.S. state prisons plus 26 semi-structured interviews with prison librarians. Arford (2013, 55) found that censored items are of two kinds. First there are materials deemed to be a "threat to the safety and security of the institution," such as the following: gang-related texts, information that could aid in escape such as a manual for locksmiths, sexually explicit materials, and material that refers to illicit activities such as tattooing, gambling, and making/using alcohol or drugs. Second, materials are censored because the content is deemed harmful to inmates' rehabilitation, such as urban fiction, true crime stories, cowboy western series such as Longarm and Lone Star, and sexually explicit materials (114). The expansive and ill-defined "counter-to-rehabilitation" category is used to censor materials that could be thought to glamorize the "criminal lifestyle" or support a criminal "mindset." This same rationale was used by nineteenth-century guardians to prevent urban youth from reading dime novels, whose get-rich-quick plots often featured glamorous highwaymen. Arford (2013, 128) describes how censorship is managed in prisons both by formal institutional policies and by informal action by guards such as "spot and seize." In the "spot and seize" maneuver, a prison guard spots a book on the library book truck or in a prisoner's hands, decides the book is harmful (because it is thought to promote a criminal mindset or it features homosexuality or criticizes the criminal justice system or offends the guard's religious beliefs), and confiscates the book. In the power hierarchy of prisons, librarians are below guards; maintaining prison discipline trumps prisoners' rights to read; and many books simply disappear.

Arford reports that when books featuring "criminal lifestyles" are censored, the banned books are much more likely to be African American urban fiction, or street literature, than crime novels written by white authors featuring the Mafia or white-collar crime. Urban fiction, which is often written by prisoners or former prisoners, features African American characters involved in drug dealing, pimping, prostitution, and murder. Donald Goines—air force enlistee at age 15, heroin addict, pimp, and armed robber—was a forerunner in the genre. Goines started writing in prison and, before being shot to death in 1974 while he was at work at his typewriter, he published 16 novels about the street life he knew. His books, which still sell more than 200,000 copies a year, are among the most requested and most censored books in American prisons, as is the whole urban fiction genre. Meagan Sweeney (2012, 125) described how a penal official burst in to stop a book discussion meeting she was leading with women incarcerated in Ohio. He had only just learned that the urban fiction novels being discussed were published by Triple Crown Publications, a firm founded by a former prisoner Vickie Stringer, who says she publishes books by prisoners because she knows "no one else will do it" (141). Sweeney was told to "collect the books and immediately remove them from the prison grounds," as if, remarked one of the discussion group members, they were "a bomb that no one can touch" (125). Another prisoner told Sweeney (2008, 668) that she should "rename [her] study 'Fear of Books.' "

Clearly, urban fiction has become a highly contested scene of reading. Hugely popular with incarcerated readers, urban fiction is praised for its compelling representations of inner-city culture and for its role in turning reluctant readers into avid readers while at the same time it is deeply feared by penal officials as "incendiary." Sweeney (2012, 140) acknowledges that she herself is uneasy about a genre that "reinforces dominant ideologies that fuel conditions of inequality" because it romanticizes drug dealers who succeed at the current game of money and power, whereas genuine literature, Sweeney thinks, should seek to change the game. Nevertheless, she ends her article, "Books as Bombs," with a rousing defense of the value of respecting readers' choices: "At a moment when our highest court has construed the denial of reading to be an 'incentiv[e] for inmate growth,' it is crucial to recognize urban books' incendiary potential in prison—not as dangerous explosives that should be removed from prisoners' hands but as powerful tools for sparking critical reflection, igniting insights, and catalyzing dialogue among incarcerated and non-incarcerated members of our community" (2008, 672).

Do Readers Need Guardians?

Usually arguments about censorship and book banning boil down to a clash of mental models that people hold of the reader. Is the reader weak minded, suggestible, easily lead into error, and requiring the strong guidance and protection of wiser people, usually the book banner? Or is the reader a person with brains and judgment, capable of independent thinking, like Satrapi's version of the seventh graders of Chicago? Book banners fear that reading "will give people ideas." The history of reading offers numerous examples of susceptible groups being protected from the harms of being given ideas: women who could be mislead by romantic novels and suffragette tracts; slaves who could be inflamed by abolitionist writing; subjects who could get republican ideas from reading Voltaire or Thomas Paine; Roman Catholics whose faith and morals could be undermined by writings on the *Index*; young readers who, according to Anthony Comstock (1883), could be snared by such "*Evil Reading*" and "traps for the young" as half-dime novels and 5- and 10-cent story papers; and prisoners who could use newly acquired knowledge to challenge racial and class inequities. The self-appointed guardians who protect the less powerful—the women, slaves, political subjects, religious faithful, and children—often create personal libraries of the prohibited books for their own enjoyment, a fact that Margaret Atwood used in *The Handmaid's Tale* (1985).

A contrary view holds that protecting people from ideas "for their own good" is harmful and ends up hurting truth itself. In his tract against book licensing and censorship, John Milton famously says in *Areopagitica* (1644) that it is as good "almost [to] kill a Man as kill a good Book; ... hee who destroyes a good Booke, kills reason it selfe." In *On Liberty* (1859), John Stuart Mill develops Milton's idea that truth emerges from the give and take of free discussion, "not without dust and heat," in which opinions are contested, corrected, and refined. Mill argues, "the only way in which a human being can make some approach to knowing the whole of a subject, is by hearing what can be said about it by persons of every variety of opinion, and studying all modes in which it can be looked at by every character of mind." Many people who say they are against censorship support freedom to read in principle, but are not so sure when it comes to specific cases. Mill comments on this inconsistency:

> Strange it is, that men should admit the validity of the arguments for free discussion, but object to their being "pushed to an extreme"; not seeing that unless the reasons are good for an extreme case, they are not good for any case. Strange that they should imagine that they are not assuming infallibility, when they acknowledge that there should be free discussion on all subjects which can possibly be *doubtful*, but think that some particular principle or doctrine should be forbidden to be questioned because it is *so certain*, that is, because *they are certain* that it is certain. To call any proposition certain, while there is any one who would deny its certainty if permitted, but who is not permitted, is to assume that we ourselves, and those who agree with us, are the judges of certainty, and judges without hearing the other side.

Freedom to Read

The freedom to read—and the individual's freedom to choose what to read—is, among other things, a political issue for citizens everywhere. In the Trump era, Atwood's prophetic novel *The Handmaid's Tale* has returned to best-seller lists, along with Sinclair Lewis's *It Can't Happen Here* (1935), Aldous Huxley's *Brave New World* (1935), George Orwell's *1984* (1948), and Ray Bradbury's *Fahrenheit 451* (1953). For readers worried about encroaching authoritarian power, these dystopian novels offer what seems like a prophetic insight into events that *are* "happening here": curtailing of women's reproductive rights, fear-mongering and hate speech directed at immigrants and other targeted groups, the surveillance state, undermining of freedom of the press and media, and the attack on language itself with government promotion of "alternative facts" and double-speak that calls to mind the slogans used in *1984*: "Ignorance is strength" and "Freedom is slavery" (Wheeler 2017).

What Libraries Can Do

1. Be advocates in every venue for readers and for their freedom to read. Support Banned Books Week. And respect readers by trusting their reading choices. Readers themselves are the experts in what they want to read and what satisfactions they are looking for from the reading experience.

To Read More

Check out the American Library Association's web pages and materials on banned books and its involvement in Banned Books Week. Banned Books Week is an annual event celebrating the freedom to read, usually held in the last week of September and sponsored by a coalition of book industry and library groups, including the Association of American Publishers, the National Council of Teachers of English, and the American Library Association. The books featured have all been targeted for removal or restriction in libraries or schools. In 2017, Banned Books Week marked its 35th anniversary. The Harry Potter series tops the American Library Association's list of the most often banned/challenged books during the decade 2000 to 2009. The tag line on buttons, book marks, stickers, and posters for Banned Books Week in 2017 is: "Words have POWER. Read a banned book."

References

Ahmed-Ullah, Noreen, and Lolly Bowean. 2013. "CPS Tells Schools to Disregard Order to Pull Graphic Novel." *Chicago Tribune*, March 15. Available at: http://articles.chicagotribune.com/2013-03-15/news/chi-cps-promises-explanation-after-graphic-novel-pulled-20130315_1_book-graphic-novel-school-libraries.

American Library Association. "Top 100 Banned/Challenged Books: 2000–2009." Available at: http://www.ala.org/bbooks/top-100-bannedchallenged-books-2000-2009.

American Library Association. 2010. *Prisoners' Right to Read*. Available at: http://www.ala.org/advocacy/intfreedom/librarybill/interpretations/prisonersrightoread.

Arford, Tammi. 2013. "Captive Knowledge: Censorship and Control in Prison Libraries." PhD diss. Northeastern University, Boston, Massachusetts.

Bosmajian, Haig A. 2006. *Burning Books*. Jefferson, NC: McFarland & Company.

Carriere, Jean-Claude, and Umberto Eco. 2011. *This Is Not the End of the Book: A Conversation Curated by Jean-Philippe de Tonnac*. Translated by Polly McLean. London: Random House.

Comstock, Anthony. 1883. *Traps for the Young*, 3rd ed. New York: Funk & Wagnalls Company.

Jenkins, Christine A. 2011. "Censorship: Book Challenges, Challenging Books, and Young Readers." In *Handbook of Research on Children's and Young Adult Literature*, 443–454. Edited by Shelby A. Wolf, Karen Coats, Patricia Encisco, and Christine A. Jenkins. New York and London: Routledge.

Peterson, Karyn M. 2013. "*Persepolis* Restored to Chicago School Libraries: Classroom Access Still Restricted." *School Library Journal*, March 22. Available at: http://www.slj.com/2013/03/books-media/persepolis-restored-to-chicago-school-libraries-classroom-access-still-restricted/.

Steinberg, Avi. 2010. *Running the Books: The Adventures of an Accidental Prison Librarian*. New York: Anchor Books.

Sweeney, Meagan. 2008. "Books as Bombs: Incendiary Reading Practices in Women's Prisons." *PMLA* 123, no. 3 (May): 666–673.

Sweeney, Meagan. 2010. *Reading Is My Window: Books and the Art of Reading in Women's Prisons*. Chapel Hill: The University of North Carolina Press.

Sweeney, Meagan. 2012. " 'Keeping It Real': Incarcerated Women's Reading of African American Urban Fiction." In *From Codex to Hypertext: Reading at the Turn of the Twenty-First Century*, 124–141. Edited by Anouk Lang. Amherst and Boston: University of Massachusetts Press.

Wheeler, Brian. 2017. "The Trump Era's Top-selling Dystopian Novels." *BBC News*, January 29. Available at: http://www.bbc.com/news/magazine-38764041.

World Prison Brief. n.d. Institute for Criminal Policy Research. Available at: http://www.prisonstudies.org/highest-to-lowest/prison_population_rate?field_region_taxonomy_tid=All.

4.5 Attracting Attention

The wealth of books now available in every category is a feast indeed, but readers are sometimes overwhelmed. Publishers and booksellers, who want to focus readers' attention on specific titles, use strategies to help readers choose: the best-seller list, prizes, catchy titles, and attractive book covers. Like flowers that use fragrance and color to attract bees, book jackets call out to readers by announcing as many elements of attraction as possible on the front and back covers. Pushing back, critics have been quick to criticize best-seller lists, book prizes, and celebrity endorsements as sad evidence of the commodification of culture. In their book on readers' advisory in North America, Juris Dilevko and Candice Magowan (2007, 9) are especially severe on market-driven trends "where discretionary reading becomes commodified and disposable entertainment, as manifested principally in genre fiction and genre nonfiction ... bestsellers, celebrity-authored books, and prize-winning titles."

Best Sellers

Why pick on best sellers? Because books have a double life: they are commodities within the cash nexus and they are sources of cultural experiences that can be informative, pleasurable, and transformative. The term "best seller" highlights the former aspect and elicits ideas of advertising budgets, hype, and hordes of lemming-like readers thoughtlessly following the crowd rather than making informed, individual decisions about reading. Profits are higher when publishers and booksellers sell a huge number of a single title rather than fewer copies apiece of many different titles. So the best seller in its aspect as commodity invites us to think about print runs, economies of scale, marketing, advertising, and big box bookstores. It is an easy transition from there to start talking about duped mass readers. In *The Late Age of Print*, Ted Striphas (2009, 58) observes wryly that "books are supposed to be treated as sacred artifacts, not as bulk merchandise.

To treat them otherwise is to fall prey to the crass trifecta of volume, efficiency, and commercialism." Right from the beginning, best sellers have been charged with being *too* popular and too much associated with the taint of "trade." By the middle of the nineteenth century, sentimental domestic novels, mostly written by and for women, were becoming so popular that Nathaniel Hawthorne complained that "America is now wholly given over to a d—d mob of scribbling women" and concluded glumly that his own books had "no chance of success while the public taste is occupied with their trash" (Hart 1950, 93).

At the heart of all accounts of best sellers are the lists. "Making the list" means appearing on one of the many best-seller lists produced since the invention of the form. The first list, which included only fiction, was produced by *The Bookman* in 1895 and appeared monthly. After 1912 *Publishers Weekly* produced both fiction and nonfiction lists. In 1942 the *New York Times* began printing its own lists, which are now considered the gold standard. A key source for finding out best-selling titles for much of the twentieth century are the compilations, decade by decade, prepared by Alice Payne Hackett while she was working for *Publishers Weekly*, the last version of which is *80 Years of Best Sellers, 1895–1975* (Hackett and Burke 1977). Michael Korda's *Making the List* (2001) covers the entire twentieth century, drawing on lists produced by *The Bookman*, *Publishers Weekly*, and the *New York Times*. An editor at Simon & Schuster for over four decades, Korda takes a personal and chatty approach to best sellers. Ten chapters, one for each decade, provide annual lists and reflections on the types of books that have proved popular over the years, many now almost totally unknown but some with staying power (e.g., Owen Wister's *The Virginian*, the number one fiction best seller in 1902, or *The Education of Henry Adams*, the top nonfiction best seller in 1919). Librarians will find this book useful in creating displays: What did people read 100 years ago or 50 years ago or in the year when such and such happened?

The lists themselves have been criticized both for the way they have been constructed and for what they show about book-selling trends. Laura Miller (2000) has pointed out the difficulties in deciding what counts as a best seller. Appearing on the list depends on speed not duration: a book with a spike in sales in a given week makes the list, whereas a book with steady sales over years may have much higher total sales but never make the list. Then there is the criticism about the low representation of women on the list. Rosie Cima (2017) provides informative visual displays of data showing representations, decade by decade, of the following: male authors and female authors who made the top 10, best-selling novels by genre, and gender ratio by decade of best-selling authors writing in various popular genres.

Instead of a single list for fiction and another for nonfiction, we now have a proliferation of best-seller lists categorized by format (hardcover, paper), audience (children, adult), nonfiction topic area (business, cookbook, self-help), and fiction genres (literary fiction, romance, crime, and so on). Fragmentation of the best-seller list into many parallel lists corresponds to the reality of a great many differing taste communities. As Elizabeth Long (1985, 31) points out that "high culture, which used to be seen as *the* culture, is now being dealt with in publishing as one specialized aspect of a less hierarchical and more fragmentary cultural totality." Janice Radway has observed that the Book-of-the-Month Club follows a similar practice of replacing a hierarchy of taste by horizontal categories, each with their own criteria of excellence: "Distinctions are made . . . within equivalent categories," notes Radway (1989, 266–267). In this value system, literary fiction doesn't trump cookbooks, leading high-culture supporters to lament what they see as a leveling down of taste.

For a present-day reader, one surprise of lists of best sellers from an earlier era is the huge range of books represented, from light fiction to "serious litera- ture." Some books have retained their popularity and achieved the canonical status conferred by being put on college syllabi, for example, Joel Chandler Harris's *Uncle Remus* (1881), Robert Louis Stevenson's *Treasure Island* (1883), Thomas Hardy's *The Mayor of Casterbridge* (1886), or Steven Crane's *The Red Badge of Courage* (1895). Others that were equally popular at the time are today almost unknown, unread, and unreadable such as John Hay's *The Bread-Winners* (1884) or Francis Marion Crawford's *A Cigarette-Maker's Romance* (1890). While ana- lysts of the best-seller phenomenon often point retrospectively to certain elements that account for popularity—religious or spiritual themes, tear-jerking emotional appeal, information and guidance, sensationalism and adventure, humor, sympa- thetic characters, happy endings, topical subject matter, congruence with readers' values and beliefs—there is nothing that all best sellers have in common except that they sell spectacularly well.

Not so, claims James W. Hall in *Hit Lit: Cracking the Code of the Twentieth Century's Bestsellers* (2012). By examining 12 mega–best sellers from *Gone with the Wind* (1936) to *The Da Vinci Code* (2003), Hall identifies common elements in these best sellers that he compares to bits of DNA code that are combined and recombined in various permutations. Common elements include the following: best sellers have a broad scope, with high stakes, a large cast of characters, and a "sweeping backdrop of epic consequence"; they explore "some controversial or divisive issue of its day"; they are full of facts so that the reader comes away hav- ing learned about some unfamiliar world; they feature some form of secret soci- ety; rebels, loners, and outcasts play a leading role as they buck conventional societal pressures; and "sexual incidents play pivotal roles" (Hall 2012, 222–223).

Looking only at the lists and analyzing the best-selling books themselves gives just one part of the story. To get a complete picture, we need to recognize that best-sellerdom takes place within a communications circuit that also includes authors, publishers, booksellers/libraries, and readers. Typically, critics who write about best sellers pick one of these nodes in the communication circuit as the dom- inant force. Giving the nod to the reader, Hart claims, "The popular author is always the one who expresses the people's minds and paraphrases what they con- sider their private feelings" (Hart 1950, 285). Elizabeth Long's interesting study of the theme of success in best-selling American novels likewise depends on the assumption that novels become best sellers "because they resonate with the values of their readers" (Long 1985, 26).

An opposed view is that the readers are powerless before the manipulations of commercial forces that have reshaped publishing, turning it from a gentlemen's literary club to a business that treats books just like any other commodity. An early and still interesting analysis of the economic forces that affect publishing and reading audiences alike is Q. D. Leavis's *Fiction and the Reading Public* 1932/1965). She used a number of research methods including sending questionnaires to best-selling authors and analyzing selected novels from the glory days of the novel in Bunyan, Fielding, Richardson, and Swift to the dismal present. The superiority of those early authors lay in the way they provide their readers with a succession of "shocks and jars." Leavis (1932/1965, 109) remarks admiringly, "The eighteenth century novelist is continually pulling up the reader, disappointing his expectations or refusing him the luxury of day-dreaming and not infrequently douching him with cold water." In her chapter on "The Disintegration of the Reading Public," Q. D. Leavis (1932/1965, 126–163) blames the economics of mass market publishing, cheap books, the Railway Library, and the serial publication of fiction for a decline that she thinks set in around the time of Dickens.

More recently, critics point to corporate acquisitions of publishing houses and the domination of the market by a few large, vertically integrated publishing companies; the increasing importance of subsidiary rights, including film and television rights, with the result that sales departments have a growing role in selecting which books get published; and the role of big box bookstores that use sophisticated computerized systems to track sales and winnow out slow-moving titles. From Adorno onwards, culture-critics have argued that multinational conglomerates use the rhetoric of "free choice" as a smoke screen to hide the fact that consumers are reduced to choosing among standardized, interchangeable products on the basis of insignificant differences. Alarmed by this concentration of power, Ursula LeGuin (2008) published an article in *Harpers* in which she criticized corporate publishers who have pushed out book-loving editors and put decision making in the hands of marketing division people, who have abandoned midlist authors and backlist books, shortchanging genuine writing in their relentless search for blockbusters and best sellers.

Studies that emphasize the corporate matrix of publishing usually end up concluding that the chase to sign up the next blockbuster homogenizes production and reduces the choices available to readers. However, economist Alan T. Sorensen (2007) investigated the impact of best-seller lists on "product variety." In his empirical research, Sorensen asked if being on the *New York Times* list causes an increase in sales; and, secondly, whether the influence of the best seller-list affects the number of titles published and, if so, in which direction. He concluded that being on the list does provide "a modest boost to sales," especially in the first few weeks after the book appears on the list, and that the boost is greatest for new authors. On the second question, the data are "less than ideal" but provide indirect evidence that "the business-stealing effects of bestseller lists are unimportant: if anything, bestseller lists appear to increase sales for both bestsellers and non-bestsellers in similar genres" (716).

Ostensibly, best-seller lists are simply a tool to track consumer behavior. However, there is good reason to think that the lists also *shape* behavior (Sorensen 2007, 715). Given the huge numbers of choices available, readers need a way to reduce overload and use the lists as a marker of quality. They may not have heard of the author or title themselves but have confidence that at least some of the many who bought the book did so on the basis of positive information about the book's quality. Some people want to read what everyone else is reading in order to be in the know about popular culture and be able to talk about it with others. And finally, once a book is on the list, bookstores display it prominently and provide discounts. However, despite the view that the cultural industries hold all the chips and can use big advertising to control readers and manufacture taste, readers still have a huge role to play in what actually gets read. Readers are unruly and unpredictable. Big budget, would-be blockbusters often fall flat, despite large advertising budgets. And readers themselves have the final say when it comes to whether books actually get read as opposed to produced, marketed, or sold.

Book Prizes

The whole point of book prizes is to attract attention, and it works. In her chapter on the Man Booker Prize in *The New Literary Middlebrow*, Beth Driscoll (2014, 119) remarks, "Prizes offer spikes of adrenaline that drive sales for the book industry." Anne Enright's *The Gathering* had sold fewer than 3,500 copies when it won the 2007 Booker and went on to pick up an additional quarter million in sales. Whereas some readers are attracted by the popularity of best sellers, others trust the discernment of literary judges to identify authors and books worth reading. And still others such as Clive (airplane pilot, age 60) from my avid readers study say they are "less inclined" to read an award-winning book: "I find that people who win prizes fit into certain categories—they have to be compatible with current political correctness. I also feel that the basis for the award of the prizes is a type of literary excellence that doesn't particularly make for enjoyable reading."

Readers who value the winnowing-out work done by discriminating judges get book suggestions by looking at the shortlists and the lists of winners of literary prizes such as the Governor General's Literary Awards and the Giller Prize in Canada, the Miles Franklin Literary Award in Australia, the National Book Award and the Pulitzer Prize in the United States, and the Man Booker Prize and the Costa Book Award in the United Kingdom. People who are trying to pick acceptable books as gifts often choose prizewinners as safe bets. Readers may, and often do, disagree with the judges over the book that eventually wins. However, longlists and shortlists, which are released well before the ultimate winner is announced, offer a manageable list of new books worth taking a flyer on. Some book clubs read all the books on the longlist for a particular prize and compare book club members' assessments with those of the judges (Poole 2003, 273). Cultural capital accrues to readers in the know about prestigious books that other people are reading. And beyond the individual winners, publicity over the awards creates a buzz about books that expands the general audience for reading, attracts readers to new books, and sometimes catapults unknowns into public attention. This broader goal is captured in the mandate of the National Book Award, which is "to celebrate the best of American literature, to expand its audience, and to enhance the cultural value of great writing in America."

Hold it right there, some critics say: What values are being rewarded here? Are book prizes good for literature and excellent writers or are they good for commerce? Isn't there something, well, nonliterary about press hype that reports "a strong field" for the Man Booker, with contenders "still tightly bunched together entering the final strait," and with bookmakers offering 7/4 odds on some "clear favorite." And isn't the fact that so-and-so just won (or, contrariwise has *never* won) the Pulitzer proof in itself of biased and faulty judging? Insider stories of any particular judging event are likely to include accounts of backbiting and conflicts of interest among the judges and trade-offs in which the winner is everyone's second choice and nobody's first choice. Then there is the complaint that books *by* women are underrepresented in the winning circle, receiving only 12 percent of the Nobel Prizes for Literature, 25 percent of the National Book Award (fiction) prizes, and 35 percent of the Man Booker Prizes (Mohdin 2016). Moreover, when it comes to the top literary prizes, books *about* women or girls or written from a female perspective almost never win, whether written by men or by women (Regan 2015). And anyway aren't there just way too many prizes?

In *The Economy of Prestige*, James English (2005) asks what it means to award cultural prizes. What is being exchanged? What is the currency? How did a series of scandals save the Booker Prize? How do we fairly assess a phenomenon that participates simultaneously in two spheres: the marketplace and the world of culture? English notes that accounts of phenomena such as prizes typically tell one of two stories. Either prizes are part of a narrative of commodification in which artists and artistic autonomy are the victims of capitalism. Or, more rarely, the story is told of "popular liberation, via the marketplace, from the tyranny of elitist coteries and gatekeepers" (12). English himself does a balanced job of paying attention to both aspects of the Janus-faced prize economy.

The prominence of literary awards began at the beginning of the twentieth century with the establishment of the Nobel Prize for Literature in 1901 and the Prix Goncourt in 1903 (Driscoll 2014, 120). English (2005, 324–327) traces the explosion of new literary awards in the twentieth century, set off by the dynamite of the Nobel Prize and rising to about 1,100 literary awards by the end of the century. He provides graphs that show that, from the 1970s on, books on the bestseller list were less and less likely to win literary awards, noting that "the awards industry has helped to shape a scale of value ever further removed from the scale of bestsellerdom" (331).

At present, literary awards divide up the book pie in every possible way: awards for authors from a particular language group or geographical area ranging from the local to the global; awards directed to books written for children, young adults, or adults; awards for work in various genres and subgenres of nonfiction and fiction (e.g., Edgar Awards for crime novels, Nebula Awards for science fiction, Bram Stoker Awards for horror, RITA Awards for romance, and Spur Awards for westerns); and awards for special author categories such as for women writers, Indigenous writers, African American writers, Jewish writers, prison writers, first-time novelists, or science writers. In *A Few Good Books*, Stephanie Maatta (2010) provides a useful chapter on book awards, which lists various significant literary awards and provides a brief history and description of some of the most important ones, including Library Association Awards such as Notable Books.

Frenzy, controversies, and scandals just add to the buzz that attracts publicity to the awards and to their winners. Commonly, whenever shortlists are announced, outrage erupts over the "snubbing" of particular authors or over the exclusion of various categories of authors such as women or minorities. Maatta (2010, 253) reports that spurned, but highly regarded, books also benefit from book award announcements "through the ensuing scandal of being ignored by the judges. These titles reap publicity for the accolades they *did not* receive." Beth Driscoll (2014, 120) considers the Man Booker Prize to be a paradigmatic example, along with Oprah Book Club (see section 4.7) and the Harry Potter phenomenon, of what she calls the "new literary middlebrow." She identifies as key features of this new middlebrow that it is middle class, feminized, and recreational. Driscoll claims that middlebrow readers are earnest, emotional, and reverential towards elite culture, but at the same time middlebrow texts are embedded in commercial distribution networks and reliant on cultural intermediaries such as the broadcast media and the Internet to organize potentially huge readerships.

This built-in tension between reverence for elite culture and desire for popular appeal erupts in repeated controversies over award nominations and winners. According to Driscoll (2014, 147), novelist Louise Doughty suggested that male academics made poor judges of the Man Booker because they have a vested interest in picking someone "as literary and obscure as possible." When John Banville's *The Sea* won over Kazuo Ishiguro's heavily favored *Never Let Me Go* in 2005, many were outraged, but Banville himself said on award night that it was reassuring that this time the award had gone to "a work of art." A few days later he remarked to *The Guardian*, "There are plenty of other rewards for middlebrow fiction. There should be one decent prize for real books" (Lyall 2005). Taking a contrary stand for readability, the 2011 chair of the committee of judges said about the shortlist, "We were looking for enjoyable books. ... We wanted people to buy these books and read them. Not buy them and admire them." Fellow judge and writer Susan Hill tweeted, "Hurrah! Man Booker judges accused of 'dumbing down.' They mean our shortlist is readable and enjoyable" (Bennett 2011). Judges, media critics, and readers duke it out over whether literary prizes should go to experimental "real books" or to readable books that sell. And because the judges change, readers who read Man Booker Prize winners year after year have a chance to read both kinds. Cynthia Ozick, commenting on a controversy over a literary prize for women writers in the *New York Times*, concluded, "For readers and writers, in sum, the more prizes the better, however they are structured, and philosophy be damned."

Covers

Surveys have repeatedly found that people say that book covers influence their book choices. In the United Kingdom, when the BookTrust survey (2013, 30) asked people to tick off all the various strategies they use to pick books to read, the top choice (40 percent) was "Blurbs/book covers," followed by

"Recommendations from friends" (33 percent), "Recommendations from family" (23 percent), and "Reviews on websites" (9 percent). Similarly, when the website *Bookbrowser* (2007) surveyed its readers to find out "What most influences you when buying a book?" 35 percent of respondents ticked off the option "Book jacket." Other strong influences included: "I like this author"—65 percent; "It has good reviews"—48 per cent; and "Recommended by a friend"—43 per cent.

Many avid readers in my study said that the cover gets them to pick the book up, but then they put it through a series of other tests. "You're not supposed to judge a book by its cover, but I do, I do!" confessed Zoe (student, age 24). She says, "The first thing I look at is the cover. And if the cover isn't really nice looking, I don't generally take the book out any further. But [if the book passes the cover test], then I read the first page and I read the last page, and then I read a couple of in-between pages." Similarly, Madeline (student, age 22) says that in choosing books she goes a lot by cover but actually is taking into account a whole interplay of factors: "Color. And if it's got a sort of catchy title—not a jingle-catchy—but words that are interesting. I buy by author and I buy by books I've heard of or by reviews."

We now think of the book jacket as a form of advertising, a poster for the book designed to attract an intended specific readership. As Alan Powers puts it in his excellent book *Front Cover* (2001), "A book jacket or cover is a selling device, close to advertising in its form and purpose, but also specific to a product that plays a teasing game of hide and seek with commerce." Powers's comment reminds us again of the special Janus-faced identity of books: both a cultural product with a special aura and a consumer good that needs to be marketed. But book jackets evolved only gradually into their current form, where every element—front, back, flaps, and spine—has a role in enticing the reader. The book jacket began in the 1830s as a plain paper wrapper intended to protect from soil the book that was expensively bound in cloth, silk or leather. Book jackets with flaps came later, possibly in the 1850s. Then, according to Steven Heller and Seymour Chwast (1995, 12) in *Jackets Required*, sometime around 1910 along came "a new promotional gimmick called a 'blurb.' " Book jackets had finally made the jump from protective casing to advertising display. Decorative elements moved from the book's binding to the book jacket. The front became an area of graphic design, the flaps became spaces for advertising copy describing and praising the book's contents, and the back was often used to list other books from the publisher's list. With the expansion of paperback publishing, these advertising elements became part of the cover itself, not the detachable wrapper. And all along, jacket design has gone hand in hand with new technologies in printing, the production of images, and distribution, including four-color printing, digital images, and computer-assisted design.

Jackets and covers, whatever else they may be, are expected to help sell books. The cover that you see on the finished book is the survivor of a long process of give-and-take, design and reworking, that involves the publisher's art director, the designer, the book's editor, sometimes the author, and of course the marketing department. A well-designed cover attracts eyes to the book; conveys the aura of the book through the felicitous patterning of image, textual elements, color, and typeface; and offers something new to be understood more fully once the reader has finished the book. In short, a good jacket tells you what kind of book it is without giving away too much. A book cover, says Knopf's recently retired senior designer Peter Mendelsund (2013), "should be a book's true face. ... It should work to entice a browser, and serve as a lasting emblem of the experience of having read a given text." In his gorgeous book *Cover*, which is, among other things, a selective collection of his own cover designs, Mendelsund (2014, 108–109) outlines 11 different functions for a book cover. It is a skin, membrane, or boundary, which is all the more helpful as "we spend more of our reading time in digital, disembodied, notional environments where texts lack differentiation, and may easily leach into one another unconstrained." It is a frame. It is a reminder because a "distinct jacket mapped to a distinct text helps index that text; identify and remind you of it." It is an information booth that "tells you what the book is: what the title is; who the author is; what the book is about; what genre it may belong to." It is a teaser, a trophy ("Just look at what I read"), and an advertising billboard. It is a translation: "The jacket is a rendition of a book; a reading of it, an enactment."

Jackets—front, back, and spines—speak a coded language that experienced readers have learned to interpret through their prolonged engagement with books. Scarlet (commercial credit analyst, age 26) says, "I choose books by the cover. I like bright covers—I don't like dark and a lot of bad things happening. I try and pick books that look happy by the cover, so bright colors on the front and happy pictures." Author Francis Spufford (2003, 3) describes how he negotiates a big science fiction bookstore: "I'm a really skilled browser, believe me, finely attuned to the obscure signals sent out by the spines of paperbacks, able to detect at speed the four or five titles in a bay that pull at me in different ways." Experienced readers know that a genre book often announces itself by particular colors and iconic graphics— Chick Lit by a hot pink cover, a squiggly font, and an illustration that might include a shoe, a handbag, a red dress, or a martini glass; Westerns by sand-colored covers and a horse and/or a man with a rifle; and so on. Novices and unengaged readers have more trouble than do old hands in gauging a book by its cover and they make more mistakes. Experienced readers, on the other hand, report a careful weighing of claims and a sophisticated balance of skepticism and willingness to be seduced by jacket inducements that call out, "Read me!"

Peter Dixon and Marisa Bortolussi (2005, 2009, 2015) have published an interesting series of research articles that investigate people's knowledge of popular genres. In "Judging a Book by Its Cover," Dixon, Bortolussi, and Mullins (2015) used a sorting task to investigate the role of genre knowledge in interpreting cues on book covers that signal genres and subgenres. Their hypothesis was that "knowledgeable readers can use a book's cover to make informed inferences about the relationship of a book to others in the same fictional genre" (31). They found, as we would expect, that subjects with a lot of genre knowledge of either science fiction or mysteries differ from low-knowledge subjects on a task involving sorting book covers. Starting with 160 books randomly selected from the larger set of books available on ereader.com in the categories of "Mystery" and "Science Fiction," Dixon and colleagues printed on laminated cards 80 book covers from each genre. Because they were interested primarily in cover art, they masked author information and other information about the book such as the publisher, tag lines, and capsule reviews but not the title. For the 80 covers in each genre, subjects were asked to sort the covers into three to seven piles, or categories, of their own choosing, based on their estimate of "themes, plots, types of characters, settings, or other aspects of the story world" (33). Subjects with high knowledge of the genre more often described the categories in terms of subgenre labels, such as " 'Chandleresque mysteries,' 'modern, neo-noir' stories, and 'applications of technology' " (42). Here is how one high-knowledge subject describes one sorted pile derived from the mystery covers: "Broadly, these covers seemed likely modern, or neo-noir, or both. The images evoked either modern atmospheres or styles. ... Several of the titles—Addiction, Blood Diamonds, Blood Orchid, for example—seemed modern because they were so abrupt—even grim. I had the impression that these stories were modern, urban and likely grim" (43).

What Libraries Can Do

1. Take advantage of the fact that different readers use different ways of browsing for good books to read, some picking best sellers, some avoiding best sellers and going for the distinction of the prize winner, and still others attracted by genre or by cover. Cater to each of these groups with strategies that appeal to their differing ways of choosing books. Piggyback on the already existing publicity provided by book publishers, best-seller lists, prizes and prize winners, and cover art.

To Read More on Covers

Check out the *Design Observer* website (designobserver.com), which showcases the winners of the "50 Books, 50 Covers" annual competition that selects the best cover for an English language book published anywhere.

References

Bennett, Catherine. 2011. "The Man Booker Judges Seem to Find Reading a Bit Hard." *The Guardian*, September 11. Available at: https://www.theguardian.com/commentis free/2011/sep/11/catherine-bennett-dumbed-down-booker-prize.

BookBrowse. 2007. "What Most Influences You When Buying a Book?" *BookBrowse Poll*, March 12. Available at: https://www.bookbrowse.com/bb_poll/index.cfm.

BookTrust. 2013. "BookTrust Reading Habits Survey 2013." Available at: https://www .booktrust.org.uk/usr/library/documents/main/1576-booktrust-reading-habits-report -final.pdf.

Cima, Rosie. 2017. "Bias, She Wrote: The Gender Balance of *The New York Times* Best Seller List." *The Pudding*, June 1. Available at: https://pudding.cool/2017/06/best -sellers/?ncid=newsltushpmgnewsThe%20Morning%20Email%20060617.

Dilevko, Juris, and Candice F. C. Magowan. 2007. *Readers' Advisory Service in North American Libraries, 1870–2005: A History and Critical Analysis*. Jefferson, NC: McFarland & Co.

Dixon, Peter, and Marisa Bortolussi. 2005. "Approach and Selection of Popular Narrative Genre." *Empirical Studies of the Arts* 23, no. 1: 3–17.

Dixon, Peter, and Marisa Bortolussi. 2009. "Readers' Knowledge of Popular Genre." *Discourse Processes* 46: 541–571.

Dixon, Peter, Marisa Bortolussi, and Blaine Mullins. 2015. "Judging a Book by Its Cover." *Scientific Study of Literature* 5, no.1: 23–48.

Driscoll, Beth. 2014. *The New Literary Middlebrow: Tastemakers and Reading in the Twenty-First Century.* Basingstoke: Palgrave Macmillan.

English, James F. 2005. *The Economy of Prestige: Prizes, Awards, and the Circulation of Cultural Value.* Cambridge, MA, and London, England: Harvard University Press.

Hackett, Alice Payne, and James Henry Burke. 1977. *80 Years of Best Sellers, 1895–1975.* New York: R. R. Bowker.

Hall, James W. 2012. *Hit Lit: Cracking the Code of the Twentieth Century's Bestsellers.* New York: Random House.

Hart, James D. 1950. *The Popular Book: A History of America's Literary Taste.* New York: Oxford.

Heller, Steven, and Seymour Chwast. 1995. *Jackets Required: An Illustrated History of American Book Jacket Design, 1920–1950.* San Francisco: Chronicle Books.

Korda, Michael. 2001. *Making the List: A Cultural History of the American Bestseller, 1900–1999.* New York: Barnes and Noble Books.

Leavis, Q. D. 1932/1965. *Fiction and the Reading Public.* London: Chatto and Windus.

LeGuin, Ursula K. 2008. "Staying Awake: Notes on the Alleged Decline of Reading." *Harpers* (February 28): 33–38. Available at: https://harpers.org/archive/2008/02/staying-awake/.

Long, Elizabeth. 1985. *The American Dream and the Popular Novel.* Boston, London, Melbourne: Routledge and Kegan Paul.

Lyall, Sarah. 2005. "His Love of Words Rivals His Contempt for Critics." *The New York Times,* November 2. Available at: http://www.nytimes.com/2005/11/02/books/his-love-of-words-rivals-his-contempt-for-critics.html?_r=0.

Maatta, Stephanie L. 2010. "Book Awards and Award-Winning Books." *A Few Good Books: Using Contemporary Readers' Advisory Strategies to Connect Readers with Books,* 253–275. New York and London: Neal-Schuman.

Mendelsund, Peter. 2013. "An Interview with Peter Mendelsund." *Porter Square Books blog,* Thursday, May 2. Available at: http://portersquarebooksblog.blogspot.ca/2013/05/interview-with-peter-mendelsund.html.

Mendelsund, Peter. 2014. *Cover.* Brooklyn, NY: powerHouse Books.

Miller, Laura J. 2000. "The Best-Seller List as Marketing Tool and Historical Fiction." *Book History* 3: 286–304.

Mohdin, Aamna. 2016. "Women Are Horribly Under-represented in the World's Top Literary Awards." *Quartz,* November 17. Available at: https://qz.com/838175/the-national-book-award-and-other-top-literary-prizes-seriously-under-represent-women/.

Ozick, Cynthia. 2012. "Prize or Prejudice." *The New York Times,* June 6. Available at: http://www.nytimes.com/2012/06/07/opinion/prize-or-prejudice.html.

Poole, Marilyn. 2003. "The Women's Chapter: Women's Reading Groups in Victoria." *Feminist Media Studies* 3, no. 3: 273–281.

Powers, Alan. 2001. *Front Cover: Great Book Jacket and Cover Design.* London: Mitchell Beazley.

Radway, Janice A. 1989. "The Book-of-the-Month Club and the General Reader: The Uses of 'Serious Fiction.'" In *Reading in America*, 259–284. Edited by Cathy N. Davidson. Baltimore and London: Johns Hopkins University Press.

Regan, Helen. 2015. "Books about Women Don't Win Top Literary Prizes and That's a Problem." *Time*, June 1. Available at: http://time.com/3902821/literature-women-nicola-griffith-female-protagonists-pulitzer-prize-underrepresentation/.

Sorensen, Alan T. 2007. "Bestseller Lists and Product Variety." *The Journal of Industrial Economics* 55, no. 4: 715–738. Available at: http://www.ssc.wisc.edu/~sorensen/papers/sorensen_JIE_2007.pdf.

Spufford, Francis. 2003. *The Child That Books Built: A Life in Reading.* London: Faber and Faber.

Striphas, Ted. 2009. *The Late Age of Print: Everyday Book Culture from Consumerism to Control.* New York: Columbia University Press.

4.6 Advising Readers

Getting personal advice on what to read is something that readers both yearn for and dread. With so many books clambering for attention, readers, especially novice readers, often need help in narrowing choices. Advice from someone who wants to instruct, impose, or proselytize is unwelcome, but avid readers are hungry for suggestions from sources they trust. Readers turn for help to friends and family members with similar tastes, and they make use of book reviews, reading lists, and tips from social media sources such as Goodreads. But sometimes these strategies fail, and readers must look for advice further afield. And this should be said at the outset: although, for simplicity's sake, books are mentioned most often here, readers' advisory has become an inclusive practice, referring to advice on material in all formats: print, eBooks, audio books, films, and music. Included in the scope of readers' advisory are both fiction and nonfiction—anything, in fact, which is read primarily for pleasure. And finally readers' advisory (RA) is needed for all age groups.

Whether book advice happens in the context of a bookstore or library or in an informal exchange between friends or family members, the elements of successful advising are the same: *start with the reader and with what the reader says about the reading experience that is desired.* Then use what you know about books and genres and their differing elements of appeal to make a match, with titles offered as suggestions that the reader "might enjoy" but has no obligation to read. Bookstores, with their long tradition of "hand-selling," have modeled helpful strategies for connecting readers with books: grouping books on shelves by genres, providing good signage, putting attractive displays in high-traffic areas, and providing staff recommendations or "shelf-talkers." They also have a long tradition of supporting the culture of reading (and book buying) by sponsoring author visits and book clubs (see section 4.7). And unlike some library staff, bookstore staff members are never heard to say to customers, "Why are you wasting your time on paranormal romance when you could be reading a really *good* book like *Jane Eyre*?"

In the library field, public libraries, in particular, increasingly recognize the centrality of readers' advisory to their mission. Schwartz and Thornton-Verma (2014) surveyed public librarians using a questionnaire developed by the *Library Journal* along with NoveList and the RUSA/CODES Readers' Advisory Research and Trends Committee. They reported that some 84 percent of respondents think that "RA is important or very important to the library's mission already." More than half said that readers' advisory had increased in importance in the last three years, with 54 percent predicting it will become even more important in the next three years.

Already three factors have, in the past 50 years, transformed readers' advisory as a service in public libraries. First, the model of reading has changed so that reading is regarded as a transaction in which the reader is an equal partner, along with the text, in making meaning. Second, and following from the first, hierarchical structures of value have been challenged: respect for readers' choices means valuing and stocking the popular genres of reading that readers enjoy. And, third, impressive developments in new professional resources and technology have given librarians tools to find materials that match readers' stated preferences. For more than 100 years of library history, people have wanted help finding their next good read. Libraries are now well positioned to embrace readers' advisory, not just as something nice to do but as an essential core service.

Recently, some academic librarians have made the case that support for pleasure reading should also be part of the mission of the academic library. Meagan Lacy (2014, 18–23) provides a concise account of the ebb and flow of readers' advisory service in academic libraries, from the nineteenth century to the present. She argues that promoting recreational reading needs to be recognized as "a part of the educational and instructional mission—not counter to it" (23). Pauline Dewan (2014) points to the consolidation of research that affirms the importance of pleasure reading in the formation of lifelong readers. Academic libraries are full of books that readers would enjoy reading for the fun of it, but, Dewan says, they are "invisible, hidden away in numerous rows on multiple floors. Faced with overwhelming choice, only the most persevering patrons find the leisure reading material they want." It is time to change that, argue a growing number of academic librarians including Dewan (2010, 2013, 2014), Elliott (2007), Gilbert and Fister (2011), Lacy (2014), Mueller and colleagues (2017), and Smith and Young (2008).

Dewan (2013) suggests that academic libraries adopt some of the proven strategies used in public libraries, specifically the following: the creation of popular reading collections; themed displays in high-traffic areas filled with inviting books that are intended to circulate; retention of book covers, which work as eye-catching posters conveying the book's appeal (see section 4.5); the creation of comfortable spaces for reading; the creation of book-themed bookmarks, lists, and reading maps; and the inclusion of RA information on the library website. In addition, some academic libraries are partnering with public libraries in One Book, One Community (OBOC) programs (see section 4.7). As Smith and Young (2008) remark, "Evidence is growing of the recognition of reading's importance by colleges and universities, some of whom have begun to ask all incoming freshman to read the same book before arriving on campus."

In public libraries, two elements are currently recognized in effective readers' advisory work: the behind-the-scenes work—sometimes called indirect support—and the direct face-to-face interaction that includes the RA interview, booktalks, and outreach programs such as sponsoring author visits and book discussion groups. Indirect support includes putting spine labels on books, shelving books into separated genre collections, creating bookmarks and annotated book lists, setting up attractive displays that are constantly replenished, creating comfortable reading areas within the library, and maintaining a space on the library's web page to highlight library RA services and alert readers to new books. Research shows that circulation increases when libraries adopt such strategies, although there has been some pushback relating to separated genre collections (Trott and Novak 2007). In any case, like the layout of the bookstore, the physical arrangement of the collection itself should help readers choose books. When such strategies are pursued, the library itself becomes a prop for the RA conversation. *Bedrock for successful implementation of both direct and indirect readers' advisory work is an understanding of readers and what they look for in a satisfying reading experience.* Therefore, this section on advising readers builds on the discussion in section 1.2 on why no two readers ever read the same book, the discussion in section 4.2 on *why* readers read, and the discussion in section 4.3 on the reading experience.

Readers' Advisory in North American Public Libraries

Readers' advisory is old enough in North America to have had two births and two periods of unfolding. The first was in the 1920s and 1930s and the second began in the early 1980s and has extended to the present. Each phase has its own classic account and rationale: Jennie Flexner's *A Readers' Advisory Service* (1934) and Joyce Saricks and Nancy Brown's *Readers' Advisory Service in the Public Library* (1989/1997/2005). The first phase of readers' advisory was part of the public library's drive to help readers pursue goals of self-education. The second phase emerged in recognition of the centrality of pleasure reading and popular culture to the public library's mission.

By the 1920s, public libraries were ready to build on 50 years of professional experience by moving confidently to fill a social need for public education in the postwar years. Readers' advisory service during this period emphasized "reading with a purpose"—systematic reading on socially significant topics for purposes of self-improvement and self-education. The emphasis was on making the public library primarily an educational institution directed toward the diffusion of knowledge (Learned 1924). Jennie Flexner's *A Readers' Advisory Service* (1934) explains how readers' advisors interviewed clients as the basis for drawing up individualized, annotated reading lists and then discussed the list with clients in follow-up interviews. These lists were designed to offer a range of viewpoints on such topics as economics, sociology, the life of Christ, or classical Greek drama, while leading the reader in orderly steps from introductory works to more complex treatments. By the 1940s, this phase of readers' advisory as adult education had lost momentum and readers' advisory was folded into adult services. The special job designation of the readers' advisor was phased out, not to reappear in adult services for another 50 years. During this period of retrenchment in adult services, readers' advisory continued to be a cornerstone of the work of children's librarians.

Bill Crowley (2004, 19) dates the contemporary revival of readers' advisory for adults in North American public libraries from 1984. This was the year of the founding of the Adult Reading Round Table (ARRT) in the Chicago metropolitan area under the leadership of such RA advocates as Ted Balcom, Merle Jacob, and Joyce Saricks. ARRT members studied popular genres of fiction and their appeal to readers. The book by Joyce Saricks and Nancy Brown entitled *Readers' Advisory Service in the Public Library* (1989) embodies the new approach to readers' advisory that emerged from the ferment of genre study. In North America, RA practitioners have largely rejected the earlier library mission of pushing readers up the reading ladder from fiction to nonfiction and from pleasure to solid instruction (Ross 2006).

A whole generation of public librarians has embraced the reader-centered values and practical guidance provided by *Readers' Advisory Service in the Public Library*. Now in its third edition as updated by Joyce Saricks (2005, 1), this indispensable guide stresses that RA service "is a patron-oriented library service for adult fiction readers"—now expanded to readers of all kinds of materials. Saricks and Brown's book, written in the first instance to provide training to readers' advisors, puts the emphasis on the quality of the reading *experience* for the reader, not on the literary quality of the book judged as an autonomous work of art. They advocate a knowledgeable, nonjudgmental approach that values all kinds of reading and takes the view that the reader, not the librarian, knows best what kind of reading experience is desired. In "We Owe Our Work to Theirs," Neal Wyatt (2014) celebrates the 25th anniversary of *Readers' Advisory Service in the Public Library* by telling the story of how this book came to be written and how Saricks and Brown developed their framework of a book's elements of appeal. Saricks and Brown had staff to train for a new library service, Wyatt (2014) explained, and they needed a framework that was "easy to learn" that could be used to "help staff work with titles they had not read." According to Wyatt, the appeal framework, described later, "needed to help an advisor quickly winnow out titles that would not satisfy readers and focus attention on a smaller group that might." In summary, Wyatt says, "Twenty-five years ago, armed with fierce curiosity, sharp intelligence, and an abiding interest in what made reading such a grand pleasure for themselves and others, Joyce Saricks and Nancy Brown changed our profession."

Reader Development

In Europe, the United Kingdom has led the way in establishing a reader-centered approach in public libraries. Rachel Van Riel is the counterpart in the European story to Saricks and Brown in America. Van Riel has been a key figure in effecting a change in public library culture, saying in essence: start with the reader, not with the book. Second-phase readers' advisory in North America and British "reader development" have a lot in common, but they began from different ends of the book/reader spectrum. Saricks and Brown worked out their appeal framework by intensive genre study as part of the Adult Reading Round Table. So they started with the books and moved toward readers. Rachel Van Riel started with readers and moved toward books. Van Riel is the director of Opening the Book, a company she founded in 1991 that provides library design, library furniture, and library training that follow from the goal of promoting literature from the reader's point of view. With a background not in librarianship but in merchandising and adult education, Van Riel introduced in 1992 the set of ideas that she called "reader development" and more expansively "audience development," which is a broader concept than readers' advisory. Reader development means "active intervention" with the following goals: to "increase people's confidence and enjoyment of reading"; to encourage readers to try something new in order to "open up reading choices"; to "offer opportunities for people to share their reading experience"; and to "raise the status of reading as a creative activity" (Van Riel et al. 2008, 14).

Briony Train, coauthor of *Reading and Reader Development: The Pleasure of Reading* (2003, 31–33), noted that, before the turn toward reader development, adult services librarians in the United Kingdom provided indirect service to the fiction reader, while children's librarians, in contrast, took an active role in providing reading advice and in organizing programs to foster the enjoyment of reading. This situation changed, starting in the late 1980s and early 1990s with a new emphasis on pleasure reading from a coalition of groups. In 1992, a conference *Reading the Future: A Place for Literature in Public Libraries* (Van Riel 1992) brought together publishers, booksellers, librarians, and arts administrators under the banner of promoting fiction reading. Delegates emphasized the need for a "large scale change in library culture," including the "[n]eed to counter the move to make literature less important than information" in libraries (Van Riel 1992, 45). In 1998 and again in 2008, the United Kingdom celebrated a "National Year of Reading," an initiative led by a coalition of partners interested in reading, including the National Literacy Trust. The energy to promote reading generated in the United Kingdom's National Year of Reading has been maintained in follow-up projects such as the National Literacy Trust's "Words for Life" campaign promoting children's reading from birth to age 11 and the Australian National Year of Reading in 2012 (Bundy 2008).

Rachel Van Riel has been a leader in reader-centered librarianship for over 25 years. In 1996, she provided an inspirational six-month training program in reader development to 10 library authority representatives in northwest England, jumpstarting a partnership called "Time to Read" (TTR) just in time to get government funding during the 1998 National Year of Reading (Mathieson 2008, 23). Rachel Van Riel, Olive Fowler, and Anne Downes, all from Opening the Book, have collaborated on *The Reader-Friendly Library Service* (2008), which provides the rationale for a reader-centered strategy and offers practical guidance on how to put it into practice in public libraries. The cornerstone is respect for readers' choices. As Van Riel and colleagues (2008, 15) put it, "reader development begins from valuing and respecting individual reading preferences; each reader is expert and judge of their own reading experiences." This means that the reader-centered librarian takes a nonjudgmental approach to reading choices, while at the same time offering readers an opportunity to take the risk of trying something new to them. Van Riel says, "The best book in the world is quite simply the one you like the best." The reader-centered approach "sells the reading experience and what it can do for the reader," not specific books or writers.

The "Opening the Book" website (openingthebook.com/resources/audience-development) highlights some of the foundational ideas of this approach. Some examples: "Making the reader visible," "Respecting other people's reading experience," "A reader-centred approach to quality," and "Opening up reading choices." The approach is non-hierarchical: "Reader development begins with an assumption of fundamental equality between readers—no one reader is more important than another—while celebrating the differences of individual reading experiences." When it comes to promotion, Van Riel advises, "Sell the sizzle not the sausage," an advertising slogan that drives home the point that book promotion should be all about the reader's experience. Instead of a booktalk or annotation that starts off, "This is the third book by prize-winning Bolivian writer so-and-so, whose previous novels addressed themes of such-and-such," Van Riel recommends telling what the book will do for the reader: "You will be thrilled, amused, riveted or challenged" (Van Riel et al. 2008, 10).

Describing the situation in Danish and Norwegian public libraries, Nanna Kann-Rasmussen and Gitte Balling (2014, 4) report that library discourse has shifted from the older idea that librarians are experts who push readers up the reading ladder to the current reader-centered idea that librarians collaborate with users to find books that meet the users' interests and needs. Kann-Rasmussen and Balling interviewed 13 librarians and managers from all six county libraries in Denmark to find out their perceptions of "the purpose and effects of readers' advisory and audience development." Interviewees supported the official view that librarians should respect readers' choices, regarding them all equal in importance. As one interviewee (C2) said: "[Readers] don't want a stern librarian slap them on the wrist and scold them for not understanding Dostoevsky" (Kann-Rasmussen and Balling 2014, 6). However, respecting readers' choices has its limits, it appears. One interviewee (D1) was uneasy about "ubiquitous bestsellers": "We should shift readers' focus away from bestsellers. Well, we make bestsellers available, but we don't have to actively promote them."

And what should librarians do when readers seem to be attracted to "bad" literature? According to interviewee B1, "We have to have the courage to take a stand, to say to a user: 'It's not bad what you like to read. We would just like to show you something else.' We have also Margit Sandemo, to my horror. This is really bad. This is real trash. But people love it.' " (Margit Sandemo is the author of a multi-generational, historical fantasy series, *The Legend of the Ice People*, in 47 volumes, about a clan whose bloodline is cursed through four centuries. One of Scandinavia's best-selling series, it was published originally in Norwegian and subsequently translated into at least eight other languages including English.) Another interviewee C1 is no fan of Sandemo either:

> We have two tables in the hall holding the books that have just been returned. We know that these books will be borrowed again right away. What sits on these tables means a lot to me. There should not be a pile of Sandemo's *The Legend of the Ice People.* I simply remove these books.

As Kann-Rasmussen and Balling (2014, 7) observe, this well-intentioned librarian struggles to reconcile two opposing values: on the one hand, respect for readers' choices, a value that she claims to embrace; on the other hand, her own "passionate relation to literature and her desire to pass good reading experiences on to users." (See section 1.2 for more on why trying to "pass on" your own good reading experiences to others seldom works.) As Diana Tixier Herald (Orr and Herald 2013, xvi) succinctly explains the "passing on" problem: "My personal mantra is: 'No two people ever read the same book.' "

Putting the Emphasis on the Quality of the Reading Experience (with Help from Professional Tools)

There is a way to resolve the apparent conflict between respecting readers' choices and recommending quality. The quality that should concern readers' advisors is *not* the quality of the book itself as judged by literary critics. It is the quality of the reading experience that results when a particular reader, with a specific reading history and set of preferences, encounters the book. As we can see from the Danish study, it can be hard to hang on to a reader-centered approach when readers are seen to prefer *The Legend of the Ice People* (or dime novels, vampire novels, paranormal romances, or any of the other denigrated genres) to Dostoevsky. Nevertheless, the reader-centered approach has largely prevailed both in Europe and in North America, in official discourse if not always in practice, because it takes into account people's reading experience and motivation for reading (Ross 1991) and because it respects readers. Neil Hollands (2017, 35) is unequivocal in his advice to readers' advisors: "First and foremost, you have to get every last hint of book shaming out of your system. . . . You can't love every author, but you're going to have to truly embrace the right of others to read what they like."

For library staff, the reader-centered approach makes the job more challenging, more scary, but also more rewarding. If you could rely on a list of "Good Books"—say the Harvard Classics or Modern Library's "100 Best Novels"—and recommend the same books to everyone, advising would be easy (and unnecessary). *But the transactional model of reading requires us to give weight to both agents in the transaction: reader and book.* Readers' advisors need, first and foremost, to take the particular reader into account. And when that happens, a hugely larger universe of potentially "good books" opens up—not just the "works of enduring literature" recommended by Dilevko and Magowan (2007, 199) as the books to be offered by readers' advisors, but also fiction and nonfiction at all levels of reading difficulty and in all genres. No wonder librarians became panicky. Cynthia Orr (Orr and Herald 2013, 16–17) reported that when she surveyed public service staff in a library that she was managing in order to find out their "most dreaded reference questions," the top three included: "Can you help me find a good book to read?" With library catalogs an awkward tool for selecting enjoyable books that respond to readers' criteria, librarians worried initially that they were expected to have read everything before they could make a recommendation.

The publication in 1982 of the first edition of Betty Rosenberg's *Genreflecting* was a precursor of the type of professional tool needed by readers' advisors in a reader-centered service that responds to readers' tastes. As Herald (Orr and Herald 2013, xvi) says in her Preface to the seventh edition, "I loved [Betty Rosenberg's first edition of] *Genreflecting* because it didn't treat the reading I enjoyed as trite, unimportant, or, heaven forbid, 'trashy.' " Through three decades, different editors, and seven editions, *Genreflecting* has focused on helping readers find books that would give them pleasure. It became the template for the Libraries Unlimited Genreflecting Advisory Series, with some 50 titles that focus variously on specific genres or audiences such as Meagan Honig's *Urban Grit: A Guide to Street Lit* (2011), Diana Tixier Herald's *Teen Genreflecting 3* (2011), Kristin Ramsdell's *Romance Fiction* (2012), or Vnuk and Donohue's *Women's Fiction* (2013).

Readers' advisory services have increasingly turned to online resources including social networking sites (Stover 2009). With catalog enrichment, the library catalog itself is becoming a much more useful resource for RA, as Mary K. Chelton (2017) has pointed out. Enterprising vendors such as LibraryThing and NoveList Select allow for the incorporation into the catalog of user-generated reviews and tags, recommendations, and series reading order information. A key resource for readers' advisors and readers alike, EBSCO's NoveList Plus is a subscription database that allows for retrieval from a subscription database currently containing over 511,000 fiction and nonfiction titles and growing by some 30,000 new titles each year. Almost 50,000 of these, or 10 percent, are audiobook titles. NoveList and NoveList Plus are searchable by author, title, and subject and include information about reading level, appeal factors, read-alikes, and more.

Excellent guides to professional tools for RA work are now available. Filling in what used to be a gap in Linda C. Smith and colleagues' standard text, *Reference and Information Services*, an all-new chapter in the fifth edition— "Readers' Advisory Services and Sources," by Neal Wyatt (2016)—is a compact, authoritative, and engaging guide to what good RA service is and does, while also providing a round-up of the best sources. In *Crash Course in Readers' Advisory*, Cynthia Orr (2015) also provides an excellent run-down on the most useful books, websites, and databases available to help librarians to approach readers' advisory work the same way that they would approach any reference question, using professional tools to help them find answers. No longer is there any excuse for readers' advisors to limit their book suggestions to the scope of their own personal reading or to put off readers who ask for a specific genre by saying, "Well, I don't know much about urban fiction/manga/westerns/steampunk."

Listening to Readers

Professional tools about the books help with half of job. The other half is to find out, through a conversation with the reader, what the *reader* thinks is an enjoyable book and what kind of reading experience the reader desires. Readers are often wary of advice, however well intentioned, when it seems that the advisor wants to sell his or her own favorites. One participant in my RA Visit Study reported how unhelpful it was to be regaled with a list of the advisor's own favorite books:

> I was wondering if she were just going to show me her own favorite books, or would she ask more questions to gauge what I prefer to read. We arrived at the stacks. She said, "Oh, here's one by Anita Shreve. And here, this is a good one too. I enjoyed this one." She handed me *Where the Heart Is* by Billie Letts. "It's good if you like romance." She had handed the book to me without really asking whether I liked romance, which I don't.

As we keep saying, what counts is the *reader's* experience of the text, not the personal favorites of the readers' advisor. Nancy Pearl said, "The first thing is that readers' advisors have to know it's not about them. We should make those little plastic bracelets and have them say, 'It's not about you' " (Ross 2014, 248).

Effective readers' advisors discover readers' tastes by inviting them to talk about their own engagement with books or authors. For many avid readers, talking about books is an enjoyable experience in itself and an extension of the pleasurable reading experience. To initiate the conversation about the reader's experience, the readers' advisor may say, "Can you tell me about a book that you've really enjoyed?" followed possibly by, "What did you enjoy most about that book?" and "What do you feel in the mood to read now?" It is also useful to ask, "What kind of book/genre/experience do you *not* enjoy?" This conversation about books—what librarians call "the readers' advisory interview"—is an indispensable element in the process of matching book to reader and should happen *before* the advisor makes any book suggestions (Ross, Nilsen, and Radford 2009, 244–245). When readers talk about books, they provide clues about the reading experience they desire. A side benefit of this readers' advisory conversation about books is that it helps readers make discoveries about themselves as readers and about their own reading preferences. Jessica E. Moyer (2008, 154–160) has helpfully reviewed the too sparse research on the readers' advisory interview—more research is needed on the RA transaction, both face-to-face and online.

Readers' advisors learn to listen closely with their ears sharpened for clues about (1) the *types of books* the reader enjoys, (2) the *reading experience* desired (see section 4.3), and (3) the *reading situation* for which the book is intended. Concerning book-based clues, does the reader use such terms as "hard-to-put-down" or "heart-warming" or "hard-hitting"? Does the reader talk about a setting so atmospheric that it infuses every aspect of the novel? Is a strong central character mentioned or does the reader talk about the complex interweaving of many characters, perhaps through several generations? Concerning the desired reading experience, does the reader want to be comforted by something familiar and reassuring or astonished and unsettled by the new? What does the reader say she does *not* enjoy? Even people who say they are omnivorous readers who read "everything" actually reject vast tracts of the book universe—for example, they may say no psychological horror, nothing with a sad ending, no sadomasochism, no unreliable narrators, and no books about orphans. And what does the reader say about the *situation* in which the book will be read? Does the reader mention needing a good beach read? Books for a friend recovering from surgery? Some discussible books as options for a book club? In the United Kingdom, Opening the Book (2008) has a book promotion site, "Take your seat," that recommends books by the situations in which they might be read—such as books to read on the train or books to be read at 3:00 a.m. when you can't sleep. In RA work, there is seldom a single right answer—there are usually many books that would suit the reader. But there are also many totally wrong answers—books that would *not* be appropriate for that particular reader. Using clues about book appeal, reading experience wanted, and reading situation gives the readers' advisor a better shot at eliminating the wrong answers and suggesting something readers will read and enjoy.

Barry Trott, Neil Hollands, and others in the Williamsburg Regional Library, Virginia, have expanded the scope of readers' advisory beyond the library's walls through the development of an asynchronous, form-based RA service (Trott 2005, 2008; Hollands 2006). Form-based readers' advisory, which takes the RA interview online, is a return to the service of the 1930s when readers received personalized lists based on what they said about reading interests. On the Williamsburg form, readers complete a reader profile that includes detailed closed questions on preferred genres, pet peeves, preferred content, and preferred tone/style/mood plus open questions asking for five favorite books and what is enjoyed about them. Many other public libraries have followed Williamsburg's lead in introducing online forms for readers' advisory. In Part 2 of *A Few Good Books*, Stephanie Maatta (2010) provides a useful round-up of technological tools that librarians can use to engage readers in virtual conversations about books through blogs, wikis, podcasting, and social cataloguing.

Appeal and Beyond

When Joyce Saricks and Nancy Brown (1997, 35–55) introduced the concept of a book's appeal factors, they gave readers' advisors a vocabulary for talking about and thinking about the elements in a book that make a difference to the reader's experience. Elaborated in two subsequent editions (Saricks 1997, 2005), "appeal" has become a foundational concept for thinking about RA work. In the transactional model of reading that underlies the concept of appeal, the reading experience depends partly on identifiable elements in the text itself and partly on what the particular reader brings to the reading experience in terms of reading skill, preferences, purpose in reading, and mood. Saricks (2005, 42) captures the two collaborative agents of book and reader by defining appeal as the "elements of books to which a reader relates." Saricks and Brown initially identified four main appeal factors—pacing, characterization, storyline, and setting/frame/tone—to which was added language or style (2005, 40–66). Storyline goes beyond plot to include narrative point of view, the amount of dialogue, and the author's treatment of the story—for example, a light-hearted romp or a bleak critique. Setting goes beyond time and place to include the density of atmospheric detail that is brought to the novel's world. Unlike a list of subject headings, an articulation of appeal elements captures the "feel" of the book and provides readers with helpful clues for assessing whether or not they are likely to enjoy a book. The appeal framework provides a scaffolding for readers' advisors, directing them to pay special attention to key phrases in readers' accounts of the books they like—"strong characters" or "fast-paced" or "world-building" or "upbeat" or "edgy"—and then translate those desirable elements into a framework that leads to other titles.

As Neal Wyatt (2007a, 40) has noted, "The concept of appeal is ... being changed and adapted by those who helped to create it and by a new group of librarians eager to help develop new thinking about how patrons react to, and interact with, what they read." Wyatt herself has been part of this adaptation, notably by her advocacy of "whole collections" RA, her elaboration of the appeal framework for application to nonfiction in *Readers' Advisory Guide to Nonfiction* (Wyatt 2007b), and her introduction of the concept of the "reading map," which is a visual map of the internal life of the book that takes into account read-arounds and read-alikes (Wyatt 2006). When Saricks and Brown wrote their first edition, they focused on fiction books as the source of pleasurable reading, but we know that many readers read nonfiction for pleasure and many prefer formats other than a print book as their source for story. The "whole collections" idea, as Wyatt envisages it, draws upon *everything*: it moves beyond fiction books to include nonfiction, audiobooks, movies, music, websites, databases—"this whole world," as she put it in an interview with me. In this interview, Wyatt described how, in her own reading, the book she read "had an internal life of its own and that internal life wasn't just appeal." Subject matter was important too and so was the perspective from which the reader wants to view that subject. Wyatt said that the last chapter of *Readers' Advisory Guide to Nonfiction* lays out this expanded world of whole collections: "It says it's not just read-alikes; it's read-arounds too. You need to create this universe that supports their reading interest that's beyond appeal."

Recently, there have been calls for readers' advisors to up their game (Beard and Thi-Beard 2008; Crowley 2014, 2015; Dali 2013, 2014, 2015). Beard and Thi-Beard (2008, 331) argue that the "bulk of the literature on RA and the bulk of its tools focus on the book as an object." To redress that imbalance, they conclude, readers' advisory service must be reconceptualized to put the reader center stage and emphasize not "the features of the books" but "the activities of the reader" (333). Keren Dali (2014, 33) recommends the adoption of the term "reading appeal," the twofold nature of which encompasses both "book-related appeal" and "reader-driven appeal," which is to say "appeal related to readers and their social environment." Taken together, Keren Dali's accumulating body of work is a rich addition to our understanding of readers' reading experience, which must underlie all RA work.

Case 16: The Four Doorways

Instead of talking about appeal elements, Nancy Pearl talks about the "four doorways." The doorway metaphor more clearly highlights the activity of the reader who is drawn into the book through one or another of the doorways. Here's how she explained it to me in an interview and what she tells students in her class on readers' advisory at the University of Washington:

Pearl: It's important to try to understand *why* people like the books that they like. That's why the doorways idea for me is so intuitively perfect. It's the same thing as the appeals, generally, but it's a terrific metaphor. Ever since I've started using that in the class, it's been smoother sailing.

Ross: How do you describe the doorways to your students?

Pearl: That every book has the same four doorways—character, language, setting, and story. But every book does not have the same size doorways. There are some books where 99 per cent of the people who love that book have entered through the very same doorway.

Ross: Streams of people all going through the plot doorway.

Pearl: Exactly. So I say, "Look at your readers." The biggest circulating fiction—and probably nonfiction too—are those story-driven books. *The Da Vinci Code*, Lee Child, mysteries, which I think are primarily plot-driven. Then the next biggest doorway in terms of the numbers of readers or in terms of the numbers of books that you have in the library collection is character. Then setting is smaller, and language is the smallest. Then I ask them to make the connections between fiction and nonfiction. So if it's story, where would you send them [to find nonfiction where the doorway is primarily story]?

Comments

In stories about reading, some authorities give the upper hand to the book, some to the reader. It is hard, if not impossible, to keep both in focus simultaneously, but both reader and book are coequal partners in the reading experience. That's why a "terrific metaphor" is needed to try to capture the reality of two active agents in a transaction where both are required for meaning making. The ratios of the four main elements of story, character, setting, and language can be used to describe the book itself. But different people may love the very same book for different reasons and so the doorways metaphor also describes individual readers and their preferred way of experiencing books. Perhaps we need more than one metaphor. Here are additional metaphors from Rebecca Solnit's *The Faraway Nearby* (2013, 51): "The object we call a book is not the real book, but its potential, like a musical score or seed. It exists fully only in the act of being read; and its real home is inside the head of the reader, where the symphony resides, the seed germinates. A book is a heart that beats only in the chest of another."

What Libraries Can Do

1. Recognize that knowledge about genres of fiction and their appeal is an important competency for public library staff. One good way to develop an understanding of appeal elements is to read five books in a new genre every year—the five-book challenge first issued by Ann Bouricius (2000). Start by reading in the genre that you have read the least and think that you don't like. The experience may surprise you.

2. Test out your own library website. Imagine that you are a reader who is checking out the library website to get suggestions for good books to read. Does the web page include specific RA pages? What information is included? Susan Burke and Molly Strothmann (2015) surveyed a random sample of 369 public libraries to get a picture of the types of RA information services being offered on their websites and found that somewhat less than one-fifth offered any RA information online. Try putting NoveList wherever it is that people go to look for book suggestions. The Williamsburg Regional Library puts it under "How Do I Find a Good Book?"

To Read More

Hornby, Susan, and Bob Glass, eds. 2008. *Reader Development in Practice: Bringing Literature to Readers*. London: Facet.

This edited collection of essays fills out the picture of reader development in the United Kingdom as it involves writers, collaborative networks, government funding, libraries, and readers. The introduction promises "a guide to how readers develop, and the impact that they can have on what libraries offer."

Moyer, Jessica E. 2008. *Research-Based Readers' Advisory*. Chicago: American Library Association.

Twelve chapters focus on various aspects of RA work, including different kinds and ages of readers; different kinds of materials (nonfiction, audiovisual); and different library activities related to readers' advisory, including the interview. Most chapters offers a double perspective, with a review of the research literature provided mostly by Jessica Moyer followed by a "librarian view" provided by expert practitioners such as Sarah Statz Cord, Kaite Mediatore Stover, Heather Booth, David Wright, Cynthia Orr, and Neil Hollands.

Saricks, Joyce G. 2009. *The Readers' Advisory Guide to Genre Fiction*, 2nd ed. Chicago: American Library Association.

An invaluable resource that provides an overview of 15 genres, including "gentle reads," "women's lives and relationships," and "literary fiction" as well as popular genres of science fiction, mysteries, romance, thrillers, historical fiction, westerns, and so on. Each chapter contains a discussion of the genre's appeal to readers, a section on key authors and subgenres, "Sure Bets," and suggestions for questions to ask in the RA interview. Neal Wyatt is preparing a third edition, which will include expanded sections on meta appeals and whole collection readers' advisory.

References

Anderson, Stephanie H., and Barry Trott. 2016. "Trends and Directions in RA Education." *Reference & User Services Quarterly* 55, no. 3: 203–209.

Beard, David, and Kate Vo Thi-Beard. 2008. "Rethinking the Book: New Theories for Readers' Advisory." *Reference & User Services Quarterly* 47, no. 4: 331–335.

Bouricius, Ann. 2000. *The Romance Readers' Advisory: The Librarian's Guide to Love in the Stacks*. Chicago: American Library Association.

Bundy, Alan. 2008. *A Nation Reading for Life: The Challenge for Australia's Public Libraries*. Melbourne: Friends of Libraries Australia. Available at: http://www.fola.org.au/docs/a_nation_reading_for_life.doc.

Burke, Susan K., and Molly Strothmann. 2015. "Adult Readers' Advisory Services through Public Library Websites." *Reference & User Services Quarterly* 55, no. 2: 132–143.

Crowley, Bill. 2004. "A History of Readers' Advisory Service in the Public Library." In *Nonfiction Readers' Advisory*, 3–29. Edited by Robert Burgin. Westport, CT: Libraries Unlimited.

Crowley, Bill. 2014. "Time to Rethink Readers' Advisory Education?" *Public Libraries* 5, no. 4: 37–43.

Crowley, Bill. 2015. "Differing Mental Models and the Futures of Libraries, Librarians, and Readers' Advisory." *Reference & User Services Quarterly* 55, no. 2: 91–94.

Dali, Keren. 2013. "Hearing Stories, Not Keywords: Teach Contextual Readers' Advisory." *Reference Services Review* 4, no. 3: 474–502.

Dali, Keren. 2014. "From Book Appeal to Reading Appeal: Redefining the Concept of Appeal in Readers' Advisory." *The Library Quarterly* 84, no. 1: 22–48.

Dali, Keren. 2015. "Readers' Advisory: Can We Take It to the Next Level?" *Library Review* 64, no. 4/5: 372–392.

Dewan, Pauline. 2010. "Why Your Academic Library Needs a Popular Reading Collection Now More Than Ever." *College & Undergraduate Libraries* 17, no. 1: 44–64.

Dewan, Pauline. 2013. "Reading Matters in the Academic Library: Taking the Lead from Public Librarians." *Reference & User Services Quarterly* 52, no. 4: 309–319.

Dewan, Pauline. 2014. "Adopting Readers' Advisory Practices in the Academic Library." *Ontario Library Association*, Open Shelf, October 14. Available at: http://www.open-shelf.ca/readers-advisory-academic/.

Dilevko, Juris, and Candice F. C. Magowan. 2007. *Readers' Advisory Service in North American Libraries, 1870–2005: A History and Critical Analysis*. Jefferson, NC: McFarland & Co.

Elliott, Julie. 2007. "Academic Libraries and Extracurricular Reading Promotion." *Reference & User Services Quarterly* 46, no. 3 (Spring): 34–43.

Flexner, Jennie. 1934. *A Readers' Advisory Service*. New York: American Association for Adult Education.

Gilbert, Julie, and Barbara Fister. 2011. "Reading, Risk, and Reality: College Students and Reading for Pleasure." *College & Research Libraries* 72, no. 5: 474–495.

Herald, Diana Tixier. 2011. *Teen Genreflecting 3: A Guide to Reading Interests*. Santa Barbara, CA: Libraries Unlimited.

Hollands, Neil. 2006. "Improving the Model for Interactive Readers' Advisory Service." *Reference & User Services Quarterly* 35, no. 3: 205–212.

Hollands, Neil. 2017. "Every Book Its Reader: Resolve to Reach More Readers." *Booklist* 113, no. 9/10: 35.

Honig, Meagan. 2011. *Urban Grit: A Guide to Street Lit*. Santa Barbara, CA: Libraries Unlimited.

Kann-Rasmussen, Nanna, and Gitte Balling. 2014. "Every Reader His Book—Every Book Its Reader? Notions on Readers' Advisory and Audience Development in Danish Public Libraries." *Journal of Librarianship and Information Science* 47, no. 3: 1–12.

Lacy, Meagan. 2014. "Slow Books in the Academic Library." In *Slow Books Revolution: Creating a New Culture of Reading on College Campuses and Beyond*, 17–29. Edited by Meagan Lacy. Santa Barbara, CA: Libraries Unlimited.

Learned, William S. 1924. *The American Public Library and the Diffusion of Knowledge*. New York: Harcourt, Brace.

LibraryThing. n.d. "Catalog Enrichment: Your Existing Catalog Made Extraordinary." Available at: http://www.librarything.com/forlibraries/handout/LTFL_ce_public .pdf.

Maatta, Stephanie L. 2010. *A Few Good Books: Using Contemporary Readers' Advisory Strategies to Connect Readers with Books*. New York: Neal-Schuman Publishers.

Mathieson, Jane. 2008. " 'Time to Read': The Rise and Rise of a Regional Partnership." In *Reader Development in Practice: Bringing Literature to Readers*, 23–38. Edited by Susan Hornby and Bob Glass. London: Facet.

Moyer, Jessica E. 2007. "Learning from Leisure Reading: A Study of Adult Public Library Patrons." *Reference & User Services Quarterly* 46, no. 4: 66–79.

Moyer, Jessica E. 2008. *Research-Based Readers' Advisory*. Chicago: American Library Association.

Mueller, Kat Landry, Michael Hanson, Michelle Martinez, and Linda Meyer. 2017. "Patron Preferences: Recreational Reading in an Academic Library." *The Journal of Academic Librarianship* 43, no. 1: 72–81.

Munro, Margaret E. 1986. "Vivid Colors of High Significance." *RQ* 25, no. 4 (Summer): 437–438.

Opening the Book. Available at: www.openingthebook.com.

Opening the Book. 2008. "Take Your Seat." *Reader2reader*. Available at: http://www .openingthebook.com/reader2reader/takeyourseat/default.aspx.

Orr, Cynthia. 2015. *Crash Course in Readers' Advisory*. Santa Barbara, CA: Libraries Unlimited.

Orr, Cynthia, and Diana Tixier Herald, eds. 2013. *Genreflecting: A Guide to Popular Reading Interests*, 7th ed. Santa Barbara, CA: Libraries Unlimited.

Ramsdell, Kristin. 2012. *Romance Fiction: A Guide to the Genre*, 2nd ed. Santa Barbara, CA: Libraries Unlimited.

Ross, Catherine Sheldrick. 1991. "Readers' Advisory Service: New Directions." *RQ* 30, no. 4: 503–518.

Ross, Catherine Sheldrick. 2006. "The Fiction Problem." In *Reading Matters: What the Research Reveals about Reading, Libraries, and Community*, 10–16. Westport, CT: Libraries Unlimited.

Ross, Catherine Sheldrick. 2014. "X-traordinary Readers." In *The Pleasures of Reading: A Booklover's Alphabet*. Santa Barbara, CA: Libraries Unlimited.

Ross, Catherine Sheldrick, Kirsti Nilsen, and Marie L. Radford. 2009. *Conducting the Reference Interview*, 2nd ed. New York: Neal-Schuman.

Saricks, Joyce G., and Nancy Brown. 1989. *Readers' Advisory Service in the Public Library*. 2nd ed., 1997. 3rd ed. 2005. Chicago and London: American Library Association.

Schwartz, Meredith, and Henrietta Thornton-Verma. 2014. "The State of Readers' Advisory." *Library Journal* 139, no. 2: 30. Available at: http://lj.libraryjournal. com/2014/02/library-services/the-state-of-readers-advisory/.

Smith, Rochelle, and Nancy J. Young. 2008. "Giving Pleasure Its Due: Collection Promotion and Readers' Advisory in Academic Libraries." *The Journal of Academic Librarianship* 34, no. 6: 520–526.

Solnit, Rebecca. 2013. *The Faraway Nearby*. New York: Penguin Books.

Stover, Kaite Mediatore. 2009. "Stalking the Wild Appeal Factor: Readers' Advisory and Social Networking Sites." *Reference & User Services Quarterly* 48, no. 3: 243–246, 269.

Time to Read. Available at: www.time-to-read.co.uk.

Train, Briony. 2003. "Reader Development." In *Reading and Reader Development: The Pleasure of Reading*, 30–57. Edited by Judith Elkin, Briony Train, and Debbie Denham. London: Fawcett Publishing.

Trott, Barry. 2005. "Advising Readers Online: A Look at Internet Based Reading Recommendation Services." *Reference & User Services Quarterly* 44, no. 3: 210–215.

Trott, Barry. 2008. "Building on a Firm Foundation: Readers' Advisory over the Next Twenty-Five Years." *Reference & User Services Quarterly* 48, no. 2: 132–135.

Trott, Barry, and Vicki Novak. 2007. "A House Divided: Two Views on Genre Separation." *Reference and User Services Quarterly* 46, no. 2: 33–38. Available at: http://rusq .org/2008/01/05/a-house-divided-two-viewson-genre-separation/.

Van Riel, Rachel, ed. 1992. *Reading the Future: A Place of Literature in Public Libraries*. London: The Arts Council of Great Britain and Library Association Publishing.

Van Riel, Rachel, Olive Fowler, and Anne Downes. 2008. *The Reader-Friendly Library Service*. Newcastle upon Tyne: Society of Chief Librarians.

Vnuk, Rebecca, and Nanette Donohue. 2013. *Women's Fiction: A Guide to Popular Reading Interests*. Santa Barbara, CA: Libraries Unlimited.

Williamsburg Regional Library. n.d. "Looking for a Good Book." [Reader profile form] Available at: http://www.wrl.org/books-and-reading/adults/looking-good-book.

Wyatt, Neal. 2006. "Redefining RA: Reading Maps Remake RA." *Library Journal*. Available at: http://lj.libraryjournal.com/2006/11/ljarchives/lj-series-redefining-ra-reading-maps-remake-ra.

Wyatt, Neal. 2007a. "An RA Big Think." *Library Journal* 132, no. 12: 40–43.

Wyatt, Neal. 2007b. *Readers' Advisory Guide to Nonfiction*. Chicago: ALA.

Wyatt, Neal. 2014. "We Owe Our Work to Theirs: Celebrating the Twenty-Fifth Anniversary of *Readers' Advisory Service in the Public Library*." *Reference & Services Quarterly* 54, no. 2: 24–30.

Wyatt, Neal. 2016. "Readers' Advisory Services and Sources." In *Reference and Information Services: An Introduction*, 666–701. Edited by Linda C. Smith and Melissa A. Wong. Santa Barbara, CA: Libraries Unlimited.

4.7 Shared Reading

Most research on reading has viewed it as a solitary activity. In fiction and in painting, the reader is often portrayed as an individual who withdraws from human society to become absorbed in a private world that others cannot share. Nevertheless, reading has *never* been a purely solitary activity. People have read books aloud to each other, given books as gifts, talked about books with family and friends, and reviewed books. In short, people have always shared reading, and now digital media are making that shared reading even more prominent. In a chapter called "Sharing" in *Book Was There*, Andrew Piper (2012, 84) remarks:

> Almost every major textual initiative today is structured around three overlapping notions of sharing: commonality, transferability, and sociability. We want other people to read the same thing we are reading (commonality); we want to be able to send other people what we are reading (transferability); and we want to be able to talk to other people about what we are reading (sociability). "Social reading" is shaping up to be the core identity ... of digital media.

Book Clubs, Reading Groups, and Mass Reading Events

Social reading happens both online and face-to-face. In the virtual world, reading is shared through online book discussion groups, through sites such as Wattpad where authors post their work-in-progress for reader feedback (see section 1.4), and through online reviews, recommendations, booklists, and personal catalogs on sites such as Amazon, Goodreads, and LibraryThing. For adults, face-to-face social reading typically happens in book discussion groups variously called "book clubs" or "reading groups"; in public readings by authors; and in One Book, One Community (OBOC) events in which everyone in the community is invited to read the same book.

The Oprah Book Club, which burst upon the scene in 1996, suddenly gave global visibility to shared reading. As Mary K. Chelton (2001, 31) noted, "When Oprah picks up a new hobby, so does a nation." And not just one nation—Oprah's Book Club was syndicated in 120 countries and at its height had an audience of some 13 million viewers. When its talk show life ended in April 2011, according to Beth Driscoll (2014, 47), Oprah's Book Club was restructured as a digital enterprise that operated through Facebook, Twitter, Goodreads, and the Oprah.com website. In the United Kingdom, the Richard and Judy Book Club had a similarly large impact on readers, book sales, and the visibility of featured authors, producing what was called the "Richard and Judy Effect" as the counterpart to the "Oprah Effect." A flurry of books, web pages, and newspaper articles appeared to announce, and wonder at, the suddenly visible phenomenon of social reading. No one knows exactly how many book clubs/reading groups there are, but the answer is clearly "a lot." Jenny Hartley began her book *Reading Groups* (2001, vii), a report of a survey of 350 such groups in the

United Kingdom, with the comment, "Reading groups are the success story of the past few years. . . . No one knows just how many there are; estimates run as high as 50,000 in Britain and 500,000 in America." More than 15 years later, Mackenzie Dawson (2017) in the *New York Post* speculated that "[m]ore than 5 million Americans belong to their own book clubs." For many public libraries, supporting book clubs and reading groups has become an important element in readers' advisory or reader development (see section 4.6). The American Library Association website maintains a concise and useful page on book discussion groups, which includes a "Quick Start Guide" on how to establish a book discussion group and keep it going successfully. Joyce Saricks (2009) provides a concise round-up of helpful resources, starting with *Booklist*'s book discussion blog, Book Group Buzz. A comprehensive guide for librarians on how to organize and run book discussion groups can be found in Lauren Zina John's *Running Book Discussion Groups* (2006).

Of course, before the burgeoning of book clubs post-Oprah, plenty of reading groups had been meeting all along to talk about books—eighteenth-century salons in Paris and nineteenth-century Women's Literary Clubs in North America are only the most well-publicized examples. The Chautauqua Literary and Scientific Circle, for example, enlisted members, mostly women, from small communities in New York, Pennsylvania, Ohio, Illinois, and Iowa, who read together in discussion groups. Elizabeth Long (1986, 1993, 2003) was the first to study North American reading groups in any serious way. Her *Book Clubs* (2003) is a fine-grained study of women's reading groups in Houston, Texas, from the nineteenth century to the present and their role in the everyday lives of women. Similarly, other historians of reading (Gregory 2001) began to see continuities between the contemporary phenomenon of women's reading groups and nineteenth-century women's clubs and literary societies whose members got together to educate themselves and incidentally acquire the organizational and public speaking skills that allowed them to agitate for causes in the public sphere such as temperance and women's suffrage. Until the 1990s, however, most group reading activity happened in the private sphere, was invisible to outsiders, left few physical traces, and remained under the radar. Typically 8 to 12 women met once a month for up to 25 years in the living rooms of group members, possibly keeping lists of the books they had read and sometimes preparing written reports on the books. Nobody outside of the group itself paid much attention.

Now, however, shared reading advertises itself. Reading groups post to websites information about themselves together with their reading lists. The book club idea provides the framework for such novels as Elizabeth Noble's *The Reading Group* (2003), Karen Joy Fowler's *The Jane Austen Book Club* (2004), Hilma Wolitzer's *Summer Reading* (2007), and Mary Ann Shaffer and Annie Barrows's *The Guernsey Literary and Potato Peel Pie Society* (2008). Azar Nafisi's *Reading Lolita in Tehran* (2003), which became a *New York Times* best seller, demonstrates that the reading group is a global phenomenon. Publishers, bookstores, and libraries recognize that catering to reading groups can be a good way to connect with readers and to promote books. For example, Penguin Random House features on its website a page for book clubs, "Bestsellers with Reading Group Guides." Enterprising bookstores and public libraries promote themselves as important resources for reading groups. Bookstores may offer discounts to reading group members, and both bookstores and libraries provide meeting spaces, keep directories of reading groups, display book club selections, and offer help with choosing books. The impact goes beyond the members of the book club itself, because other customers and library patrons use book club selections as recommendations for their own reading.

The Social Infrastructure of Reading

In *Book Clubs: Women and the Uses of Reading in Everyday Life* (2003, 8–11), Elizabeth Long emphasizes what she calls the "social infrastructure of reading." Reading is learned within a web of social relations, starting with the bedtime story and continuing in classrooms through teacher-directed routines. Older readers learn how to make sense of extended text in the context of what Stanley Fish (1980) has called "interpretive communities" who share a set of norms and procedures. An interpretive community might be embodied in a literature class, a graduate seminar, or a long-established reading group but could also be derived from cultural authorities such as book reviewers, literary critics, and judges of literary awards. Readers learn which kinds of texts are valued by the culture at large and which are not. They know, for example, that romances and westerns are *not* valued; in contrast, reading Man Booker prizewinners confers prestige and cultural capital. As Elizabeth Long (1993, 192) puts it, "Collective and institutional processes shape reading practices by authoritatively defining what is worth reading and how to read it." So learning how to read, what to read, and how to interpret what is read is socially mediated.

Readers now have multiple channels for finding out what other people think about books—from face-to-face talk with other readers to reading online posts, lists of best sellers and prizewinners, and reviews by book experts and by ordinary readers. The increasing prominence of reader-generated reviews on Amazon and Goodreads has democratized the process of recommendation and challenged the cultural authority of expert readers. For some, it is an additional pleasure when the book they are reading is simultaneously being read by many others. Benedict Anderson (1983/1991) coined the term "imagined community" to explain how people who have never met each other can feel part of the same community. In particular, he was interested in the way that people reading books, newspapers, and novels can feel themselves part of a large group of invisible other readers, who are simultaneously reading the same newspaper article or book. Two widely publicized and linked phenomena, to be described next, have given visibility to the concept of an imagined community of readers: Oprah's Book Club and its counterpart in the United Kingdom, the Richard & Judy Book Club, and the large number of mass reading events that have followed from Nancy Pearl's "One Book, One City" program.

Imagined Communities and the "Talking Life" of Books

Oprah's book club gave an enormous boost to the sense of a global community of connected readers. *Salon Books'* New York editorial director Laura Miller (2002) claimed that "Winfrey's book club represented a kind of supercharged word of mouth" that every day reached an audience who trusted her recommendations because they felt they had a personal relationship with her. Professional taste-makers huffed that Oprah appealed to easy sentiment, trafficked in popular wisdom, and soothed readers by telling them what they expected to hear. And any-way by what authority did a celebrity talk show host tell other people what to read? Critics claimed that her book choices, which often feature strong women who tri-umph over adversity, are schmaltzy and one-dimensional, but if she does happen to pick a good book, she picks it for the *wrong* reason, and if she happens to pick a good book for the right reason, her followers are reading it in the *wrong way*. This turf war was being fought over who has the cultural authority to define what to read and how to read it. Oprah told readers, most of them women, that they needn't feel intimidated by *Song of Solomon* or *Anna Karenina*. Feeling them-selves part of an intimate reading community, millions of women accepted Oprah's call to get the whole country reading again.

Oprah offered her daytime television audience what Cecilia Konchar Farr (2005, 41) has called "reading lessons." Books such as Toni Morrison's *Song of Solomon* are not easy reads, Oprah told her viewers, but the pay-off can be life changing. Her own story, which she often shared with her audience, makes the case for transformative power of reading: "Starting off as a poor and lonely kid growing up in Kosciusko, Mississippi, she ended up a national icon" (Ross 2009, 650). Many who accepted Oprah's reading challenge had not read a novel since leaving school, but Oprah promised big rewards: pleasure, the satisfaction of seri-ous learning, and the possibility of personal transformation. *Song of Solomon*, she told viewers, is about, among other things, "the ways we discover, all of us, who and what we are" (Hall 2003, 658). Encouraging readers not to give up on Toni Morrison's *Paradise*, she said, "When you finish this book, you will know that you have really accomplished something because it is a great journey. . . . Once you accomplish reading this book, then you are a *bona fide* certified reader" (Farr 2005, 40–41). Oprah advised her viewers that proper reading should engage both mind and heart: "You don't read this book just with your head. You have to open your whole self up. It's a whole new way of experiencing reading and life" (Farr 2005, 47). In *Reading Oprah*, Farr (2005) claimed that Oprah's Book Club has changed the way that America reads. Part of that change is the high visibility she brought to shared reading and to talking about experiences with books. Farr (2005, 1) begins her introductory chapter, "Oprah's Reading Revolution," with an epigraph from Toni Morrison: "Reading is solitary, but that's not its only life. It should have a talking life, a discourse that follows." Farr emphasizes Oprah's role as a teacher of reading, not just "get[ting] American reading again," but teach-ing readers about the "talking life" of books.

The second significant phenomenon in the shared reading story is the One Book, One Community (OBOC) idea. In 1998, Nancy Pearl, then-executive director of the Washington Center for the Book at the Seattle Public Library, and her colleague Chris Higashi launched the city-wide program, "If All of Seattle Read the Same Book" (now called "Seattle Reads"). This high-profile event was the prototype for the many OBOC events to follow, including the NEA Big Read, discussed later. The Seattle model included the following elements: ongoing publicity to raise excitement for the program, public library acquisition and circulation of 1,000 or more copies of the chosen book, programming relating to the book and the book's topic, outreach on their web page to local book clubs offering to reserve book group kits, a downloadable "Reading Group Toolbox" for the chosen book that includes author information and discussion questions, and the high point of an author visit (Fuller and Rehberg Sedo 2013, 178).

By 2002, the American Booksellers Association's publication *Bookselling This Week* reported that over 50 cities, countries, or states had begun OBOC programs. Sponsorship and funding of these programs vary considerably, from a modest low-budget event celebrating a town's birthday to a nationwide, multi-year, splashy program such as the Big Read, sponsored by the National Endowment for the Arts (NEA). Initiated in 2006 to counter what the NEA considered to be an implosion of "literary reading" in America (see sections 3.1 and 4.1), the Big Read made grants to 1,200 projects in its first 10 years, supporting community-wide programs in which 4.2 million Americans have participated. For the 2017–2018 competition, a community applying for a grant has a list of 28 books—novels, short story collections, and books of poetry—from which to choose one book as the focus of its shared reading program. NEA director of literature Amy Stolls (2016) said that "one of our guiding principles for the NEA Big Read" is: " 'Give 'em something to talk about' … for in addition to reading a book, you can find deep enjoyment in debating its merits, discussing its themes, and hearing what others have to say about it. That's one of the wonderful things about a group of people reading one book—connecting." What lies behind this sudden burgeoning of shared reading programs, which have extended their reach through the amplification of mass media and sponsorship funding? To find out, Danielle Fuller in the United Kingdom and DeNel Rehberg Sedo in Canada undertook in 2005–2008 an interdisciplinary research project to investigate what they called "mass reading events," or MREs (Fuller and Rehberg Sedo 2012). An MRE is like a book club on steroids, existing on the much larger scale of city, region, or nation. For their study, which they called "Beyond the Book," they drew on the online questionnaire responses of more than 3,500 readers and on fieldwork studies of eight OBOC programs and two nation-wide mass-mediated events: Richard & Judy's Book Club, broadcast on daytime television in the United Kingdom, and Canada Reads, broadcast on the Canadian Broadcasting Corporation's Radio 1. Fuller and Rehberg Sedo (2016, 135) estimated that by 2015 there were more than 500 OBOC programs taking place each year around the world in the United States, Canada, Britain, Europe, Singapore, and Australia. Why so popular? Fuller and Rehberg Sedo (2016, 144) argue that different kinds of pleasures and relationships are afforded by shared reading experiences at different scales and different levels of intimacy. They quote Lynn, a woman in her 50s from Waterloo, Ontario, who said:

> I think some communities are intimate and I consider my book club
> to be intimate and ... I reveal myself to them. But this One Book
> One Community gives me a whole other social network that is part
> of the warp and the woof of holding a community together. I can
> carry that book with me into a restaurant or to have a cup of coffee
> and somebody will stop and say, I read that book.

In *Reading Beyond the Book*, Fuller and Rehberg Sedo (2013) examine mass
reading events in detail, dedicating individual chapters to various facets of the
phenomenon, including the role of mass media, sponsorship money, the workers
who organize and promote mass reading events, the books that are chosen, and
the readers themselves.

Taken together, these two linked phenomenon—the Oprah Book Club and
the OBOC programs—are part of a larger shift in cultural ideas of how to value literature: not as cultural artifacts to be reverenced but as sources of pleasure that
speak directly to readers' personal concerns. Jim Collins in *Bring on the Books
for Everybody* identifies the Oprah phenomenon, together with the growing influence of reader-generated reviews on Amazon and Goodreads, as forces in the
democratization of taste and the popularization of literary culture. Previously, cre-
dentialized reading experts guided readers' choices on what books are worth reading and how to read them in the "right way." Collins (2010, 183) argues that Oprah
has encouraged readers to view reading as "a process of self-empowerment that no
longer depends on acquiring the right sort of pedigree or professional training."
Readers are encouraged to think that they don't need to attend a graduate seminar
in order to read novels by Tolstoy, Melville, Woolf, and Austen "because reading
pleasure itself has been so thoroughly redefined. They are different novels now,
because readers are encouraged to read them as primers or guidebooks rather than
expressions of transcendent literary genius—it's all about how you *read* them."

The July 2006 issue of *O, The Oprah Magazine* includes a piece by Geoffrey
Sanborn, "How to Read a Hard Book," that advises readers not to be intimidated into
believing that "the classics" such as *Moby-Dick* should be treated with reverence and
read for arcane, hidden meanings that only English professors can reveal. Instead
you, the reader, should "[l]isten with nothing more than ordinary human curiosity
to the voice that begins speaking to you"—a voice that "wants above all else ... to
be in a meaningful relationship with you." Tellingly, reading guides appearing at
the back of would-be book club choices often pose questions that invite readers to
consider how the book achieves this "meaningful relationship," whether through
relatable characters or through incidents that resonate in readers' own lives.

This way of reading novels as equipment for living rather than as aesthetic
artifact has produced a predictable backlash. Joe Queenan (2012, 44) grumps:

> I have always had an aversion to book clubs. I have always had an
> aversion of people who belong to book clubs. I would rather have
> my eyelids gnawed on by famished gerbils than join a book
> club. ... Book discussion clubs have almost nothing to do with read-
> ing. This may be why they so rarely choose good books. ... One of
> the things about book clubs I find extremely annoying is those
> "Questions for Discussion" that appear at the back of books.

Reading Groups

To turn from mass reading events to the smaller scale of groups that meet in living rooms across the country, we can ask: Who belongs to reading groups and what motivates people to join them? It turns out that reading groups attract people who share a love of book discussion, but that the groups vary in many other respects. In the survey of 350 UK reading groups reported by Jenny Hartley (2001, 155), 69 percent were all-women groups, 27 percent were mixed male and female, and 4 percent were all men. Some groups are quite new, but others have been going for upwards of 25 years. Some meet in public spaces and participation is open to all comers—in the UK survey, 6 percent of groups reported meeting in libraries; 16 percent met in other public spaces such as pubs, bars, restaurants, fitness centers or "a quiet corner of the Royal Festival Hall." A large majority or 80 percent met in members' homes (Hartley 2001, 10). When meetings are held in private houses, membership is by invitation only, typically with new members recruited from friends of existing members. Some groups pick their books a whole year in advance, often at the last meeting of the year before breaking for the summer. Others prefer the flexibility of picking books as they go along.

Variety in book clubs extends to the management of the discussion itself. In the nineteenth-century book clubs that Elizabeth Long (2003, 68) reports on, each woman took turns presenting a book at a meeting, spending long hours in advance preparing a report that analyzed the book as a literary artifact. Contemporary reading groups tend to be less formal. Some well-to-do groups hire a professional reading group leader, as portrayed in Hilma Wolitzer's novel *Summer Reading* (2007), in which a group of women living in the Hamptons answer a newspaper advertisement: "Enhance your summer with the company of great books. Retired professor of literature will lead the way." More often, book club members share among themselves the job of leading the discussion, with each member taking a turn to lead the talk about a given book. And some groups are self-regulating, with no designated group leader but with many members able to step in to perform whatever role may be needed to get everyone involved, making comments such as "Madeline, you haven't yet said what you thought about the ending" or "I was intrigued by Jason's idea about menace in this book and would like to hear what others think" or "Getting back to the book itself, did anyone else besides me find that it was hard to become engaged because the main character is so unappealing?"

Some groups treat the book discussion as if it were a well-structured graduate seminar, and others prefer casual, free-flowing conversation that wanders off the chosen book to other books or to personal topics. And finally some book clubs prefer to read popular genres such as romance or detective fiction, reject the graduate seminar model out of hand, and refuse to privilege an analytical discussion of the book itself. In her critical ethnography of a romance reading group, Linda Griffin (1999, 144, 160) describes how the group members she observed resisted attempts by a bookstore employee and would-be group discussion leader to have a focused discussion in "an orderly fashion," preferring instead to exchange books and provide brief recommendations ("What did you think of Barbara Delinsky's book?" "That was great." "I loved that one.").

Choosing Books

Reading groups who say they read "everything" typically exclude whole categories such as plays, poetry, avant-garde fiction, and popular genres of fiction (unless they are a specialized group that has been deliberately formed to focus on one of these categories). The majority of books chosen by reading groups are what booksellers call literary fiction, leavened with a sprinkling of classics and nonfiction titles. Although the chosen books may be best sellers or award winners, many such books are considered poor book club choices—not sufficiently discussible, or too literary and bleak. Certain high-profile books such as Paula Hawkins's *The Girl on the Train* turned up on many reading group lists because readers enjoy reading what other people are reading. But reading groups also pride themselves on *not* following the herd and often choose little-known gems. As Jenny Hartley (2001, 66–67) points out, reading groups are fiercely independent and maverick: they want to have their own identity, which they confirm through individual choices that are *not* on everyone else's list. Of the 1,160 titles mentioned by the reading groups in the UK survey, 882, or 76 percent, had been read by one group only.

A new category has emerged known as the "book club" book. These books have almost nothing in common except for two things: they have at least one character that readers can care about, and they are capable of generating discussion. The consensus among book club experts and members alike is that a good book club book must be "discussible," a quality more likely to found in some genres than in others. According to Long (2003, 118), "No mainstream group considers romances, for example, to be discussible." The ReadingGroupGuides.com website advises, "You want the perfect book: one that's not too easy, not too hard, that will hold the interest of a diverse group of readers and will also inspire a lively discussion." A page turner that is a "good read" for a solitary reader may not lead to a good discussion. On the other hand, a book so difficult, long, or unengaging that readers can't force their way through it before the meeting also dampens discussion. Reading group members say that a key pleasure of book discussions is the discovery, which happens repeatedly, of how radically other people's experiences with a book can differ from their own. This means that the ideal book needs to be complex enough to support differing responses and interpretations. Books don't need to be well liked, or liked by everyone, to sustain a good discussion. In fact, when some members love a book such as Helen Macdonald's *H Is for Hawk* and others hate it, the differing responses spark a real debate. On the social media site Goodreads, a Listopia feature, "Best for Book Clubs," invites members to suggest and vote on books "that your group has read that led to a lively discussion, whether people loved or hated them." The top five books listed in 2017 were Kathryn Stockett's *The Help*, Khaled Hosseini's *The Kite Runner*, Sara Gruen's *Water for Elephants*, Markus Zusak's *The Book Thief*, and Harper Lee's *To Kill a Mockingbird*.

Books that distance the reader from the main characters are often rejected or disliked. A question commonly asked in group reading guides goes something like, "Which of the characters did you most identify with or feel closest to?"

If the answer is "none of them," then it is usually game over for that book. Jenny Hartley (2001, 132–133) says that there is a "striking consensus" in the comments made by reading groups that they put a high premium on "empathy, the core reading-group value. . . . The failure of reader-character empathy is what doomed Beryl Bainbridge's *Every Man for Himself*, the title itself so anti-group in its sentiments." Joan Bessman Taylor (2012, 154), who for five years was a participant observer in six "open-to-the-public adult recreational book groups" in the United States, reported that character development was the key to reader engagement. One reader was quoted as expressing a common view: "The characters have to be described well enough. I have to care what happens to them."

Book Talk

Knowing how to talk about books is a learned skill. For some, as already noted, the reading group is an extension of the graduate English seminar, where participants have been taught to discuss the literary elements of tone, narrative point of view, imagery, foreshadowing, patterned language, and so on. However, some potential book club members worry that what they would say about the book might not be the *right* things. Shelley (age 26, student), an interviewee in my study of avid readers, said, "Yeah, I would love to join a book club." But she hasn't joined one so far because she is worried her book talk won't measure up: "I'm so afraid to join one because I'm afraid that the people in it would know a lot about books and be very well read. And the things I would have to say about them probably wouldn't sound too intelligent. I still have this really bad fear that when I read something, I don't understand it as much as other people." Recognizing the commercial advantage of providing a common language to talk about books, many publishers produce "reading guides" as a marketing tool. These guides, which provide information about the author and lists of questions intended to foster discussion, are often printed in the back of the book itself and are available online on publishers' websites and elsewhere. ReadingGroupGuides.com brings together in a single place over 4,300 downloadable reading group guides, which the book's publisher pays to have included on the site (Fuller and Rehberg Sedo 2011, 189).

The questions provided in the reading group guides are clues to what publishers think makes a book discussible. But they also reflect competing discourses about what literature is supposed to do for its readers and how it should be evaluated. In an interesting analysis of reading guide questions, Anna S. Ivy (2011) examines how such questions "reflect and/or define a set of reading practices" (160). Elizabeth Long (2003, 145–146) notes that although reading groups defer to cultural authorities in their book choices, they tend to be more subversive in their actual discussions: "Participants talk about books with deep engagement, but very differently than literary professionals do, and they sometimes interpret characters and evaluate novels with marked disregard for critics' opinion. . . . [W]omen often expand on an opinion by discussing their personal reasons for making a certain interpretation, using the book for self-understanding and revelation of the self to other participants rather than for discovery of meaning within the book." Linsey Howie (2011, 142) agrees that sharing personal issues in a supportive environment was a valued part of the reading group experience that she studied in eastern Australian, as women "welcomed the free exchange of ideas whether or not these ideas were strictly related to the text in question."

In a nutshell, reading group guides draw upon heterogeneous discourses. Sometimes it is graduate seminar talk, where students are supposed to examine key features of the text itself. And sometimes it is encounter group talk, where participants are encouraged to read books as a catalyst for self-discovery. Both types of talk may occur at the same meeting. The reading guide for Anthony Doerr's *All the Light We Cannot See* begins with the first kind of question, asking about literary technique and theme: "The book opens with two epigraphs. How do these quotes set the scene for the rest of the book?" For the second kind of question that asks discussants to relate elements in the book to their own lives and social world, consider this question from a reading group guide on Ann Patchett's *Commonwealth*: "Among other things, Holly is attempting to find inner peace. To what extent does childhood experience determine who we become?" Ivy (2011, 166) notes that reading guides often ask readers to imagine how they themselves would have behaved, were they in a particular character's situation. It is easy, however, to see how such questions invite parody: "Were you Emma Bovary/Isabel Archer/Anna Karenina/Lady Macbeth, what would you do differently?" In fact, book clubs often ignore the reading guide questions, finding them unhelpful—too specific, too much like homework questions in English class, too much like an encounter group, or too wide of the mark in terms of their own experience of the book. As another option, the American Library Association's page, "Book Discussion Groups: Quick Start Guide" suggests some all-purpose questions, which I have very freely adapted here:

- How easy was it for you to get into this book? What features in the book itself helped you to become engaged/hindered your engagement?
- Is the book's title the kind that normally would attract you? Once you finished the novel, what was your understanding of the significance of the title?
- Is there anything particular in this book that moved you deeply or made you think about something in a new way?
- Were you convinced by the characters? *Why* do you think he/she/they did what they did? Which character(s) do you find yourself still thinking about after you have finished the book?
- Does this book convey a strong sense of place or atmosphere? How important is the setting to your experience of the book?
- Who is telling this story? How is your experience of the book affected by the way the story was told (e.g., first-person or third-person narration, single or multiple narrators, chronological unfolding or jumps in time)?
- How satisfied were you with the ending?

- How important to your enjoyment is the author's use of language? Can you provide a specific example that stood out for you?
- What, if anything, surprised you in reading this book?
- What other books does this one remind you of—and why?

While directing attention to elements of plot, character, theme, setting, and language, these questions also offer opportunities to readers to talk about their individual reading experiences, to make connections between the fictional world and their own lives, and to connect the current book to the verbal universe of other books.

Reading groups that meet regularly for a long time with the same members gradually teach themselves a common language for talking about books. With each new book that they read, they develop a set of commonly shared literary experiences that can function as a fixed point for comparison with a new book ("Well, at least it's not as bad as *The Beans of Egypt, Maine!*" or "It was okay but it was no *The Invention of Wings*"). In *Reading Lolita in Tehran*, Azar Nafisi (2003, 21) illustrates the development of a commonly shared language of literary allusions with the example of "upsilamba," a made-up word from Nabokov's *Invitation to a Beheading* that the reading group came to associate with creativity and freedom: "*Upsilamba* became part of our increasing repository of coded words and expressions, a repository that grew over time until gradually we had created a secret language of our own."

What Makes Book Discussion Groups So Popular?

"The real, hidden subject of a book group discussion is the book group members themselves," Margaret Atwood is quoted as saying in the epigraph to Elizabeth Noble's novel *The Reading Group* (2003). Atwood's insight is the theme of Karen Joy Fowler's *The Jane Austen Book Club*, which is a novel about how readers engage with fiction. The five women and one man who are members of the "Central Valley/River City all-Jane-Austen-all-the-time book club" meet to discuss the six Jane Austen novels but end up talking about themselves, each seeing the novels through the lens of her or his own life. In a successful reading group, the opportunity to discuss the book and the opportunity to meet socially with group members are almost equally balanced as draws. Here is what reading group members say about what they value in book club membership:

- It enlarges your literary horizons by introducing you to new authors and unfamiliar genres that you would never have read on your own.
- It is mind-expanding, helping you stretch because you get a deeper understanding of the book when you talk with others.
- It provides an opportunity to hear a diversity of perspectives and opinions and compare your own responses to the book with those of others. The discussion itself elevates the book, often making it seem like a different and more complex book.

- It is a way of learning about yourself and about other group members because people reveal a lot about themselves when they discuss their responses to books.
- It gets you reading in a more reflective way.
- It provides a valuable social experience—a way of meeting a diverse group of congenial people who become friends.

And there is an extra bonus. According to a study by Kamy Ooi and Chern Li Liew (2011), being in a book club develops readers, making them more self-aware about the kind of reader they are. In their study based on face-to-face semi-structured interviews with 12 adult fiction readers who are book club members, Ooi and Liew (2011, 759) found that being in a book club "influenced the type of fiction the interviewees chose to read *outside* the club." Participants said that, having been introduced to a new author in the book club, they read other books by that same author. But they also said that being in a book club changed the way that they picked fiction titles in general, making some readers more discerning and selective and others more adventurous.

Research Tells Us

Five doctoral theses have examined women's reading groups in five different settings: the eastern seaboard of Australia (Howie 1998); Houston, Texas (Griffin 1999); St. Louis, Missouri (Gregory 2001); Vancouver, British Columbia (DeNel Rehberg Sedo 2004); and Midwestern United States (Taylor 2007). Studying St. Louis women's literary societies in the late nineteenth and early twentieth centuries and comparing them with contemporary book clubs in St. Louis, Gregory says, "The evidence shows that book clubs have changed in their group structure, methods of accumulating cultural capital and the arbitration of taste, and in women's use of the clubs for affiliation, accommodation and resistance." However, some things have not changed. The researchers found that women use book clubs to achieve social, intellectual, and spiritual growth. Howie found that the "ritual" of the book club provided a safe, women-only space for personal change and self-understanding. Rehberg Sedo found that there is an interpretive community dimension to a reading group that unfolds over time. In the romance reading group that Griffin studied, members also found validation through social interaction with other romance readers who shared their love of a genre that is widely stigmatized and denigrated. Taylor, who studied three all-female groups, two mixed gender groups, and one all-male group, was interested in understanding book clubs as a social practice involving various strategies for the negotiation of meaning.

What Libraries Can Do

1. Cater to reading groups. Make the local library the first place that reading group members turn to when they want a space to meet or

suggestions for appropriate books to read or copies of the chosen book or background information on the book and its author.

2. Create an area in your library where you have assembled the tools to help people start a book club and then find suitable books for their group. This can be as simple as several shelves, with clear signage, that display books relevant to book club membership. Many books and other resources are now available that cater to this audience.

To Read More

Beyond the Book. Available at: http://www.beyondthebook.bham.ac.uk/.
The Beyond the Book project is a UK/Canadian research collaboration of Danielle Fuller and DeNel Rehberg Sedo on mass reading events. Its website posts a lot of useful information related to community reading programs.

References

American Booksellers Association. 2002. "Following Seattle's Read: Citywide Book Clubs Sprout Up throughout the US." *Bookselling This Week*, March 13. Available at: http://news.bookweb.org/news/306.html.

American Library Association. n.d. "Book Discussion Groups: Quick Start Guide." Available at: http://libguides.ala.org/bookdiscussiongroups/startguide.

Anderson, Benedict. 1983; rev. ed. 1991. *Imagined Communities: Reflections on the Origins and Spread of Nationalism.* London and New York: Verso.

Chelton, Mary K. 2001. "When Oprah Meets E-mail: Virtual Book Clubs." Reference & User Services Quarterly 41, 1: 31-36.

Collins, Jim. 2010. *Bring on the Books for Everybody: How Literary Culture Became Popular Culture.* Durham, NC: Duke University Press.

Dawson, Mackenzie. 2017. "The 10 Titles Book Clubs Are Buzzing About in 2017." *New York Post*, January 14. Available at: http://nypost.com/2017/01/14/the-10-titles-book-clubs-are-buzzing-about-in-2017/.

Driscoll, Beth. 2014. *The New Literary Middlebrow: Tastemakers and Reading in the Twenty-First Century.* Basingstoke: Palgrave Macmillan.

Farr, Cecilia Konchar. 2005. *Reading Oprah: How Oprah's Book Club Changed the Way America Reads.* Albany: State University of New York Press.

Fish, Stanley. 1980. *Is There a Text in This Class? The Authority of Interpretive Communities.* Cambridge, MA: Harvard University Press.

Fowler, Karen Joy. 2004. *The Jane Austen Book Club.* New York: Putnam.

Fuller, Danielle, DeNel Rehberg Sedo, and Claire Squires. 2011. "Marionettes and Puppeteers? The Relationship between Book Club Readers and Publishers." In *Reading Communities from Salons to Cyberspace*, 181–199. Edited by DeNel Rehberg Sedo. New York and Houndmills, UK: Palgrave Macmillan.

Fuller, Danielle, and DeNel Rehberg Sedo. 2012. "Mixing It Up: Using Mixed Methods to Investigate Contemporary Cultures of Reading." In *From Codex to Hypertext: Reading at the Turn of the Twenty-First Century*, 234–251. Edited by Anouk Lang. Amherst and Boston: University of Massachusetts Press.

Fuller, Danielle, and DeNel Rehberg Sedo. 2013. *Reading beyond the Book: The Social Practices of Contemporary Literary Culture.* New York: Routledge.

Fuller, Danielle, and DeNel Rehberg Sedo. 2016. "Fun . . . and Other Reasons for Sharing Reading with Strangers: Mass Reading Events and the Possibilities of Pleasure." In *Plotting the Reading Experience: Theory/ Practice/ Politics*, 133–147. Edited by Paulette Rothbauer, Kjell Ivar Skjerdingstad, Lynne (E. F.) McKechnie, and Knut Oterholm. Waterloo, ON: Wilfred Laurier University Press.

Goodreads. 2017. "Best for Book Clubs." *Listopia*. Available at: https://www.goodreads .com/list/show/19.Best_for_Book_Clubs.

Gregory, Patricia Lehan. 2001. "Women's Experience of Reading in St. Louis Book Clubs (Missouri)." PhD diss., Saint Louis University, St. Louis, Missouri.

Griffin, Linda Coleman. 1999. "An Analysis of Meaning Creation through the Integration of Sociology and Literature: A Critical Ethnography of a Romance Reading Group." PhD diss., University of Houston and Rice University, Texas.

Hall, R. Mark. 2003. "The 'Oprahfication' of Literacy: Reading Oprah's Book Club." *College English* 65, no. 6: 646–667.

Howie, Linsey. 1998. "Speaking Subjects: A Reading of Women's Book Groups." PhD diss., Latrobe University, Bundora, Australia.

Howie, Linsey. 2011. "Speaking Subjects: Developing Identities in Women's Reading Communities." In *Reading Communities from Salons to Cyberspace*, 140–158. Edited by DeNel Rehberg Sedo. New York and Houndmills, UK: Palgrave Macmillan.

Ivy, Anna S. 2011. "Leading Questions: Interpretive Guidelines in Contemporary Popular Reading Culture." In *Reading Communities from Salons to Cyberspace*, 159–180. Edited by DeNel Rehberg Sedo. New York and Houndmills, UK: Palgrave Macmillan.

John, Lauren Zina. 2006. *Running Book Discussion Groups: A How-to-Do-It Manual for Librarians*. New York: Neal-Schuman.

Long, Elizabeth. 1986. "Women, Reading, and Cultural Authority: Some Implications of the Audience Perspective in Cultural Studies." *American Quarterly* 38, no. 4: 591–612.

Long, Elizabeth. 1993. "Textual Interpretation as Collective Action." In *The Ethnography of Reading*, 180–211. Edited by Jonathan Boyarin. Berkeley and Los Angeles: University of California Press.

Long, Elizabeth. 2003. *Book Clubs: Women and the Uses of Reading in Everyday Life*. Chicago and London: University of Chicago Press.

Miller, Laura. 2002. "After Oprah." *Salon Books*, April 18.

National Endowment for the Arts (NEA). "NEA Big Read." Available at: http://www .neabigread.org/.

Noble, Elizabeth. 2003. *The Reading Group*. London: Hodder & Stoughton.

Ooi, Kamy, and Chern Li Liew. 2011. "Selecting Fiction as Part of Everyday Life Information Seeking." *Journal of Documentation* 67, no. 5: 748–772.

Piper, Andrew. 2012. *Book Was There: Reading in Electronic Times*. Chicago and London: The University of Chicago Press.

Poole, Marilyn. 2003. "The Women's Chapter: Women's Reading Groups in Victoria." *Feminist Media Studies* 3, no. 3: 273–281.

Queenan, Joe. 2012. *One for the Books*. New York: Viking.

ReadingGroupGuides. n.d. "Choosing What to Read." Available at: http://www.reading groupguides.com/choosing-what-to-read.

Rehberg Sedo, DeNel. 2004. "Badges of Wisdom: Reading Clubs in Canada." PhD diss., Simon Fraser University, Vancouver, British Columbia.

Richard & Judy Book Club. Available at: http://www.richard andjudy.co.uk/home.

Ross, Catherine Sheldrick. 2009. "Reader on Top: Public Libraries, Pleasure Reading, and Models of Reading." *Library Trends* 57, no. 4 (Spring): 632–656.

Sanborn, Geoffrey. 2006. "How to Read a Hard Book." *O, The Oprah Magazine*, July. Available at: http://www.oprah.com/omagazine/How-to-Read-a-Hard-Book/2.

Saricks, Joyce. 2009. "At Leisure: Leading Book Discussions." *Booklist* 106.1 (September 1): 37.

Stolls, Amy. 2016. "The NEA Big Read Gets a Makeover." *National Endowment for the Arts blog*, July 13. Available at: https://www.arts.gov/art-works/2016/nea-big -read-gets-makeover.

Taylor, Joan Bessman. 2007. "When Adults Talk in Circles: Book Groups and Contemporary Reading Practices." PhD diss., University of Illinois at Urbana-Champaign, Illinois.

Taylor, Joan Bessman. 2012. "Producing Meaning through Interaction: Book Groups and the Social Context of Reading." In *From Codex to Hypertext: Reading at the Turn of the Twenty-First Century*, 142–158. Edited by Anouk Lang. Amherst and Boston: University of Massachusetts Press.

4.8 Reading and Therapeutic Practices

There is nothing new in the idea that reading is potentially therapeutic, capable of improving mental health and well-being. In his *Autobiography* (1873), John Stuart Mill described how at the age of 20 he experienced a mental crisis—"a dull state of nerves," during which he "seemed to have nothing left to live for." He attributed his recovery to reading Wordsworth: "What made Wordsworth's poems a medicine for my state of mind, was that they express . . . states of feeling, and of thought coloured by feeling, under the excitement of beauty" (Ross 2014, 63). Recently we have been hearing about "book cures" and "book apothecaries." In *The Novel Cure* (2013), British bibliotherapists Susan Elderkin and Ella Berthoud prescribe 751 novels for whatever ails you A to Z from abandonment to zestlessness. Suffering from anxiety? Try *The Book of Disquiet* by Fernando Pessoa. For a broken leg, pick up Johanna Spyri's *Heidi*. In Nina George's best selling *The Little Paris Bookshop* (2015, 28), bookseller Monsieur Perdu claims that "a book is both medic and medicine at one. It makes a diagnosis as well as offering therapy." From his book barge on the Seine that he has named Literary Apothecary, Perdu matches customers with exactly the book they need to be reading. Inspired by Monsieur Perdu, Penguin Random House (2015) posted a blog, "Let the Book Apothecary Pick Out Your Next Read!" The healing power of reading is a firmly established trope in popular culture and more recently has become the focus of research. This section looks at the various approaches to reading as a therapeutic practice and at the models of reading that underpin such approaches.

Most therapeutic reading is not prescribed. In the course of reading widely for pleasure, many individual readers say that they encounter something that intersects with their lives in ways that gives them comfort, strength, insight, or blueprints for living—what I have called "finding without seeking" (see section 4.2). Going a step further, some books, including self-help titles, are specifically written—and self-selected by readers—to provide help in coping with challenges relating to mood, addictions, marital problems, life crises, and so on. But in special cases, books are prescribed as a form of therapy. In July 2013, the British government announced a new program, *Reading Well Books on Prescription,* to be described in more detail later, which has partnered with public libraries to make available across England a core list of 30 recommended books that take a cognitive behavioral approach to overcoming various common mental health problems such as anxiety, mood disorders, chronic pain, stress, relationship problems, and eating disorders (Reading Agency 2013).

Similarly, for the majority of readers in book clubs, social reading has benefits of the "finding without seeking" variety. Book club members say that they joined their book club for pleasure and sociality, but participation in the club helped them at a time of personal crisis. In such cases, the therapeutic benefits flow from the combined experience of reading the books on one's own and of discussing the book with others in the supportive context afforded by a close-knit group (see section 4.7). Will Schwalbe's book club for two—himself and his mother, who is dying of cancer—described in *The End of Your Life Book Club* (2012) is a specialized example of therapeutic benefits in an informal book club setting (see section 4.3 for a discussion of Schwalbe's reading memoir). Recently, however, there has been a push, especially in the United Kingdom, for reading groups with therapeutic goals to be established in hospitals, prisons, nursing homes, hostels, and mental health drop-in centers.

So how does reading work its therapeutic magic? Joseph Gold (2002) has argued that the ability to read literature is an adaptive human behavior. Writing out of his experience as an English professor and family therapist, Gold claims that stories have healing power by helping human beings find balance. Reading other people's stories allows people to step outside of their own story long enough to decide what they want to change about it (Gold 2002, 126). A person who is trapped in the same disabling story—for example, "My parents didn't love me" or "I must be a bad person, or else this abuse would not have happened to me"—can rewrite their story by grafting into it new experience derived from literature. Similarly, in her book about reading in prison, *Reading Is My Window,* Meagan Sweeney (2010, 3) says that "reading generates possibilities for prisoners to reenvision and rescript their lives—to view their experiences in relation to broader social and historical contexts and to glimpse different horizons as they engage with others' stories."

The burgeoning field of therapeutic reading has called forth various efforts at bibliographic control in order to map different parts of the domain. *Self-Help That Works* by John C. Norcross and colleagues (2013) is a comprehensive guide written for laypersons and mental-health professionals that evaluates some 2,000 self-help titles in 41 categories from abuse and addictions to violent youth and women's issues. In the library field, Keren Dali (2015) has produced a guide for librarians on bibliotherapy, a term in use for more than a hundred years to refer to an intervention that involves prescribing books to improve mental health. With funding from a Carnegie-Whitney Award from the American Library Association, Keren Dali (2015) has produced an online bibliography, "Biblio or Therapy: An Annotated Bibliography on Bibliotherapy for Librarians," that summarizes research on bibliotherapy published in the medical and library fields up to 2015.

Individual Readers on Prescription

Health professionals sometimes recommend books for clients to read on their own as a way of getting insight into particular problems. When Joan C. Chrisler and Heather M. Ulsh (2001) surveyed the 249 members of the Association for Women in Psychology who were identified as clinicians in the membership directory, they asked whether the therapists ever recommended to clients any self-help books and, if so, which ones. The majority of respondents (93 percent) said that they regularly recommended self-help books and they supplied 800 titles. There was a wide scatter, but 28 books were mentioned repeatedly, which the authors called "clinical best sellers." The top five, still in print in new editions, have demonstrated their staying power: *The Courage to Heal: A Guide for Women Survivors of Child Sexual Abuse* by Ellen Bass, 1988 (recommended by 83); *The Dance of Anger* by Harriet Lerner, 1986 (recommended by 74); *The Dance of Intimacy* by Harriet Lerner, 1989 (45); *Fat Is a Feminist Issue* by Susie Orbach, 1978 (33); and *The Drama of the Gifted Child* by Alice Miller, 1997 (21).

In England, the therapeutic use of prescribed books has expanded from an individual practice to a large, country-wide, government-sponsored and funded program. In 2013 the Reading Agency (2013, 2016) launched a program, *Reading Well Books on Prescription*, to help people "manage their mental health and wellbeing by providing access to accredited self-help reading through English public libraries." This model of bibliotherapy uses targeted self-help books that use a cognitive behavioral therapy (CBT) framework. The program is a partnership involving the following: the reading agency that chooses the books on the reading lists based on advice from mental health professionals and also produces pamphlets and publicity; the health professionals who are encouraged to prescribe the books to clients; and the 97 percent of public libraries in England that stock the books on the lists and make them freely available. The core of the initial scheme, which focused on "common mental health conditions" of adults, is the reading list of books, endorsed by health professionals. Three new *Books on Prescription* booklists have expanded the program's scope into the following areas: dementia; mental health conditions of young people such as ADHD, autism spectrum disorders, bullying, mood swings, and self-harm; and long-term conditions such as fatigue, pain, arthritis, diabetes, and heart disease. Since its launch in 2013, the program cumulatively has reached some 635,000 people. About one-third of the participants were referred by a health care professional and the rest were self-referred. The Reading Agency (2016, 21) analyzed surveys of users and program prescribers of the Reading Well program and suggested "repositioning of the scheme as less a resource that is 'prescribed' and more a public health intervention, supporting self-management of health conditions, and potentially a first step for people in seeking other sources of support."

Two Models of Therapeutic Reading

The terms "Books on Prescription" and "Cure," though catchy, suggest a model of reading in which books are pills. In discussions of bibliotherapy from the 1930s onward, the book-as-pill analogy has engendered turf wars between librarians and physicians and a lot of cautions that "bibliotherapy should be prescribed as carefully as medications" by qualified therapists who alone could select the "correct" book on the basis of "the patient's identified problems" (Jack and Ronan 2008, 168). Bibliotherapists were warned that they must "know each book and understand its action as thoroughly as the physician seeks to know the ingredients and actions of a medical prescription" (Gottschalk 1948, 54). According to Sweeney (2008, 306–310), from the 1950s through the 1970s in the United States, the prison library was described as comparable to a "pharmacy in a hospital." The job of the bibliotherapist was to foster social compliance in an essentially passive reader by means of the careful selection of texts and close monitoring to correct faulty interpretations. But despite the exclusion from the prison library of a wide array of inappropriate and potentially harmful materials including the "classics," the reading cures often backfired (see section 4.4 on prison reading). Sweeney (2008, 310) says that prisoners "managed to thwart penal authorities' control by attempting to fulfill their own reading desires, which often focused on developing their racial and class consciousness rather than complying with state-defined rehabilitative goals." In the book-as-pill model, outcomes are supposed to be predictable because the passive reader consumes messages that are already *in* the book. But the unruly readers described by Sweeney construct their own meanings of resistance. A more helpful model of what actually happens during reading has been developed by reader response theorists, who describe reading as a transaction between active readers and texts. Readers construct meanings, not predictable in advance, and produce interpretations in ways that reflect their own interests as well as their own knowledge about how texts work and how the world works.

In contrast to the text-based model of books as pills, Sociologist Paul Lichterman (1992, 423) embarked on his study of self-help reading using a reader-response model according to which "self-help readers construct meanings through their reading." He conducted in-depth interviews on self-help reading with six men and nine women. When Lichterman (1992, 430) asked his interviewees to tell him what they found good about self-help books, "most of the readers spoke in terms of gleaning a 'nugget' in the books." One interviewee, Sheila, told him, "You might only get maybe one or two sentences out of one of these books, that really apply to you in a way that you say, 'that's it. Aha!' And if you can apply that to your life, you've learned a tremendous thing." Unlike the patient who swallows the entire pill, ordinary readers don't feel obligated to read every word of a book, but skip over parts that don't speak to their personal situations. They give extra weight to other parts, reading and rereading the passages—"the one or two sentences"—that resonate. In this way, readers take a generic book written to address a problem shared by millions and individualize it to suit their own needs, creating their own version. In an attempt to answer the question of how self-help books may actually help readers, various observers turn to metaphor. Lichterman's readers describe themselves as gleaners and as miners of self-help materials to find the occasional gold nugget. Bergsma (2008, 356) speculates that maybe self-help books work more like travel guides: "Most readers will not follow the book page by page, but will study parts of the book and will select some travel options they would have never heard of without the book." All three of these metaphors of gleaning, mining nuggets, and selecting travel options put the reader in charge of meaning making.

Perspectives on Bibliotherapy

Therapeutic outcomes from reading have become a research focus. A researcher with a long-standing interest in bibliotherapeutic practices in the United Kingdom, Liz Brewster (2008, 2009, 2016; Brewster, Sen, and Cox 2013) has produced an impressive body of work, building on her doctoral dissertation, which used participant observation and interviews to study a range of bibliotherapy programs. Brewster (2009, 400) distinguishes between two types of bibliotherapy: (1) "self-help bibliotherapy," which uses nonfiction self-help books, often recommended by medical practitioners and targeted to address particular problems (the model used in *Books on Prescription*), and (2) "creative bibliotherapy," which uses fiction and poetry with individuals or groups to promote mental health through guided book discussion (the model used by the Shared Reading program in Liverpool, described later). She reported that readers who participate as *users* of bibliotherapy programs have a different understanding of the term "bibliotherapy" than the one held by the *providers* of bibliotherapy service. According to Brewster, "Service providers were often more focused on the type of text used, while readers were concerned about the outcome of the intervention" (2016, 167). The text-based *Books on Prescription* program matches books to people on the basis of the problem experienced: for example, books on depression for people who are depressed. In the view of the service providers, the prescribed books help by providing targeted information, the information helps by increasing the reader's understanding of the problem, and that helps by triggering a change in behavior. According to Brewster (2016, 174), the users of bibliotherapy programs, in contrast, have a much more inclusive understanding of what elements do the therapeutic work. Program participants who were asked to provide a definition of bibliotherapy "were very clear that therapeutic effect could be found in any text that a person found useful when experiencing distress." Brewster (2016, 174–178) also found that "informational bibliotherapy," in which readers increase their knowledge and understanding of their particular problem, was only one of several ways that reading can be therapeutic. Other therapeutic elements offered by reading are as follows:

- An "individual emotional connection with a work of imaginative literature" in which a reader experiences comfort or the reassurance that they are not alone when they read about a fictional character who has experienced a similar problem and survived.
- A source of distraction or escape in which readers are transported to "a very safe world." (See section 4.2 on reading for escape.)
- A "social discussion of texts in a group environment" in which the benefit is conferred by the combination of reading the book and

discussing it in a group setting, facilitated by a discussion leader. (See section 4.7.)

Therapeutic Shared Reading

For a successful example of Liz Brewster's category of "creative bibliotherapy" that uses poetry and fiction in a small-group setting, we can turn to the Shared Reading program by The Reader Organization in Liverpool, a charity founded by Jane Davis and "dedicated to bringing serious literature from all ages to often hard-to-reach communities" (Davis and Magee n.d., 11). Led by volunteer discussion leaders who are given training by The Reader Organization, over 200 groups meet weekly in homeless hostels, dementia care homes, mental health drop-in centers, drugs and alcohol rehabilitation centers, and refugee centers with the goal of improving health and well-being. The model of reading underpinning this program is transactional, where meaning is cocreated by readers. Jane Davis explicitly rejects the book-as-targeted-pill model: "Our belief in not giving group members targeted self-help books is a major structural principle: what literature offers is the opportunity for people to discover a relation to the book rather than the book narrowly proposing it. Deeper, wider, and richer resources are offered within the broadly human realm than are offered through the medicalised 'self-help' pigeonhole" (Billington 2011, 72). Three elements crucial to the therapeutic outcome are mutually interactive and reinforcing: the work of serious literature that is shared, the group leader, and the group dynamic (Billington 2011, 71–72).

Unlike in traditional book clubs where the book is read in advance, in shared reading meetings, the facilitator and sometimes volunteering group members read aloud from the chosen texts—short poems, short stories, plays, or chapters from novels—within a session that lasts about an hour and a half. Long novels such as Tolstoy's *Anna Karenina* or Dickens's *Great Expectations* may take months to read aloud (Billington 2011, 70). The read-aloud feature makes literature accessible to people who do not, or cannot, read much on their own. Open-ended discussion is encouraged, and the aloud reading may be interrupted by participants who wish to share thoughts and immediate responses. The Reader's website says, "The charity's weekly read aloud groups have taken Shakespeare to supermarkets, poetry to prisons and Hardy to hospitals." An evaluative report on the Shared Reading program by Philip Davis and Fiona Magee (n.d.) called "What Literature Can Do" provides many concrete examples and statements from participants to make the case that hearing "serious literature," especially poetry, read aloud in a group setting brings about change and breakthroughs in self-understanding.

According to University of Liverpool researcher Josie Billington (2011, 70), "The virtue of the shared reading-aloud model is its inclusiveness: even people who cannot read—whether through literacy difficulties or neurological disorders, or impaired vision—can participate meaningfully." The goal is not to increase literacy *per se* but to make reading "a creative, social life-enhancing activity in with the shared experience of literature is an important element" (2011, 70). Works of "serious literature"—for example, Shakespeare, nineteenth-century realist novels, contemporary middlebrow material such as Alan Bennett's *The Uncommon Reader*—are chosen rather than "misery memoirs," because they are thought to offer models of human thinking and feeling (2011, 70). In reading literature, group members, as a matter of course, recognize aspects of their own experience in the distanced, and therefore safe, framework provided by story. The shared story elicits personal narratives from group members and gives them a language through which they can tell a new story about themselves.

Reading Groups in Prison

Professors of English at the University of Roehampton Jenny Hartley and Sarah Turvey already knew a lot about reading groups before they began facilitating reading groups for prisoners (see section 4.7). They had collaborated on a survey-based study of 350 reading groups in England, which was reported in *Reading Groups* (Hartley 2001). In that project, they found that belonging to a reading group offered readers both a safe space for sharing personal stories and a sense of connectedness to a wider culture (Hartley and Turvey 2013, 9). Thinking that reading groups could similarly benefit people in prison, Hartley and Turvey set up and ran four prison reading groups, with a structure much like that used by reading groups in the general community: participants choose the book, everyone reads the book in advance, and the group meets monthly for an hour or so to discuss the book and choose the next book. Participation is voluntary, the focus is on reading for pleasure, and, crucially, books are *chosen* by the participants, not prescribed. Hartley and Turvey had run the initial four prison reading groups for 10 years when, in 2010, funding from the Arts and Humanities Research Council allowed them to expand the Prison Reading Groups (PRG) project. By 2016, it was supporting over 45 groups in more than 30 male and female prisons. A new partnership in 2016 with The Booker Prize Foundation will support the creation of 10 new reading groups. With the expansion of groups came the need for new models and formats, as prison librarians and volunteers developed programs tailor-made for different groups: read-ahead and read-aloud; monthly and weekly meetings; mainstream reading materials and prisoners reading their own writing aloud to the group. The PRG model has gone global. Dr. Carol Finlay, who consulted with Hartley and Turvey, has borrowed from the PRG model in setting up in 2009 the Toronto-based charity, Book Clubs for Inmates (BCFI), which supports some 30 volunteer-run book clubs in federal penitentiaries across Canada. In *The Prison Book Club*, Ann Walmsley (2015) describes her experience running a BCFI book club for 18 months at the Collins Bay Institution in Kingston, Ontario.

From their previous research on reading groups and their own experience running four prison reading groups, Hartley and Turvey were committed to the principle of choice and made it a cornerstone when the PRG project expanded. Choosing the book was very important for community reading group members. Hartley and Turvey felt that it could be even more important in prison, where prisoners have very few opportunities to choose any aspects of their life. In their report on the PRG project, *What Books Can Do behind Bars*, Hartley and Turvey (2013, 13) say, "Our watchword throughout the project has been choice. . . . This means choice in both how the group should run, and what it should read." To help with book selection, group facilitators bring in single copies of books, book reviews, prize shortlists, publishers' catalogues, and Amazon descriptions. Among other things, prisoners learn how one might choose a book that they might enjoy. Books chosen by prison groups are more diverse than those borrowed from prison libraries and resemble book choices of community reading groups, including, for example, Russo's *Nobody's Fool*, Haddon's *Curious Incident of the Dog in the Night-Time*, McCarthy's *The Road*, Collins's *The Hunger Games*, Larson's *The Girl with the Dragon Tattoo*, Simpson's *Touching the Void*, Spiegelman's *Maus*, Donoghue's *Room*, Coelho's *The Alchemist*, and King's *Misery* (Hartley and Turvey 2013, 54–55). Hartley and Turvey (2013, 21) stress that although everyone in the reading group—prison group members, librarians, and volunteers—do learn a lot, there is no secret agenda: "Our groups are to do first of all with pleasure: the pleasure of reading and of talking about books."

References

Bergsma, Ad. 2008. "Do Self-Help Books Help?" *Journal of Happiness Studies* 9: 341–360.

Billington, Josie. 2011. " 'Reading for Life': Prison Reading Groups in Practice and Theory." *Critical Survey* 23, no. 3: 67–85.

Brewster, Liz. 2008. "The Reading Remedy: Bibliotherapy in Practice." *APLIS* 21, no. 4 (December): 172–177.

Brewster, Liz. 2009. "Books on Prescription: Bibliotherapy in the United Kingdom." *Journal of Hospital Librarianship* 9, no. 4: 399–407.

Brewster, Liz. 2016. "More Benefit from a Well-Stocked Library Than a Well-Stocked Pharmacy: How Do Readers Use Books as Therapy?" In *Plotting the Reading Experience: Theory/ Practice/ Politics*, 167–182. Edited by Paulette Rothbauer, Kjell Ivar Skjerdingstad, Lynne (E.F.) McKechnie, and Knut Oterholm. Waterloo, ON: Wilfrid Laurier University Press.

Brewster, Liz, Barbara Sen, and Andrew Cox. 2013. "Mind the Gap: Do Librarians Understand Service User Perspectives on Bibliotherapy?" *Library Trends* 61, no. 3: 569–586.

Chrisler, Joan C., and Heather M. Ulsh. 2001. "Feminist Bibliotherapy: Report on a Survey of Feminist Therapists." *Women & Therapy* 23, no. 4: 71–84.

Dali, Keren. 2015. "Biblio or Therapy: An Annotated Bibliography on Bibliotherapy for Librarians." Available at: https://bibliotherapyforlibrarians.wordpress.com/.

Davis, Philip, and Fiona Magee. n.d. *What Literature Can Do*. The University of Liverpool. Available at: http://www.thereader.org.uk/wp-content/uploads/2017/06/What-Literature-Can-Do.pdf.

Elderkin, Susan, and Ella Berthoud. 2013. *The Novel Cure: An A-Z of Literary Remedies*. Edinburgh: Canongate.

Gold, Joseph. 2002. *The Story Species: Our Life-Literature Connection*. Markham, ON: Fitzhenry and Whiteside.

Gottschalk, L. A. 1948. "Bibliotherapy as an Adjuvant in Psychotherapy." In *Bibliotherapy Sourcebook*, 48–58. Edited by E. J. Rubin. Phoenix, AZ: Oryx Press.

Hartley, Jenny. 2001. *Reading Groups*. Oxford: Oxford University Press.

Hartley, Jenny, and Sarah Turvey. 2013. *Prison Reading Groups: What Books Can Do behind Bars: Report on the Work of PRG 1999–2013*. Available at: https://prisonreadinggroupscouk.files.wordpress.com/2016/03/what-books-can-do-behind-bars.pdf.

Jack, Sarah J., and Kevin R. Ronan. 2008. "Bibliotherapy: Practice and Research." *School Psychology International* 29, no. 2: 161–182.

Lichterman, Paul. 1992. "Self-Help Reading as Thin Culture." *Media, Culture & Society* 14: 421–447.

Norcross, John C., Linda F. Campbell, John M. Grohol, John W. Santrock, Florin Selagea, and Robert Sommer. 2013. *Self-Help That Works: Resources to Improve Emotional Health and Strengthen Relationships*, 4th ed. New York: Oxford University Press.

Penguin Random House. 2015. "Let the Book Apothecary Pick Out Your Next Read!" *The Perch: The Penguin Random House Blog*, June 29. Available at: http://www.penguinrandomhouse.com/blog/2015/06/29/let-the-book-apothecary-pick-out-your-next-read/.

The Reader Organization. Available at: https://www.theguardian.com/books/booksblog/2012/jun/27/reader-organisation-mutual-improvement-society-modern.

Reading Agency. 2013. "Reading Well Books on Prescription Launches." Available at: http://readingagency.org.uk/news/media/reading-well-books-on-prescription-launches.html.

Reading Agency. 2016. *Reading Well Books on Prescription Evaluation 2015–16*. BOP Consulting, November. Available at: https://tra-resources.s3.amazonaws.com/uploads/entries/document/1886/161111_TRA_RWBoP_Y3_Evaluation_Final.pdf.

Ross, Catherine Sheldrick. 2014. *The Pleasures of Reading: A Booklover's Alphabet*. Santa Barbara, CA: Libraries Unlimited.

Schwalbe, Will. 2012. *The End of Your Life Book Club: A Mother, a Son, and a World of Books*. London: Two Roads.

Sweeney, Meagan. 2008. "Reading and Reckoning in a Women's Prison." *Texas Studies in Literature and Language* 50, no. 3: 304–328.

Sweeney, Meagan. 2010. *Reading Is My Window: Books and the Art of Reading in Women's Prisons*. Chapel Hill: The University of North Carolina Press.

Walmsley, Ann. 2015. *The Prison Book Club*. Toronto, ON: Viking.

Coda:
Reading Becomes You

At an American Library Association (ALA) mid-summer conference, a packet of 50 bookmarks was on sale in the ALA store bearing the message "Reading Becomes You." Of course, it is a pun. Reading shows you off in a flattering light—just as wearing a becoming article of clothing does. But more importantly, reading enters into you and *becomes you*. You are what you read and, through reading, you discover who you are. All the stories, all the plots, all the words, all the fictional people, all the information about people and places encountered in books—they settle into your memory, layer upon layer, to be drawn upon later.

As myths about reading yield to new research-based insights, we now know quite a lot about what reading is and does. We know that reading begins almost at birth and is a lifelong activity, fostered by the pleasure of the reading experience itself. What reading means to an individual reader changes over the course of a reading life, as more books and stories and materials make up the reader's repertoire. We also know that it is never too late to start reading for pleasure. Although the best predictor of adult reading is having read for pleasure as a child, a significant minority are late comers to voluntary reading, often introduced to reading pleasure by a mentor. The gift of reading can best be given by another reader, often a family member, teacher, librarian, or friend, who models the joy of reading. We know that our understanding of reading for pleasure needs to be sufficiently inclusive to encompass a variety of formats from codex and comics to eBooks to audiobooks as well as a variety of activities from a baby's chiming in on patty-cake to an older reader "lost in a book" or sharing reading experiences with others on social media sites or in book clubs.

The research on reading is reassuring for librarians, parents, and teachers alike. For librarians, it legitimates what you are doing to support reading for pleasure and the provision of story in all formats as a central function of a public library. For parents, the research confirms that you have unrecognized expertise and quite naturally do the things that research has shown to be critical: reading stories aloud in a risk-free environment where stories are enjoyable occasions, not tests. Everyone can stop worrying over the quality of the books that readers choose: the best book is the one that the reader loves and wants to read. Choices evolve over a lifetime, depending on the readers' reading skill and what else is going on in readers' lives. For community members, the research confirms that the activities that booklovers do naturally all the time anyway—giving books as gifts, borrowing books from the library for family members, and talking about books with friends—are important in keeping others among the community of readers. For teachers, the research confirms the importance of making time for voluntary free reading, by which we mean giving readers the chance to *choose* what they want to read. It also confirms the value of reading aloud, not just in the early years of elementary school but right on into high school.

A Reading Gift: Eleven Novels That Celebrate the Reading Experience

Readers sometimes talk about "reading their way into reading." Having read one good book, they want to start on another one right away, so as to repeat the pleasurable experience. Here are 11 novels that in one way or another celebrate reading so persuasively that, having read one of them, you may want to drop everything and immerse yourself in another good book.

Calvino, Italo. 1981/2015. *If on a Winter's Night a Traveller.* Translated by William Weaver. London: Vintage.

A dazzling turn on reading that starts, "You are about to begin reading Italo Calvino's new novel. . . . Relax. Concentrate." Chapters about the main characters' quest for an ideal reading experience alternate with the first chapters of different novels that correspond to the readers' varying descriptions of their preferred types of fiction such as "I prefer novels . . . that bring me immediately into a world where everything is precise, concrete, specific."

Carey, Mike, Peter Gross, Todd Klein, Chris Chuckry, and Jeanne McGee. 2009–2015. *The Unwritten.* 11 vols. New York: DC Comics/Vertigo.

This meta-fictional fantasy comic weaves literary works, folktales, and pop culture that frame Tom Taylor's quest to find out who he is: Is his father really the best-selling author Wilson Taylor? Throughout 11 volumes and a graphic novel, the art is cleverly inspired by well-known literary images and storylines. Beginners and avid readers will enjoy traveling through history, visiting sites where boundaries between reality and fiction blur.

Dahl, Roald. 1988. *Matilda.* London: Puffin Books. Illustrated by Quentin Blake.

There are some Very Bad People in this book, especially Miss Trunchbull, the bullying headmistress who hates children and can "liquidize [them] like a carrot in a kitchen blender." She meets her match in Matilda, the five-and-a-half-year-old reader *extraordinaire*, who has a knack for thinking up and executing clever revenge plots. A mood-booster and good read-aloud book for all ages—and with the added bonus of wonderful comic-style illustrations by Quentin Blake.

Leavitt, Martine. 2012. *My Book of Life by Angel.* Toronto: Groundwood/House of Anansi.

Reduced to turning tricks in Vancouver's seedy Downtown East Side where girls and women are mysteriously disappearing, 16-year-old Angel is paid by one of her johns to read Book 9 of Milton's *Paradise Lost.* By turns harrowing and hopeful, this powerful YA novel is told in free verse in Angel's voice. Angel is quite literally saved by books: "I breathed in the books, / the good smell a million books make, / the bookstore was my home."

Rushdie, Salman. 1990. *Haroun and the Sea of Stories.* London: Granta Books.

A children's story with crossover appeal for adults, this multilayered fable is about storytelling itself. An exuberant, fantastical, and story-affirming *tour de force*.

Shaffer, Mary Ann, and Annie Burrows. 2008. *The Guernsey Literary and Potato Peel Pie Society*. New York: Random House.

A chance letter in 1946 from a Guernsey man she has never met connects London writer Juliet Ashton with an entire community in Guernsey, who are gradually recovering from the grim, wartime Nazi occupation. This feel-good, epistolary novel of survival and resilience includes quirky characters; a spur-of-the-moment book club; a writer and her London publisher; and a great many letters that are by turns amusing, sad, engaging, and informative about wartime conditions.

Sloan, Robin. 2012. *Mr. Penumbra's 24-Hour Bookstore*. New York: Picador/ Farrar, Straus and Giroux.

This exuberant quest story involves a fellowship of friends in a Google-meets-fifteenth-century-typesetting world. Sloan said, "I wrote this book because it's the one I wanted to read, and I tried to pack it full of the things I love: books and bookstores; design and typography; Silicon Valley and San Francisco; fantasy and science fiction; quests and projects."

Walton, Jo. 2010. *Among Others*. New York: Tor.

Fans of vintage SF/Fantasy will get lots of reading suggestions in this coming-of-age, life-affirming story set in 1979–1980 and featuring magic, Welch-speaking fairies, a very bad mother, libraries, a SF book club, and a 15-year-old outsider from Wales who tells the story. In diary form, Mori relates what happens after her life is blown apart in a car crash and she is packed off to live "among others" in a posh boarding school in England, which, she thinks glumly, "is just like Enid Blyton showed it."

Zafón, Carlos Ruiz. 2001/4. *The Shadow of the Wind* (The Cemetery of Forgotten Books, #1). Translated by Lucia Graves. New York and London: Penguin.

In 1945 in Barcelona, when Daniel is almost 11, his father takes him to the Cemetery of Forgotten Books—a gothic structure with labyrinthine passageways crammed with bookshelves—and says that Daniel must choose a book and make sure that it never disappears. Daniel picks Julian Carax's *The Shadow of the Wind* and then gradually discovers that someone is systematically burning all Carax's books. A wild ride through gothic territory involving crumbling ruins, torture, prisons, young love, best friends, a trickster, ghosts, betrayal, an antiquarian bookstore, and books.

Zevin, Gabrielle. 2014. *The Storied Life of A.J. Fikry*. Algonguin Books.

Before everything changes, A. J. Fikry is a curmugeony, 39-year-old widower and owner of a failing bookstore who rants at a publisher's sales rep: "I do not like post-modernism, postapocalyptic settings, postmortem narrators, or magic realism . . . children's books, especially ones with orphans." This story about the transformative power of books and community includes an island, a stolen rare book, an orphan, a book club, and references to 50 titles from *Anne of Green Gables* to David Foster Wallace's *Infinite Jest*—enough variety to tempt every reader.

Zusak, Markus. 2005. *The Book Thief*. New York: Knopf.

This story is about a parentless girl who steals a book, is adopted by a German family during the dark days of Nazi book burnings, learns how to read, steals more books, and discovers the power of words. Grim and darkly humorous, the novel is narrated by Death, who says of Leisel, "When she came to write her story, she would wonder exactly when the books and the words started to mean not just something, but everything."

For the avid reader, reflecting on the experience of reading is a pleasure in itself—which accounts for the popularity of fiction that features reading. It also explains the mini-boom in books by readers who have published reading memoirs about their personal engagement with books. We hope that you, our readers, find this book useful in your own reflections on reading, an activity that can provide an endlessly renewable source of pleasure over a lifetime.

Name and Subject Index

The notation "work cited" after an author's name indicates an annotated entry of a work that has been recommended in a To Read More *section or in the* Coda.

Title Index

About the Authors

CATHERINE SHELDRICK ROSS is dean and professor emerita of the Faculty of Information and Media Studies at the University of Western Ontario, where she taught graduate courses on pleasure reading and reference services. Her most recent books include Libraries Unlimited's *The Pleasures of Reading: A Booklover's Alphabet* and, with Kirsti Nilsen, *Communicating Professionally: A How-To-Do-It Manual for Librarians*, Third Edition. She is the recipient of NoveList's Margaret E. Monroe Library Adult Services Award (2013), awarded by the Reference and User Services Association (RUSA).

LYNNE (E. F.) McKECHNIE is professor at the Faculty of Information and Media Studies at the University of Western Ontario, where she teaches graduate courses in library materials, services for children, and research methods. She practiced as a children's librarian for almost 20 years before becoming an academic. She is the coeditor of *Plotting the Reading Experience: Theory/Practice/Politics*. Her latest research project, funded by an ALISE/OCLC research grant, explored children's perspectives on e-reading.

PAULETTE M. ROTHBAUER is associate professor at the Faculty of Information and Media Studies at the University of Western Ontario, where she teaches graduate courses in library materials and services for teens as well as reference. She is the coeditor of *Plotting the Reading Experience: Theory/Practice/Politics*. Her latest research project is exploring the meaning of reading among older adults.